COLLECTED PAPERS OF KENNETH J. ARROW

Volume **1** Social Choice and Justice

COLLECTED PAPERS OF KENNETH J. ARROW

Social Choice and Justice

The Belknap Press of Harvard University Press
Cambridge, Massachusetts   1983

This book is printed on acid-free paper,
and its binding materials have been chosen
for strength and durability.

Library of Congress Cataloging in Publication Data

Arrow, Kenneth Joseph, 1921–
  Collected papers of Kenneth J. Arrow.

  Includes bibliographical references and index.
  Contents: v. 1. Social choice and justice.
  1. Welfare economics—Addresses, essays, lectures.
  2. Social choice—Addresses, essays, lectures.
  3. Social justice—Addresses, essays, lectures.
  4. Distributive justice—Addresses, essays, lectures.
  I. Title.
HB846.A7725 1983   330.1   83-2688
ISBN 0-674-13760-4 (v.1)

To the memory of Harold Hotelling, who encouraged my entrance into the field of economics, bolstered my limited self-confidence, and set the example of human concern combined with analytic rigor that I have always attempted to follow

Preface

My work in economics took its original cast from the depression, during which I grew to maturity; from my personal interest in mathematics, and especially in logic and the goal of coherence; and most particularly from my early fascination with the new concepts of mathematical statistics. My ideal in those days was the development of economic planning, a task which I saw as synthesizing economic equilibrium theory, statistical methods, and criteria for social decision making. I was content to work on the separate pieces of this task and not seek a premature synthesis. Naturally, my concepts and directions were partially altered by my own development and by changes in the world and in economic science as a whole.

General equilibrium theory tells us that every economic activity is connected with every other one. In principle, therefore, my implicit program included any interesting economic question; in practice, I felt open to a variety of outside stimuli to work on specific tasks. The current literature and events of the day raised more than enough particular problems to which I felt I could contribute useful solutions. The tasks of economic theory include but are certainly not confined to the abstract development of very broad principles. Indeed, even to one whose interests are largely theoretical, specific problems have frequently suggested new general principles. Thus, my work contains both successive developments of large themes and much that is opportunistic and specific.

This first volume draws together my papers on social choice. Policy implications have been the direct or indirect concern of economists throughout the history of the subject. For while it is possible to study economic phenomena from a purely descriptive or positivistic viewpoint, there are few economists who do so — or who have ever done so. When I was a graduate student, it was fashionable to sneer at the medieval idea of "just price" (nowadays, students never even hear of it, or of any economic concept more than thirty years old); but a glance at any contemporary journal will find articles on pricing to ensure economic efficiency, the modern version of the same idea.

Recommending a policy is making a choice, and the inevitable question arises, by what criteria should a choice be made? While the subject abuts closely on philosophers' theories of justice, in fact the only philosophical influence has been that of classical utilitarianism — which is, to a large extent, the work of economists.

The particular circumstances that led to my own viewpoint on social choice are recounted in the headnote to Chapter 1 of this volume. The theory is more systematically expounded in my 1951 monograph *Social Choice and Individual Values* (2nd ed., 1963). Still, most of the basic elements are to be found in Chapters 1, 3, and 4 here, along with comments on newer developments; relations with the systematic theories of justice and economic welfare developed by I. M. D. Little, John Rawls, and Robert Nozick; and studies of other problems at the foundations of policy analysis.

The papers that follow are among those I have published in technical journals, or as chapters in various types of collections, or as separate pamphlets. (Portions of books of which I was primary author are not included.) I am grateful to the various publishers for their permission to reproduce these materials as part of the present volume. The papers have been edited lightly and, where necessary, brought up to date by the insertion of bracketed material. A few have been supplied with headnotes, to give the reader some insight into the circumstances that motivated the writing.

I should like to express my thanks to Michael Aronson of Harvard University Press for instigating this collection, and to Vivian Wheeler for her patient and meticulous editing of the papers. I am grateful also to Mike Barclay and Robert Wood for their preparation of the index.

Contents

1   A Difficulty in the Concept of Social Welfare[1]

Most of my research over the years has focused on the workings of the general equilibrium system — its logic, its potentialities, and its shortcomings both descriptively and normatively. It started therefore from an accepted tradition; while my individual research topics were frequently matters of chance and circumstance, I have pursued the overall agenda in a reasonably deliberate fashion. My work on social choice, however, did not come out of prolonged scrutiny of a previously recognized problem. It seemed to be more a concept that took possession of me — and had been trying to for some time.

While an undergraduate and even while in high school, I had been fascinated by mathematical logic, first through the popular writings of Bertrand Russell and later from more advanced works.

1. This paper is based on research carried on at the RAND Corporation, a project of the United States Air Force, and at the Cowles Commission for Research in Economics, and is part of a longer study, *Social Choice and Individual Values* [Cowles Commission Monograph No. 12. New York: Wiley, 1951]. A version was read at the December 1948 meeting of the Econometric Society. I am indebted to A. Kaplan, University of California at Los Angeles, and J. W. T. Youngs, Indiana University, for guidance in formulating the problem, and to A. Bergson and A. G. Hart, Columbia University, and T. C. Koopmans, Cowles Commission and the University of Chicago, who read the manuscript and made valuable comments on both the presentation and the meaning. Needless to say, any error or opacity remaining is the responsibility of the author.

Among the concepts that I found there were those pertaining to relations, in particular transitivity and orderings. This interest was reinforced by my good fortune of having a course in the calculus of relations from Alfred Tarski. Trapped in this country by the outbreak of World War II, he was teaching at the City College of New York as a visiting professor. (Ironically, the vacancy existed because a New York court had forbidden the appointment of Russell on grounds of immorality.)

When I started studying economic theory, I recognized right away that consumer indifference maps were merely orderings with special properties of continuity and convexity; but simple translation of known results into another language was not very stimulating.

When in 1946 I began a grandiose and abortive dissertation aimed at improving on John Hicks's *Value and Capital,* one of the obvious needs for generalization was the theory of the firm. What if it had many owners, instead of the single owner postulated by Hicks? To be sure, it could be assumed that all were seeking to maximize profits; but suppose they had different expectations of the future? They would then have differing preferences over investment projects. I first supposed that they would decide, as the legal framework would imply, by majority voting. In economic analysis we usually have many (in fact, infinitely many) alternative possible plans, so that transitivity quickly became a significant question. It was immediately clear that majority voting did not necessarily lead to an ordering. In view of my aims, I reacted to this result as a nuisance, not as a clue for further study. Besides, I was convinced that what we presently call the Condorcet paradox was not new. I am at a loss to identify the source of my belief, now that I know the previous literature, since I could not possibly have seen any of this obscure material prior to 1946.

Opportunity knocked again when Hicks gave a lecture at Columbia University, probably in the fall of 1946. He was developing an ordinal approach to interpersonal comparisons; A was defined to be "better off" than B if A preferred his/her own commodity bundle to B's and B also preferred A's bundle to his/her own. As far as I know, Hicks never published the idea, and it was proposed again in modified form by Duncan Foley twenty years later. Hicks recognized that the relation "better off" might be incomplete (A and B might each prefer his or her own bundle to the other's). I went a step further and noted that the relation is not necessarily transitive — that is, one could easily have A better off than B, B better off than C, and C better off than A. I did no more with this observation than raise it as a question at Hicks's lecture.

Sometime in the winter of 1947–48 my mind again turned involuntarily to voting. This time I happened to start with a political context and thought of parties arrayed in a natural left-right ordering. Then majority voting indeed implied an ordering of the alternatives. Within a month I found the same idea in a paper by Duncan Black in the *Journal of Political Economy*. Unlike some other examples of multiple discovery, this one still surprises me. The mathematics after all could have been carried out by Condorcet; and there had been no active body of literature raising comparable questions.

Even this fleeting and, as it turned out, unnecessary study seemed to me to be a self-indulgent deviation from the necessary path of better economic theory and improved statistical methods. I was invited for the summer of 1948 to the then-new RAND Corporation, which was trying to develop game theory as a tool for analysis of international relations and military conflict. During one of the coffee breaks (which frequently provided more intense intellectual challenge than the work in one's own office), Olaf Helmer, one of several logicians at RAND, told me he was troubled by the foundations of this application. Game theory was based on utility functions for individuals; but when applied to international relations, the "players" were countries, not individuals. In what sense could collectivities be said to have utility functions? I told him that economists had thought about the question and that it had been answered by Abram Bergson's notion of the social welfare function. Helmer asked me to write an exposition, showing how the social welfare function could serve as the payoff function for an international game.

I quickly perceived that the ordinalist viewpoint, which I had fully adopted, implied that the only preference information that could be transmitted across individuals was an ordering. Social welfare could only be an aggregate of orderings. I already knew that majority voting, a plausible way of aggregating preferences, was unsatisfactory; a little experimentation suggested that no other method would work in the sense of defining an ordering. The development of the theorems and their proofs then required only about three weeks, although writing them as a monograph (*Social Choice and Individual Values*) took many months. My dissertation adviser, Albert Hart, consented to my change of topic. Later, at the invitation of Earl Hamilton, editor of the *Journal of Political Economy,* I prepared the following paper as a brief exposition of my results.

In a capitalist democracy there are essentially two methods by which social choices can be made: voting, typically used to make "political" decisions, and the market mechanism, typically used to make "economic" decisions. In the emerging democracies with mixed economic systems (Great Britain, France, and Scandinavia) the same two modes of making social choices prevail, though more scope is given to the method of voting and to decisions based directly or indirectly on it and less to the rule of the price mechanism. Elsewhere in the world, and even in smaller social units within the democracies, the social decisions are sometimes made by single individuals or small groups and sometimes (more and more rarely in this modern world) by a widely encompassing set of traditional rules for making the social choice in any given situation, for example, a religious code.

The last two methods of social choice, dictatorship and convention, have in their formal structure a certain definiteness absent from voting or the market mechanism. In an ideal dictatorship, there is but one will involved in choice; in an ideal society ruled by convention, there is but the divine will or perhaps, by assumption, a common will of all individuals concerning social decisions, so that in either case no conflict of individual wills is involved. The methods of voting and of the market, on the other hand, are methods of amalgamating the tastes of many individuals in the making of social choices. The methods of dictatorship and convention are, or can be, rational in the sense that any individual can be rational in his choice. Can such consistency be attributed to collective modes of choice, where the wills of many people are involved?

It should be emphasized here that the present study is concerned only with the formal aspects of the foregoing question. That is, we ask if it is formally possible to construct a procedure for passing from a set of known individual tastes to a pattern of social decision making, the procedure in question being required to satisfy certain natural conditions. An illustration of the problem is the following well-known "paradox of voting." Suppose there is a community consisting in three voters, and this community must choose among three alternative modes of social action (such as disarmament, cold war, or hot war). It is expected that choices of this type have to be made repeatedly, but sometimes not all of the three alternatives will be available. In analogy with the usual utility analysis of the individual consumer under conditions of constant wants and variable price-income situations, rational behavior on the part of the community would mean that the community orders the three alternatives according to its collective preferences once for all and then chooses in any given case that alternative among those actually available which stands highest on this list. A natural way of arriving at the collective preference scale would be to say that one alternative is preferred to another if a majority of the community prefers the first alternative to the second — that is, would choose the first over the second if those were the only two alternatives.

Let A, B, and C be the three alternatives, and 1, 2, and 3 the three individuals. Suppose individual 1 prefers A to B and B to C (and therefore A to C), individual 2 prefers B to C and C to A (and therefore B to A), and individual 3 prefers C to A and A to B (and therefore C to B). Then a majority prefers A to B, and a majority prefers B to C. We may therefore say that the community prefers A to B and B to C. If the community is to be regarded as behaving rationally, we are forced to say that A is preferred to C. But, in fact, a majority of the community prefers C to A. So the method just outlined for passing from individual to collective tastes[2] fails to satisfy the condition of rationality as we ordinarily understand it. Can we find other methods of aggregating individual tastes which imply rational behavior on the part of the community and which will be satisfactory in other ways?[3]

If we adopt the traditional identification of rationality with maximization

---

2. It may be added that the method of decision sketched above is essentially that used in deliberative bodies, where a whole range of alternatives usually comes up for decision in the form of successive pairwise comparisons. The phenomenon described in the text can be seen in a pure form in the disposition of the proposals before recent Congresses for federal aid to state education, the three alternatives being no federal aid, federal aid to public schools only, and federal aid to both public and parochial schools.

3. The problem of collective rationality has been discussed by Frank H. Knight, but chiefly in terms of the sociopsychological prerequisites; see "The Planful Act: The Possibilities and Limitations of Collective Rationality," in *Freedom and Reform* (New York: Harper & Bros., 1947), pp. 335–69, esp. pp. 346–65).

of some sort, then the problem of achieving a social maximum derived from individual desires is precisely the problem which has been central to the field of welfare economics.[4] However, the search for a clear definition of optimum social welfare has been plagued by the difficulties of interpersonal comparisons. The emphasis, as is well known, has shifted to a weaker definition of optimum, namely, the determination of all social states such that no individual can be made better off without making someone else worse off. As Bergson, Lange, and Samuelson have argued, though, the weaker definition cannot be used as a guide to social policy; the second type of welfare economics is only important as a preliminary to the determination of a genuine social maximum in the full sense.

For instance, under the usual assumptions, if there is an excise tax imposed on one commodity in the initial situation, it can be argued that the removal of the tax accompanied by a suitable redistribution of income and direct tax burdens will improve the position of all individuals in the society. But there are, in general, many redistributions which will accomplish this end, and society must have some criterion for choosing among them before it can make any change at all. Further, there is no reason for confining the range of possible social actions to those which will injure no one as compared with the initial situation, unless the status quo is to be sanctified on ethical grounds. All we can really say is that society ought to abolish the excise tax and make some redistribution of income and tax burdens; but this is no prescription for action unless there is some principle by which society can make its choice among attainable income distributions—that is, a social indifference map.

Voting can be regarded as a method of arriving at social choices derived from the preferences of individuals. Another such method, of more specifically economic content, is the compensation principle, as proposed by Kaldor:[5] in a choice between two alternative economic states x and y, if there is a method of paying compensations under state x such that everybody can be made better off in the state resulting from making the compen-

---

4. See P. A. Samuelson, *Foundations of Economic Analysis* (Cambridge, Mass.: Harvard University Press, 1947), chap. 8; A. Bergson (Burk), "A Reformulation of Certain Aspects of Welfare Economics," *Quarterly Journal of Economics,* 52 (1938), 310–34; O. Lange, "The Foundations of Welfare Economics," *Econometrica,* 10 (1942), 215–28; M. W. Reder, *Studies in the Theory of Welfare Economics* (New York, 1947), chaps. 1–5.

5. N. Kaldor, "Welfare Propositions of Economics and Interpersonal Comparisons of Utility," *Economic Journal,* 49 (1939), 549–652; see also J. R. Hicks, "The Foundations of Welfare Economics," *Economic Journal,* 49 (1939), 698–701, 711–12.

sations under x than they are in state y, then x should be chosen in preference to y, *even if the compensation is not actually paid.* Apart from the ethical difficulties in the acceptance of this principle,[6] there is a formal difficulty which was pointed out by Scitovsky:[7] it is possible that simultaneously x should be preferred to y and y be preferred to x. Just as in the case of majority voting, this method of aggregating individual preferences may lead to a pattern of social choice which is not a linear ordering of the social alternatives. Note that in both cases the paradox need not occur; all that is said is that there are preference patterns which, if held by the individual members of the society, will give rise to an inconsistent pattern of social choice. Unless the trouble-breeding individual preference patterns can be ruled out by a priori assumption, both majority voting and the compensation principle must be regarded as unsatisfactory techniques for the determination of social preferences.

The aim of this chapter is to show that these difficulties are general. For *any* method of deriving social choices by aggregating individual preference patterns which satisfies certain natural conditions, it is possible to find individual preference patterns which give rise to a social choice pattern which is not a linear ordering. In particular, this is very likely to be the case if, as is frequently assumed, each individual's preferences among social states are derived purely from his personal consumption-leisure-saving situation in each.[8] It is assumed that individuals act rationally, in the sense that their behavior in alternative situations can be described by an indifference map. It is further assumed that utility is not measurable in any sense relevant to welfare economics, so that the tastes of an individual are completely described by a suitable preference pattern or indifference map.

Definitions and Notation

Preferences and Choice

In this chapter I shall be interested in the description of preference patterns both for the individual and for society. It will be convenient to represent

---

6. See W. J. Baumol, "Community Indifference," *Review of Economic Studies,* 14 (1946–47), 44–48.

7. T. Scitovsky, "A Note on Welfare Propositions in Economics," *Review of Economic Studies,* 9 (1942), 77–88.

8. See, for example, Samuelson, *Foundations of Economic Analysis,* pp. 222–24; Bergson, "Certain Aspects of Welfare Economics," pp. 318–20; Lange, "The Foundations of Welfare Economics," p. 216.

preference by a notation not customarily employed in economics, though familiar in mathematics and particularly in symbolic logic. We assume that there is a basic set of alternatives which could conceivably be presented to the chooser. In the theory of consumers' choice, each alternative would be a commodity bundle; in the theory of the firm, each alternative would be a complete decision on all inputs and outputs; in welfare economics, each alternative would be a distribution of commodities and labor requirements. These alternatives are mutually exclusive; they are denoted by small letters, *x, y, z* . . . On any given occasion the chooser has available to him a subset *S* of all possible alternatives, and he is required to choose one out of this set. The set *S* is a generalization of the well-known opportunity curve; thus, in the theory of consumer's choice under perfect competition, it would be the budget plane. It is assumed further that the choice is made in the following way.

Before knowing the set *S*, the chooser considers in turn all possible pairs of alternatives, say *x* and *y*, and for each pair he makes one and only one of three decisions: *x* is preferred to *y*, *x* is indifferent to *y*, or *y* is preferred to *x*. The decisions made for different pairs are assumed to be consistent with one another, so that, for example, if *x* is preferred to *y* and *y* to *z*, then *x* is preferred to *z*; similarly, if *x* is indifferent to *y* and *y* to *z*, then *x* is indifferent to *z*. Having this ordering of all possible alternatives, the chooser is now confronted with a particular opportunity set *S*. If there is one alternative in *S* which is preferred to all others in *S*, then the chooser selects that one alternative.[9]

Preference and indifference are relations between alternatives. Instead of working with two relations, I find it more convenient to use a single relation, "preferred or indifferent." The statement, "*x* is preferred or indifferent to *y*," will be symbolized by *xRy*. The letter *R*, by itself, will be the name of the relation and will stand for a knowledge of all pairs such that *xRy*. From our previous discussion we have, for any pair of alternatives *x* and *y*, either that *x* is preferred to *y* or *y* to *x* or that the two are indifferent. That is, we have

---

9. It may be that there is a subset of alternatives in *S*, such that the alternatives in the subset are each preferred to every alternative not in the subset, while the alternatives in the subset are indifferent to one another. This case would be one in which the highest indifference curve which has a point in common with a given opportunity curve has at least two points in common with it (the well-known case of multiple maxima). In this case, the best thing to say is that the choice made in *S* is the whole subset; the case discussed in the text is one in which the subset in question, the choice, contains a single element.

assumed that any two alternatives are comparable. But this assumption may be written symbolically,

AXIOM 1. *For all x and y, either xRy or yRx.*

Note that Axiom 1 is presumed to hold when $x = y$, as well as when x is distinct from y, for we ordinarily say that x is indifferent to itself for any x, and this implies xRx. Note also that the word "or" in the statement of Axiom 1 does not exclude the possibility of both xRy and yRx. That word merely asserts that at least one of the two events must occur; both may.

The property mentioned above of consistency in the preferences as between different pairs of alternatives may be stated more precisely as follows: if x is preferred or indifferent to y and y is preferred or indifferent to z, then x must be either preferred or indifferent to z. In symbols:

AXIOM 2. *For all x, y, and z, xRy and yRz imply xRz.*

A relation satisfying both Axiom 1 and Axiom 2 is termed a weak ordering, or sometimes simply an ordering. It is clear that a relation having these two properties taken together does create a ranking of the various alternatives. The adjective "weak" refers to the fact that the ordering does not exclude indifference; that is, Axioms 1 and 2 do not exclude the possibility that for some distinct x and y, both xRy and yRx.

It might be held that the two axioms in question do not completely characterize the concept of a preference pattern. For example, we ordinarily feel that not only the relation R but also the relations of (strict) preference and of indifference satisfy Axiom 2. It can be shown that by defining preference and indifference suitably in terms of R, it will follow that all the usually desired properties of preference patterns obtain.

DEFINITION 1. *xPy is defined to mean not yRx.*

The statement *"xPy"* is read "x is preferred to y."

DEFINITION 2. *xIy means xRy and yRx.*

The statement *"xIy"* is read "x is indifferent to y." It is clear that P and I, so defined, correspond to the ordinary notions of preference and indifference, respectively.

LEMMA. *(a) For all x, xRx,*
   (b) If xPy, then xRy.
   (c) If xPy and yPz, then xPz.

(d) If xIy and yIz, then xIz.
(e) For all x and y, either xRy or yPx.
(f) If xPy and yRz, then xPz.

All these statements are intuitively self-evident from the interpretations placed on the symbols.

For clarity, we shall avoid the use of the terms "preference scale" or "preference pattern" when referring to R, since we wish to avoid confusion with the concept of preference proper, denoted by P. We shall refer to R as an "ordering relation" or "weak ordering relation" or, more simply, as an "ordering" or "weak ordering." The term "preference relation" will refer to the relation P.

Suppose that we know the choice which would be made from any given pair of alternatives; that is, given two alternatives x and y from which the chooser must select, we know whether he would take x or y or remain indifferent between them. Since choosing x from the pair x, y implies that x is preferred to y, and similarly with a choice of y, a knowledge of the choice which would be made from any two given alternatives implies a knowledge of the full preference scale; from earlier remarks, this in turn implies a knowledge of the choice which would be made from any set of alternatives actually available. Hence, one of the consequences of the assumption of rational behavior is that the choice from any collection of alternatives can be determined by a knowledge of the choices which would be made from pairs of alternatives.

The Ordering of Social States

In the present study the objects of choice are social states. The most precise definition of a social state would be a complete description of the amount of each type of commodity in the hands of each individual, the amount of labor to be applied by each individual, the amount of each productive resource invested in each type of productive activity, and the amounts of various types of collective activity (such as municipal services, diplomacy and its continuation by other means, and the erection of statues to famous men). It is assumed that each individual in the community has a definite ordering of all conceivable social states in terms of their desirability to him. It need not be assumed here that an individual's attitude toward different social states is determined exclusively by the commodity bundles which accrue to his lot under each. The individual may order all social states by whatever standards he deems relevant. A member of Veblen's leisure class might order the states solely on the criterion of his relative income standing in each; a believer in the equality of man might order them in accordance with some measure of income equality. Indeed, since, as mentioned above, some of the components of the social state, considered as a vector, are collective activities, purely individualistic assumptions are useless in analyzing such problems as the division of the national income between public and private expenditure. The present notation permits perfect generality in this respect. Needless to say, this generality is not without its price. More information would be available for analysis if the generality were restricted by a prior knowledge of the nature of individual orderings of social states. This problem will be touched on again.

In general, then, there will be a difference between the ordering of social states according to the direct consumption of the individual and the ordering when the individual adds his general standards of equity (or perhaps his standards of pecuniary emulation).[10] We may refer to the former ordering as reflecting the *tastes* of the individual and the latter as reflecting his *values.* The distinction between the two is by no means clear-cut. An individual with aesthetic feelings certainly derives pleasure from his neighbor's having a well-tended lawn. Under the system of a free market, such feelings play no direct part in social choice; yet, psychologically, they differ only slightly from the pleasure in one's own lawn. Intuitively, of course, we feel that not all the possible preferences which an individual might have ought to count; his preferences for matters which are "none of his business" should be irrelevant. Without challenging this view, I should like to emphasize that the decision as to which preferences are relevant and which are not is itself a value judgment and cannot be settled on an a priori basis. From a formal point of view, one cannot distinguish between an individual's dislike of having his grounds ruined by factory smoke and his extreme distaste for the existence of heathenism in Central Africa. There are probably not a few individuals in this country who would regard the former feeling as irrelevant for social policy and the latter as relevant, though the majority would probably reverse the judgement. I merely wish to emphasize here that we must look at the entire system of values, including values about values, in seeking for a truly general theory of social welfare.

It is the ordering according to values which takes into account all the

---

10. This distinction has been stressed to me by M. Friedman, University of Chicago.

desires of the individual, including the highly important socializing desires, and which is primarily relevant for the achievement of a social maximum. The market mechanism, however, takes into account only the ordering according to tastes. This distinction is the analogue, on the side of consumption, of the divergence between social and private costs in production which has been developed by Pigou.[11]

As for notation, let R_i be the ordering relation for alternative social states from the standpoint of individual i. Sometimes, when several different ordering relations are being considered for the same individual, the symbols will be distinguished by adding a superscript. Corresponding to the ordering relation R_i, we have the (strict) preference relation P_i and the indifference relation I_i. If the symbol for the ordering has a prime or second attached (R_i', R_i''), then the corresponding symbols for preference and indifference will have the prime or second attached also.

Similarly, society as a whole will be considered provisionally to have a social ordering relation for alternative social states, which will be designated by R, sometimes with a prime or second. Social preference and indifference will be denoted by P and I, respectively, primes or seconds being attached when they are attached to the relation R.

Throughout this analysis it will be assumed that individuals are rational, by which is meant that the ordering relations R_i satisfy Axioms 1 and 2. The problem will be to construct an ordering relation for society as a whole which is also to reflect rational choice making, so that R also will be assumed to satisfy Axioms 1 and 2.

The Social Welfare Function

Formal Statement of the Problem of Social Choice

I shall largely restate Bergson's formulation of the problem of making welfare judgments[12] in the terminology here adopted. The various arguments of his social welfare function are the components of what I have here termed the "social state," so that essentially he is describing the process of

---

11. A. C. Pigou, *The Economics of Welfare* (London: Macmillan & Co., 1920), pt. 2, chap. 6. For the analogy see Samuelson, *Foundations of Economic Analysis,* p. 224; Reder, *Theory of Welfare Economics,* pp. 64–67; G. Tintner, "A Note on Welfare Economics," *Econometrica,* 14 (1946), 69–78.

12. Bergson, "Certain Aspects of Welfare Economics."

assigning a numerical social utility to each social state, the aim of society then being described by saying it seeks to maximize the social utility or social welfare subject to whatever technological or resource constraints are relevant — or, put otherwise, it chooses the social state yielding the highest possible social welfare within the environment. As with any type of behavior described by maximization, the measurability of social welfare need not be assumed; all that matters is the existence of a social ordering satisfying Axioms 1 and 2. As before, all that is needed to define such an ordering is to know the relative ranking of each pair of alternatives.

The relative ranking of a fixed pair of alternative social states will vary, in general, with changes in the values of at least some individuals; to assume that the ranking does not change with any changes in individual values is to assume, with traditional social philosophy of the Platonic realist variety, that there exists an objective social good defined independently of individual desires. This social good, it was frequently held, could be best apprehended by the methods of philosophic inquiry. Such a philosophy could be and was used to justify government by elite, secular or religious, although the connection is not a necessary one.

To the nominalist temperament of the modern period the assumption of the existence of the social ideal in some Platonic realm of being was meaningless. The utilitarian philosophy of Jeremy Bentham and his followers sought instead to ground the social good on the good of individuals. The hedonist psychology associated with utilitarian philosophy was further used to imply that each individual's good was identical with his desires. Hence, the social good was in some sense to be a composite of the desires of individuals. A viewpoint of this type serves as a justification of both political democracy and laissez-faire economics, or at least an economic system involving free choice of goods by consumers and of occupations by workers.

The hedonist psychology finds its expression here in the assumption that individuals' behavior is expressed by individual ordering relations R_i. Utilitarian philosophy is expressed by saying for each pair of social states that the choice depends on the ordering relations of all individuals, that is, depends on $R_1, \ldots, R_n$, where n is the number of individuals in the community. Put otherwise, the whole social ordering relation R is to be determined by the individual ordering relations for social states, $R_1, \ldots, R_n$. We do not exclude here the possibility that some or all of the choices between pairs of social states made by society might be independent of the preferences of certain particular individuals, just as a function of several variables might be independent of some of them.

DEFINITION 3. *By a "social welfare function" will be meant a process or rule which, for each set of individual orderings $R_1, \ldots, R_n$ for alternative social states (one ordering for each individual), states a corresponding social ordering of alternative social states, R.*

As a matter of notation, we shall let R be the social ordering corresponding to the set of individual orderings $R_1, \ldots, R_n$, the correspondence being that established by a given social welfare function; if primes or seconds are added to the symbols for the individual orderings, primes or seconds will be added to the symbol for the corresponding social ordering.

There is some difference between the concept of social welfare function used here and that employed by Bergson. The individual orderings which enter as arguments into the social welfare function as defined here refer to the values of individuals rather than to their tastes. Bergson supposes individual values to be such as to yield a social value judgment leading to a particular rule for determining the allocation of productive resources and the distribution of leisure and final products in accordance with individual tastes. In effect, the social welfare function described here is a method of choosing which social welfare function of the Bergson type will be applicable, though of course I do not exclude the possibility that the social choice actually arrived at will not be consistent with the particular value judgments formulated by Bergson. But in the formal aspect the difference between the two definitions of social welfare function is not too important. In Bergson's treatment the tastes of individuals (each for his own consumption) are represented by utility functions, that is, essentially by ordering relations; hence, the Bergson social welfare function is also a rule for assigning to each set of individual orderings a social ordering of social states. Further, as already indicated, no sharp line can be drawn between tastes and values.

A special type of social welfare function would be one which assigns the same social ordering for every set of individual orderings. In this case, of course, social choices are completely independent of individual tastes, and we are back in the Platonic case.

For simplicity of exposition, it will be assumed that the society under study contains only two individuals and that the total number of conceivable alternatives is three. Since the results to be obtained are negative, the latter restriction is not a real one; if it turns out to be impossible to construct a social welfare function which will define a social ordering of three alternatives, it will a fortiori be impossible to define one which will order more alternatives. The restriction to two individuals may be more serious; it is conceivable that there may be suitable social welfare functions which can be defined for three individuals but not for two, for example. In fact, this is not so, and the results stated in this chapter hold for any number of individuals. However, the proof will be considerably simplified by considering only two.

We shall not ask, in general, that the social welfare function be defined for every logically possible set of individual orderings. On a priori grounds we may suppose it known that preferences for alternative social states are formed only in a limited set of ways, and the social welfare function need only be defined for individual orderings formed in those ways. For example, we may suppose (and later on will suppose) that each individual orders social alternatives according to his own personal consumption under each (the purely individualistic case). Then the social welfare function need be defined only for those sets of individual orderings which are admissible, in the sense of being consistent with our a priori assumptions about the empirical possibilities.

CONDITION 1. *The social welfare function is defined for every admissible pair of individual orderings, R_1, R_2.*

Condition 1, it should be emphasized, is a restriction on the form of the social welfare function, since we are requiring that for some sufficiently wide range of sets of individual orderings, the social welfare function give rise to a true social ordering.

Positive Association of Social and Individual Values

Since we are trying to describe social "welfare" and not some sort of "illfare," we must assume that the social welfare function is such that the social ordering responds positively to alterations in individual values — or at least not negatively. Hence, we may state the following condition:

CONDITION 2. *If an alternative social state x rises or does not fall in the ordering of each individual without any other change in those orderings and if x was preferred to another alternative y before the change in individual orderings, then x is still preferred to y.*

The Independence of Irrelevant Alternatives

Just as for a single individual, the choice made by society from any given set of alternatives should be independent of the very existence of alternatives outside the given set. For example, suppose an election system has been devised whereby each individual lists all the candidates in order of his preference, and then, by a preassigned procedure, the winning candidate is derived from these lists. (All actual election procedures are of this type, although in most the entire list is not required for the choice.) Suppose an election is held with a certain number of candidates in the field, each individual filing his list of preferences, and then one of the candidates dies. Surely, the social choice should be made by taking each of the individual's preference lists, blotting out completely the dead candidate's name, and considering only the orderings of the remaining names in going through the procedure of determining the winner. That is, the choice to be made among the set of surviving candidates should be independent of the preferences of individuals for the nonsurviving candidates. To assume otherwise would be to make the result of the election dependent on the obviously accidental circumstance of whether a candidate died before or after the date of polling. Therefore, we may require of our social welfare function that the choice made by society from a given set of alternatives depend only on the orderings of individuals among those alternatives. Alternatively stated, if we consider two sets of individual orderings such that, for each individual, his ordering of those particular alternatives under consideration is the same each time, then we require that the choice made by society be the same if individual values are given by the first set of orderings as if they are given by the second.

CONDITION 3 *(independence of irrelevant alternatives). Let R_1, R_2, and R_1', R_2' be two sets of individual orderings. If, for both individuals i and for all x and y in a given set of alternatives S, xR_iy if and only if $xR_i'y$, then the social choice made from S is the same whether the individual orderings are R_1, R_2, or R_1', R_2'.*

The reasonableness of this condition can be seen by consideration of the possible results in a method of choice which does not satisfy Condition 3, the rank-order method of voting frequently used in clubs.[13] With a finite number of candidates, let each individual rank all his candidates, that is, designate his first-choice candidate, second-choice candidate, and so on. Let preassigned weights be given first, second, and additional choices, the higher

---

13. This example was suggested by a discussion with G. E. Forsythe, National Bureau of Standards.

weight to the higher choice, and then let the candidate with the highest weighted sum of votes be elected. In particular, suppose there are three voters and four candidates, x, y, z, and w. Let the weights for first, second, third, and fourth choices be 4, 3, 2, and 1, respectively. Suppose that individuals 1 and 2 rank the candidates in the order x, y, z, and w, while individual 3 ranks them in the order z, w, x, and y. Under the given electoral system, x is chosen. Then, certainly, if y is deleted from the ranks of the candidates, the system applied to the remaining candidates should yield the same result, especially since, in this case, y is inferior to x according to the tastes of every individual; but, if y is in fact deleted, the indicated electoral system would yield a tie between x and z.

The condition of the independence of irrelevant alternatives implies that in a generalized sense all methods of social choice are of the type of voting. If S is the set consisting of the two alternatives x and y, Condition 3 tells us that the choice between x and y is determined solely by the preferences of the members of the community as between x and y. That is, if we know which members of the community prefer x to y, which are indifferent, and which prefer y to x, then we know what choice the community makes. Knowing the social choices made in pairwise comparisons in turn determines the entire social ordering and therewith the social choice made from any set of alternatives. Condition 2 guarantees that voting for a certain alternative has the usual effect of making surer that that alternative will be adopted.

Condition 1 says, in effect, that as the set of alternatives varies and individual orderings remain fixed, the different choices made shall bear a certain type of consistent relation to one another. Conditions 2 and 3, on the other hand, suppose a fixed set of alternatives and say that for certain particular types of variation in individual values, the various choices made have a certain type of consistency.

The Condition of Citizens' Sovereignty

We wish to assume that the individuals in our society are free to choose, by varying their values, among the alternatives available. That is, we do not wish our social welfare function to be such as to prevent us, by its very definition, from expressing a preference for some given alternative over another.

DEFINITION 4. *A social welfare function will be said to be imposed if for some pair of distinct alternatives x and y, xRy for any set of individual orderings R_1, R_2, where R is the social ordering corresponding to R_1, R_2.*

In other words, when the social welfare function is imposed, there is some pair of alternatives x and y such that the community can never express a preference for y over x no matter what the tastes of both individuals are, indeed even if both individuals prefer y to x; some preferences are taboo. (Note that, by Definition 1, asserting that xRy holds for all sets of individual orderings is equivalent to asserting that yPx never holds.) We certainly wish to require of our social welfare function the condition that it not be imposed in the sense of Definition 4; we wish all choices to be possible if unanimously desired by the group.

CONDITION 4. *The social welfare function is not to be imposed.*

Condition 4 is stronger than need be for the present argument. Some decisions, as between given pairs of alternatives, may be assumed to be imposed. All that is required really is that there be a set S of three alternatives such that the choice between any pair is not constrained in advance by the social welfare function.

It should also be noted that Condition 4 excludes the Platonic case discussed above. It expresses fully the idea that all social choices are determined by individual desires. In conjunction with Condition 2 (which ensures that the determination is in the direction of agreeing with individual desires), Condition 4 expresses the same idea as Bergson's Fundamental Value Propositions of Individual Preference, which state that of two alternatives between which all individuals but one are indifferent, the community will prefer one over the other or be indifferent between the two according as the one individual prefers one over the other or is indifferent between the two.[14] Conditions 2 and 4 together correspond to the usual concept of consumers' sovereignty; since we are here considering values rather than tastes, we might refer to them as expressing the idea of citizens' sovereignty.

The Condition of Nondictatorship

A second form of social choice not of a collective character is the choice by dictatorship. In its pure form this means that social choices are to be based

---

14. Bergson, "Certain Aspects of Welfare Economics," pp. 318–20. His Fundamental Value Propositions of Individual Preference are not, strictly speaking, implied by Conditions 2 and 4 (in conjunction with Conditions 1 and 3), although something very similar to them is so implied; see Consequence 1 below. A slightly stronger form of Condition 2 than that stated here would suffice to yield the desired implication.

solely on the preferences of one man. That is, whenever the dictator prefers x to y, so does society. If the dictator is indifferent between x and y, presumably he will then leave the choice up to some or all of the other members of society.

DEFINITION 5. *A social welfare function is said to be "dictatorial" if there exists an individual i such that for all x and y, xP_iy implies xPy regardless of the orderings of all individuals other than i, where P is the social preference relation corresponding to those orderings.*

Since we are interested in the construction of collective methods of social choice, we wish to exclude dictatorial social welfare functions.

CONDITION 5 *(nondictatorship). The social welfare function is not to be dictatorial.*

We have now imposed five apparently reasonable conditions on the construction of a social welfare function. These conditions are of course value judgments and could be called into question; taken together, they express the doctrines of citizens' sovereignty and rationality in a very general form, with the citizens being allowed to have a wide range of values. The question is that of constructing a social ordering of all conceivable alternative social states from any given set of individual orderings of those social states, the method of construction being in accordance with the value judgments of citizens' sovereignty and rationality as expressed in Conditions 1–5.

The Possibility Theorem for Social Welfare Functions

The Range of Possible Individual Orderings

For simplicity we shall impose on the individual preference scales two conditions which in fact have almost invariably been assumed in works on welfare economics: (1) each individual's comparison of two alternative social states depends only on the commodities he receives (and labor he expends) in the two states, that is, he is indifferent as between any two social states in which his own consumption-leisure-saving situations are the same or at least indifferent to him; (2) in comparing two personal situations in one of which he receives at least as much of each commodity (including leisure and saving as commodities) and more of at least one commodity than in the other, the individual will prefer the first situation. Suppose that among the possible alternatives there were three, none of which gave any individual at least as much of both commodities as any other. For example, suppose that there are two individuals and a total of ten units of each of two commodities. Consider three alternative distributions described by the following tabulation:

	Individual 1		Individual 2	
Alternative	Commodity 1	Commodity 2	Commodity 1	Commodity 2
1	5	1	5	9
2	4	2	6	8
3	3	3	7	7

The individualistic restrictions imposed do not tell us anything about the way either individual orders these alternatives. Under the individualistic assumptions there is no a priori reason to suppose that the two individuals will not order the alternatives in any given way. In the sense of our discussion earlier, all individual orderings of the three alternatives are admissible. Condition 1 therefore requires that the social welfare function be defined for all pairs of individual orderings, R_1, R_2.

The Possibility Theorem

Some consequences will be drawn from Conditions 1–5 for the present case of a social welfare function for two individuals and three alternatives. It will be shown that the supposition that there is a social welfare function satisfying those conditions leads to a contradiction.

Let x, y, and z be the three alternatives among which choice is to be made, for example, three possible distributions of commodities. Let x' and y' be variable symbols which represent possible alternatives (in other words, range over the values x, y, z). Let the individuals be designated as 1 and 2, and let R_1 and R_2 be the orderings by 1 and 2, respectively, of the alternatives x, y, z. Let P_1 and P_2 be the corresponding preference relations, so that, for instance, $x'P_1y'$ means that individual 1 strictly prefers x' to y'.

CONSEQUENCE 1. *If $x'P_1y'$ and $x'P_2y'$, then $x'Py'$.*

Another way of saying this is that if both prefer x' to y', then society must prefer x' to y'.

Proof. By Condition 4 there are orderings R_1' and R_2', for individuals 1 and 2, respectively, such that in the corresponding social preference $x'P'y'$. Form R_1'' from R_1' by raising x', if need be, to the top, while leaving the relative positions of the other two alternatives alone; form R_2'' from R_2' in the same way. Since all we have done is raise alternative x' in everyone's esteem while leaving the others alone, x' should still be preferred to y' by society in accordance with Condition 2, so that $x'P''y'$. But, by construction, both individuals prefer x' to y' in the orderings R_1'', R_2'', and society prefers x' to y'. Since, by Condition 3, the social choice between x' and y' depends only on the individual orderings of those two alternatives, it follows that whenever both individuals prefer x' to y', regardless of the rank of the third alternative, society will prefer x' to y', which is the statement to be proved.

CONSEQUENCE 2. *Suppose that for some x' and y', whenever $x'P_1y'$ and $y'P_2x'$, $x'Py'$. Then, for that x' and y', whenever $x'P_1y'$, $x'Py'$.*

That is to say, if in a given choice the will of individual 1 prevails against the opposition of 2, then individual 1's views will certainly prevail if 2 is indifferent or if he agrees with 1.

Proof. Let R_1 be an ordering in which $x'P_1y'$, and let R_2 be any ordering. Let R_1' be the same ordering as R_1, while R_2' is derived from R_2 by depressing x' to the bottom while leaving the relative positions of the other two alternatives unchanged. By construction, $x'P_1'y'$, $y'P_2'x'$. By hypothesis, $x'P'y'$, where P' is the social preference relation derived from the individual orderings R_1', R_2'. Now the only difference between R_1', R_2' and R_1, R_2 is that x' is raised in the scale of individual 2 in the latter as compared with the former. Hence, by Condition 2 (interchanging the R_i's and the R_i''s) it follows from $x'P'y'$ that $x'Py'$. In other words, whenever R_1, R_2 are such that $x'P_1y'$, then $x'Py'$.

CONSEQUENCE 3. *If $x'P_1y'$ and $y'P_2x'$, then $x'Iy'$.*

That is, if the two individuals have exactly opposing interests on the choice between two given alternatives, then society will be indifferent between the alternatives.

Proof. Suppose the consequence is false. Then, for some orderings R_1 and R_2 and for some pair of alternatives x' and y', we would have $x'P_1y'$, $y'P_2x'$, but not $x'Iy'$. In that case, either $x'Py'$ or $y'Px'$. We will suppose $x'Py'$ and show that this supposition leads to a contradiction; the same reasoning would show that the assumption $y'Px'$ also leads to a contradiction.

Without loss of generality it can be assumed that x' is the alternative x, $y' = y$. Then we have, for the particular orderings in question, xP_1y, yP_2x, and xPy. Since the social choice between x and y depends, by Condition 3, only on the individual choices between x and y, we must have

(1-1)   whenever xP_1y and yP_2x, xPy.

It will be shown that (1-1) leads to a contradiction.

Suppose individual 1 prefers x to y and y to z, while individual 2 prefers y to z and z to x. Individual 2 then prefers y to x. By (1-1) society prefers x to y. Also, both prefer y to z; by Consequence 1, society prefers y to z. Since society prefers x to y and y to z, it must prefer x to z. Therefore, we have exhibited orderings R_1, R_2 such that xP_1z, zP_2x, but xPz. Since the social choice between x and z depends only on the individual preferences for x and z,

(1-2)   whenever xP_1z and zP_2x, xPz.

Now suppose R_1 is the ordering y, x, z, and R_2 the ordering z, y, x. By Consequence 1, yPx; by (1-2) xPz, so that yPz. By the same reasoning as before,

(1-3)   whenever yP_1z and zP_2y, yPz.

If R_1 is the ordering y, z, x, and R_2 the ordering z, x, y, it follows from Consequence 1 and (1-3) that zPx and yPz, so that yPx. Hence,

(1-4)   whenever yP_1x and xP_2y, yPx.

If R_1 is the ordering z, y, x, and R_2 the ordering x, z, y, then from Consequence 1 and (1-4), zPy and yPx, so that zPx.

(1-5)   Whenever zP_1x and xP_2z, zPx.

If R_1 is the ordering z, x, y, and R_2 is x, y, z, then, using (1-5), zPx and xPy, so that zPy.

(1-6)   Whenever zP_1y and yP_2z, zPy.

From (1-1) it follows from Consequence 2 that whenever xP_1y, xPy. Similarly, from (1-1) to (1-6) it follows that for any pair of alternatives x', y', whenever $x'P_1y'$, then $x'Py'$. That is, by Definition 5, individual 1 would be a dictator. This is prohibited by Condition 5, so (1-1) must be false. Therefore, Consequence 3 is proved.

Now suppose individual 1 has the ordering x, y, z, while individual 2 has the ordering z, x, y. By Consequence 1,

(1-7) xPy.

Since yP_1z, zP_2y, it follows from Consequence 3 that

(1-8) yIz.

From (1-7) and (1-8), xPz. But also xP_1z, zP_2x, which implies xIz by Consequence 3. It cannot be that x is both preferred and indifferent to z. Hence the assumption that there is a social welfare function compatible with Conditions 1–5 has led to a contradiction.

Put another way, if we assume that our social welfare function satisfies Conditions 2 and 3 and we further suppose that Condition 1 holds, then either Condition 4 or Condition 5 must be violated. Condition 4 states that the social welfare function is not imposed; Condition 5 states that it is not dictatorial.

POSSIBILITY THEOREM. *If there are at least three alternatives which the members of the society are free to order in any way, then every social welfare function satisfying Conditions 2 and 3 and yielding a social ordering satisfying Axioms 1 and 2 must be either imposed or dictatorial.*[15]

The Possibility Theorem shows that if no prior assumptions are made about the nature of individual orderings, there is no method of voting which will remove the paradox of voting discussed earlier, neither plurality voting nor any scheme of proportional representation, no matter how complicated. Similarly, the market mechanism does not create a rational social choice.

Some Implications for the Formation of Social Welfare Judgments

Interpretation of the Possibility Theorem

Interpretation of the Possibility Theorem is given by examination of the meaning of Conditions 1–5. In particular, it is required that the social ordering be formed from individual orderings and that the social decision

---

15. The negative outcome expressed in this theorem is strongly reminiscent of the intransitivity of the concept of domination in the theory of multiperson games; see John von Neumann and Oskar Morgenstern, *Theory of Games and Economic Behavior* (2nd ed.; Princeton University Press, 1947), pp. 38–39.

between two alternatives be independent of the desires of individuals involving any alternatives other than the given two (Conditions 1 and 3). These conditions taken together serve to exclude interpersonal comparison of social utility either by some form of direct measurement or by comparison with other alternative social states. Therefore, the Possibility Theorem can be restated as follows:

If we exclude the possibility of interpersonal comparisons of utility, then the only methods of passing from individual tastes to social preferences which will be satisfactory and which will be defined for a wide range of sets of individual orderings are either imposed or dictatorial.

The word "satisfactory" in the foregoing statement means that the social welfare function does not reflect individuals' desires negatively (Condition 2) and that the resultant social tastes shall be represented by an ordering having the usual properties of rationality ascribed to individual orderings (Condition 1 and Axioms 1 and 2).

In view of the interpretations we have placed on the conditions for a social welfare function, we can also phrase the result this way: If consumers' values can be represented by a wide range of individual orderings, the doctrine of voters' sovereignty is incompatible with that of collective rationality.

If we wish to make social welfare judgments which depend on all individual values (that is, are not imposed or dictatorial), then we must relax some of our conditions. It will continue to be maintained that there is no meaningful interpersonal comparison of utilities and that the conditions implied by the word "satisfactory" are to be accepted.[16] The only condition that remains to be eliminated is the one stating that the method of forming a social ordering would work properly for a wide range of sets of individual orderings. That is, it must be supposed that it is known in advance that the individual orderings $R_1, \ldots, R_n$ for social actions satisfy certain conditions more restrictive than those hitherto introduced.

A Reflection on the New Welfare Economics

The so-called new welfare economics has concentrated on determination of the totality of social states which have the property that any change which

---

16. The only part of the last-named conditions that seems to me to be at all in dispute is the assumption of rationality. The consequences of dropping this assumption are so radical that it seems worthwhile to explore the consequences of maintaining it.

benefits one individual injures another—"maximal states," in Lange's terminology. In particular, this problem has usually been analyzed under the assumption that individual desires for social alternatives are formed in the individualistic way we have previously considered. But if the only restrictions we wish to impose on individual tastes are those implied by the individualistic assumptions, then, as we have seen, no satisfactory social welfare function is possible when there is more than one commodity. Since the only purpose of the determination of the maximal states is as a preliminary to the study of social welfare functions, the customary study of maximal states under individualistic assumptions is pointless. There is, however, a qualification which should be added. It is conceivable that if further restrictions are added to the individualistic ones, a social welfare function will be possible. Any state which is maximal under the combination of individualistic and other restrictions will certainly be maximal if only individualistic restrictions are imposed on the individual orderings. Hence, if the proper handling of the social welfare problem is deemed to be the imposition of further restrictions in addition to the individualistic ones, then the social maximum in any given situation will be one of the maximal elements under the combined restrictions and hence one of the maximal elements under individualistic conditions. It is therefore not excluded that the current new welfare economics will be of some use in restricting the range in which we must look for the social maximum.

The failure of purely individualistic assumptions to lead to a well-defined social welfare function means, in effect, that there must be a divergence between social and private benefits if we are to be able to discuss a social optimum. Part of each individual's value system must be a scheme of socioethical norms, the realization of which cannot, by their nature, be achieved through atomistic market behavior. These norms, further, must be sufficiently similar among the members of the society to avoid the difficulties outlined above.

A One-Commodity World

The insufficiency of the individualistic hypotheses to permit the formation of a social welfare function has hinged on the assumption that there was more than one commodity involved. An investigation of the one-commodity case may be of interest to bring out more clearly the issues involved.

In a one-commodity world, if we make the same two assumptions as when we began our discussion of the Possibility Theorem, there is for any given individual only one possible ordering of the social states. He orders various social states solely according to the amount of the one commodity he gets under each. In such a situation the individual orderings are not variables; Conditions 2, 3, and 4 become irrelevant, since they relate to the variation in the social ordering corresponding to certain specified types of changes in the individual orderings. Condition 5 (nondictatorship) becomes a much weaker restriction, though not completely irrelevant. Any specification of a social ordering which does not coincide completely with the ordering of any one individual will be a social welfare function compatible with all the conditions.

For example, for each fixed total output we might set up arbitrarily an ordering of the various distributions, then order any two social states with different total outputs in accordance with the total output and any two social states with the same total output according to the arbitrary ordering. This sets up a genuine weak ordering which does not coincide with the ordering of any one individual. For let x and y be two states with total outputs s and t, respectively, and apportionments s' and t', respectively, to the given individual. If $s > t$, but $s' < t'$, then society prefers x to y, while the individual prefers y to x.

The qualitative nature of the difference between the single- and multi-commodity cases makes any welfare arguments based on implicit assumption of a single commodity dubious in its applicability to real situations. The fundamental difficulty is that in a world of more than one commodity, there is no unequivocal meaning to comparing total production in any two social states save in terms of some standard of value to make the different commodities commensurable; and usually such a standard of value must depend on the distribution of income. In other words, there is no meaning to total output independent of distribution, that is, of ethical judgments.

Distributional Ethics Combined with Individualism

We may examine briefly a set of assumptions about individual values which seem to be common to those who feel that the new welfare economics is applicable in a fairly direct way to the solution of specific economic problems. It is assumed that there are (1) an accepted (let us say, unanimously accepted) value judgment that if everybody is better off (more precisely, if everybody is at least as well off and one person better off) in one social state than another *according to his tastes,* then the first social state is preferred to the second; and (2) a universally accepted ordering of different possible welfare distributions in any given situation. The latter value judgment usually takes an egalitarian form.

This ethical schema is quite explicit in the work of Bergson; the second value judgment is contained in his Propositions of Relative Shares.[17] The same set of ethics underlies the compensation principle of Kaldor and Hicks. Subsequent proposals made by Johnson and Modigliani for meeting the problem of the increased cost of food due to European demand seem to have been based on value judgments (1) and (2) above.[18] To prevent the inequitable shift in real income to farmers, it was proposed that an excise tax should be imposed on food, accompanied by a per capita subsidy to consumers. Under the assumption that the supply of agricultural goods is completely inelastic, the tax would be absorbed by the farmers while the subsidy would have no substitution effects at the margin, so that the marginal rate of substitution for any pair of commodities would be the same for all consumers and hence the first value judgment would be fulfilled. The taxes and subsidies perform a purely distributive function and can be so arranged as to restore the status quo ante as near as may be, though actually the payment of a per capita subsidy implies a certain equalizing effect.

The value judgments are assumed here to hold for any individual. Note that even to state these judgments we must distinguish sharply between values and tastes. All individuals are assumed to have the same values at any given instant of time, but the values held by any one individual will vary with variations in the tastes of all. Our previous arguments as to the nonexistence of social welfare functions were based on the diversity of values; do they carry over to this particular kind of unanimity?

The actual distribution of welfare dictated by the second value judgment cannot be stated simply in money terms. As Samuelson points out, such a value judgment is not consistent with any well-defined social ordering of alternative social states.[19] The distribution of real income, for a given environment, must vary with individual tastes. Thus, for a given set of individual tastes (as represented by the ordering relations of all individuals, each for his own consumption) and a given environment, there is a given distribution of purchasing power (somehow defined); then exchange under

17. Bergson, "Certain Aspects of Welfare Economics."

18. D. G. Johnson, "The High Cost of Food—A Suggested Solution," *Journal of Political Economy,* 56 (1948), 54–57; Modigliani's proposals are contained in a press release of the Institute of World Affairs, New York, October 1948.

19. Samuelson, *Foundations of Economic Analysis,* p. 225.

perfectly competitive conditions proceeds until an optimum distribution is reached. The given distribution of real income and the individual tastes uniquely determine the final outcome, which is a social state. Therefore, the given ethical system is a rule which selects a social state as the choice from a given collection of alternative distributions of goods as a function of the tastes of all individuals. If, for a given set of tastes, the range of social alternatives varies, we expect that the choices will be consistent in the sense that the choice function is derivable from a social weak ordering of all social states.

Thus, the ethical scheme discussed in this section, which we may term the *Bergson social welfare function,* has the form of a rule assigning a social ordering to each possible set of individual orderings representing tastes. Mathematically, the Bergson social welfare function has, then, the same form as the social welfare function we have already discussed; though, of course, the interpretation is somewhat different, in that the individual orderings represent tastes rather than values and in that the whole function is the end product of certain values assumed to be unanimously held rather than a method of reconciling divergent value systems. If the range of tastes is not restricted by a priori considerations (except that they must be truly tastes in that they refer only to an individual's own consumption, however that may be defined), then indeed, the Bergson social welfare function is mathematically isomorphic to the social welfare function under individualistic assumptions. Hence the Possibility Theorem is applicable here; we cannot construct a Bergson social welfare function (we cannot satisfy value judgments 1 and 2) which will satisfy Conditions 2–5 and which will yield a true social ordering for every set of individual tastes. Essentially, the two value judgments amount to erecting individualistic behavior into a value judgment. It is not surprising, then, that such ethics can be no more successful than the actual practice of individualism in permitting the formation of social welfare judgments.

It must of course be recognized that the meaning of Conditions 2–5 has changed. The previous arguments for their validity assumed that the individual orderings represented values rather than tastes. It seems obvious that Conditions 2, 4, and 5 have the same intrinsic desirability under either interpretation. Condition 3 is perhaps more doubtful. Suppose there are just two commodities, bread and wine. A distribution deemed equitable by all is arranged, with the wine lovers getting more wine and less bread than the abstainers get. Suppose now that all the wine is destroyed. Are the wine lovers entitled, because of that fact, to more than an equal share of bread?

The answer is, of course, a value judgment. My own feeling is that tastes for unattainable alternatives should have nothing to do with the decision among the attainable ones; desires in conflict with reality are not entitled to consideration; so that Condition 3, reinterpreted in terms of tastes rather than of values, is a valid value judgment — to me at least.

References for Headnote

Arrow, K. J. *Social Choice and Individual Values.* Cowles Commission Monograph No. 12. New York: Wiley, 1951.

Black, D. "On the Rationale of Group Decision-Making." *Journal of Political Economy,* 56 (1948):23–34.

Foley, D. "Resource Allocation and the Public Sector." *Yale Economic Essays,* 7 (1967).

Hicks, J. R. *Value and Capital.* London: Oxford University Press, 1939 (1st edition).

2   Little's Critique
of Welfare Economics

Prescriptions for economic policy have been an integral and, indeed, controlling part of the economist's activities since the days of Jean Bodin. Such recommendations can be interpreted as assertions that the proposed changes will increase "the welfare of society," and therefore, by implication, involve a knowledge both of the consequences of the proposal for economic behavior and of the relation between such behavior and social welfare. Since Adam Smith, the central proposition has been that welfare can best be increased by relying on competition and self-interest, though exceptions to this rule were first given prominence by Marshall.[1] In this century a considerable literature has arisen dealing with the more precise and logical interpretation of these propositions. The discussion has taken several directions: (1) What is the meaning of increasing or maximizing "community welfare"? Both of the words in quotation marks lead to problems. (2) What are the precise statements of the "optimum" conditions? (3) What are the circumstances under which these conditions do not coincide with the operations of perfect competition? (4) What are the implications of the answers to (2) and (3) for practical economic policy,

---

1. That is, within the framework of orthodox theory. Of course, there had always been objectors, particularly among Continental authors, to the desirability of competition.

Reprinted from *American Economic Review,* 41 (1951):923–934.

including the choice between capitalism and socialism and the proper economic policies under each?

Little's new [in 1950] book[2] has much to say about all these four major issues of welfare economics, but particularly about the first. His fundamental thesis is that the policy recommendations of current work on welfare economics cannot be taken as a safe guide to action because they tend to disregard the problem of distribution of income and because the empirical assumptions are usually unrealistic. Supplemental to the major theme is a contrapuntal figure in the bass to the effect that the terminology used by welfare economists has strong emotive connotations, so that statements which are really logical deductions from doubtful postulates appear to be injunctions to action.

The earlier part of Little's book is devoted to a critical examination of some of the philosophical problems in the formulation of welfare economics, such as the meaning of welfare and its relation to choices actually made by individuals, the possibility and meaning of interpersonal comparisons and their relation to social welfare judgments, and the role of income distribution in welfare judgments. Two particular problems attract most of Little's attention: (1) If the effects of a policy only appear over time, while at the same time the tastes of members of the society are changing, how can we have a criterion for an increase in welfare? (2) How are judgments of increase in social welfare related to ethical propositions on the one hand and to the distribution of happiness (real income) among individuals on the other? In connection with this analysis there is a thorough examination of the view of the utilitarians and of the various schools of the "new welfare economics."

On the basis of these philosophical considerations, Little proceeds to develop a set of sufficient conditions for an increase in welfare which take into account ethical views on income distribution. (He argues that establishing criteria—necessary and sufficient conditions—is too ambitious a task.) These conditions are related to the well-known compensation principle. On the basis of them, he then reexamines the usual optimum conditions for a welfare optimum (for example, equality of marginal rates of substitution among different individuals) and argues that because some of the empirical assumptions needed for their derivation are not met, the usual

---

2. I. M. D. Little, *A Critique of Welfare Economics* (Oxford, Clarendon Press, 1950), 276 pp.

policy implications drawn from them are not to be accepted. He then examines a number of specific policy issues, such as pricing policy for nationalized enterprises, criteria for making indivisible investments, and the gains from foreign trade, partly in the light of his previous arguments and partly with a view to issues of practical possibilities.[3]

As can already be seen from the brief summary given above, and as will be seen further below, the author has courageously faced the inherent difficulties in the subject matter and has thought perceptively and intelligently about them. The relation between welfare and actual behavior of the individual, the role of ethical judgments in welfare economics, the necessity and difficulties of incorporating distributive considerations into policy recommendations, and the choices to be made when not all of the standard optimal conditions can be satisfied are real and major difficulties in the application of economic theory to life. The sole fact that the right questions have been raised would make the book worth careful reading.

But the book is provoking as well as provocative — provoking because of its lack of rigorous thinking and its polemic and repetitious style. The specific conclusions, I believe, do not follow in any very logical way from the premises, and I feel that they are distinctly less acceptable than even the doubtful results of the current doctrine. There is indeed a strong tendency to derogate precision in thought; as a result, many statements are made which are based neither on rigorous reasoning nor on careful empirical observations. Conversely, many of the so-called failures of current welfare economics could easily be remedied by deriving new formulas and others could be resolved by empirical inquiry.

In the following sections I will take up in turn: (1) Little's philosophical discussion of the underlying concepts of welfare theory; (2) his proposed new set of criteria for an increase in welfare; and (3) his discussion of the standard "optimum" conditions and of the policy implications of welfare economics, particularly with regard to decisions on indivisible investments and marginal-cost pricing.

*   *   *

---

3. Little also has a revised version of the theory of consumer behavior, based on Samuelson's concept of "revealed preference," of which he makes some terminological use throughout the book, and an interesting discussion of the problem of evaluation of real national income. For lack of space these points will not be discussed here.

Little is at his best in discussing some of the philosophical problems in the formulation of welfare economics.[4] As noted earlier, he raises two principal questions in this sphere: (1) the relation between overt choice and welfare; (2) the meaning of the distribution of welfare among individuals.

He points out that it requires a definite value judgment to assume that when an individual is in a chosen position, he is in a higher state of welfare. For one thing, there is obviously no logical necessity for giving any respect whatever to individual desires; that we all do so is the result of a certain cultural pattern of ethics. Also, of course, it might well be argued that the overt behavior of individuals in the marketplace does not reflect their "true" preferences in some sense, though this is, in another sense, an empirical proposition rather than a value judgment — or would be if we could define "true" preferences. But Little's principal stress is on a somewhat different point. Following Samuelson's technique of "revealed preference," Little argues that an individual has moved to a better position if he can now afford to buy the goods he bought earlier, but does not. If, however, the individual's preference pattern has shifted in the meantime, the criterion proposed is inapplicable.

It seems to me that the argument is more relevant to the question of determining from price-quantity data alone whether or not an improvement has taken place in time than to the usual theoretical issue of comparing two alternative *potential* situations with all preference maps known. However, it is of some importance to observe that if any proposed policy takes time to carry out, one must take account of possible changes in tastes, not only spontaneous ones but more especially the changes associated with aging. In the long run, of course, the Keynesian dictum applies; we really cannot speak of any one individual as being made better off by a policy which takes fifty years to work out, since most individuals will not be around to enjoy the benefits.[5]

Formally, this difficulty may be avoided by the same device which Hicks

---

4. Little's chapters 1, 3, 4, 5 and parts of 6 and 7.

5. Little also includes changes in tastes caused by external relations in consumption, such as pecuniary emulation. These, of course, have long been recognized as a special problem even within the frame of ordinary static welfare economics, and are not in the same class as the dynamic changes of tastes. See M. W. Reder, *Studies in the Theory of Welfare Economics* (New York, Columbia University Press, 1947), pp. 64–67; G. Tintner, "A Note on Welfare Economics," *Econometrica,* Vol. 14 (Jan., 1946), pp. 69–78. Little later errs in the statement of the modification of the "optimum" conditions in this case; see below.

has used to "dynamize" the theory of consumer's choice:[6] the welfare of an individual must depend not only on his present but also on his planned future consumption for the remainder of his life. We must even include the intended welfare of his heirs in the utility function of an individual; otherwise, how can we explain capital accumulation? Then a recommended policy should be accepted only if its effect on all the future consumptions is such as to raise the resultant utility. This "solution" implies, of course, that each decision is made with full awareness of all its implications for the future.

Little, however, rejects the development of a dynamic welfare economics on the grounds that it cannot lead to any definite conclusions. This position seems somewhat unsatisfactory; because a field has not yet been successfully explored, it hardly follows that it cannot be. It is a legitimate criticism of static welfare economics that it does not take account of such time elements; but to assess the seriousness of the criticism, one must have some sort of dynamic model of welfare economics, if only to serve as a standard of comparison.

As a resolution of the problem raised by changing tastes, Little makes the interesting suggestion that the welfare pertains to "average men" of various social groups, say, to individuals of a given age. While Little does not elaborate too much, this position seems to me to be motivated by a postulate of symmetry; all individuals are the same from the social viewpoint, so that a transformation of society which amounts to interchanging the positions of individuals (in all relevant senses) would leave invariant the social welfare. Then social or economic welfare would depend only on the statistical joint frequency distribution of real income and those variables, such as age and marital status, which affect tastes. It is, I believe, presupposed that tastes (preference maps) are in fact almost completely determined by the listed variables; otherwise we could hardly ascribe a consistent preference pattern to each of the social *groups* defined by the various values of the variables.

After discussing the relation between choice and welfare for the individual, Little raises the problem of the distribution of welfare among individuals. He argues that if by "real income" is meant "happiness," then there is nothing wrong with interpersonal comparisons, at least qualitative ones of the form "A is happier than B." Happiness or satisfaction is a relatively

---

6. J. R. Hicks, *Value and Capital,* 2nd ed. (Oxford, Clarendon Press, 1946), chap. 18.

objective concept, and such comparisons can be made as descriptive and not as value judgments by inferring mental states from objective behavior. In any case, happiness is by no means to be identified with social welfare, which is definitely a question of ethical judgments. From this point of view he agrees with the position first advanced in Bergson's remarkable paper.[7] There, as Little points out, we see a distinctly different position from the utilitarian, which would hold social welfare to be a sum of individual happinesses and therefore an objective, if not readily measurable, quantity.

In the course of the discussion he argues that many economists seem to have thought they were making objective statements about increasing welfare when in fact they were making value judgments, and that their statements had important effects because of the emotive significance of the words they used. A charge such as this, especially when repeated rather frequently, should be supported by a bill of particulars. No examples are cited, and while I do not doubt that some economists may have been misled by their own terminology, I do not believe in fact that there are many such economists, nor that there have been serious effects on either thought or action.

Little's general conclusion seems to be the same as Bergson's; we start with a value judgment that one situation is better than another if everyone is better off in the second case than in the first, and in any given context we can order welfare distributions according to our value judgments. Now if individual choices have no external economies or diseconomies, and if we say nothing about the range of possible individual tastes, then, as I have shown elsewhere,[8] the above viewpoint is contradictory to some very reasonable value judgments. The answer is that individual estimates of social welfare must be included in the individual's utility function; that is, the social distribution of real income, as seen by the individual, is a good which enters on a par with other commodities. Hence, we *must* have a certain type of external relation in individual choices. I think this will lead to the conclusion that making everyone better off need not be a social improvement if it distorts the income distribution sufficiently.

The hard problem, it seems to me, arises at the point where Little and

---

7. A. Bergson (Burk), "A Reformulation of Certain Aspects of Welfare Economics," *Quart. Jour. Econ.*, Vol. 52 (Feb., 1938), pp. 310–34.

8. *Social Choice and Individual Values*, Cowles Commission Monograph No. 12 (New York, John Wiley and Sons, 1951), pp. 71–73.

everyone else stop. It is all very well to say that the effects of a proposed change on income distribution must be taken into account in deciding on the desirability of the change, but how do we describe a distribution of real income? Admittedly, the choice between two income distributions is the result of a value judgment, but how do we even formulate such judgments?

They cannot, strictly speaking, be made in terms of money income alone, as Little himself points out (he gives an excellent refutation of Lerner's argument to the contrary). Since individuals have different tastes, equal money incomes cannot always mean equal real incomes. For suppose that in an initial situation the equivalence did hold. Then certainly we can find a shift in relative prices which will make some people worse off and others better off, keeping money incomes and the general price level constant, so that in the second situation equal money incomes will no longer coincide with equal real incomes. This difficulty is a very real one. The only way out that I can see is to carry through Little's suggestion that welfare is to be interpreted in terms of "average men." If we assume that tastes are almost completely determined by a few objectively determinable variables, such as age, sex, marital status, and geographic location, then welfare judgments will be based on the joint distribution of those variables and money income; an individual will be identified, from the social point of view, by the values of those variables.

Little, however, goes still further. He repeatedly assumes that it is meaningful to compare two situations with respect to their relative income distributions even when total income has changed. No operational interpretation of this comparison is indicated. Presumably the equivalence of two income distributions means that in some sense the *relative* utilities of different individuals are the same in the two situations. This implies, as far as I can see, the existence of some measure of utility which possesses an interpersonally comparable cardinal significance. We have already seen that money income cannot serve as the utility measure. Even if we agree with Little that "happiness" or utility is interpersonally comparable in an ordinal sense (*A* is better off than *B*), I do not see any natural cardinal measure of real income to be used in forming Little's relative income distributions.

It would, of course, be very useful to be able to compare welfare distributions independently of total income. The aim is the reciprocal of the justly criticized Kaldor-Hicks approach:[9] where Kaldor and Hicks seek to com-

---

9. See W. J. Baumol, "Community Indifference," *Rev. Econ. Stud.,* Vol. 14, No. 1 (1946–

pare different production levels independently of income distributions, Little wants to compare different distributions independently of income. I am afraid that, desirable though such separation would be from the viewpoint of simplification, no such separation is likely to be valid. We come back to Bergson's original formulation of the social welfare function; we simply must rank in order of preference *absolute* welfare distributions and we cannot simplify the comparison in any way by analyzing such a distribution into "total income" and "relative income distribution."[10]

Little's conclusions from his discussion of welfare distribution are somewhat contradictory. On the one hand, he concludes that the concept of an "ideal" distribution is meaningless because of the vagueness involved in the concept of distribution; on the other hand, he believes that it is possible to compare any two distributions independently of total real income.[11] It would certainly seem that if we can make the second statement, we can find a distribution which is better than any other (apart from some technical mathematical problems of the existence of a maximum).

On the basis of his philosophical analysis, Little seeks to establish a set of sufficient conditions for an increase in welfare.[12] Because they seem to represent such an important step forward, I should like to examine them at considerable length. The discussion may be found somewhat technical and can be skipped with only slight loss of continuity.

Little starts from the well-known Kaldor-Hicks criterion: we should change from situation *A* to situation *B* if there is some redistribution of the goods in the second situation which will make everyone better off than in situation *A*. He objects to this criterion on two grounds: (1) that it ignores income distribution and (2) that it leads to the paradoxical conclusion, first pointed out by Scitovsky in his brilliant paper,[13] that it can be recommended

---

47), pp. 44–48; N. Kaldor, "Welfare Propositions of Economics and Interpersonal Comparisons of Utility," *Econ. Jour.,* Vol. 49 (Sept., 1939), pp. 549–52; J. R. Hicks, "The Foundations of Welfare Economics," *Econ. Jour.,* Vol. 49 (Dec., 1939), pp. 698–701, 711–712.

10. The above discussion is not meant to be rigorous and cannot be, since the proposition treated does not seem capable of a rigorous formulation. I have been, in effect, seeking unsuccessfully to restate Little's comparisons in a meaningful form.

11. Actually, as we shall see, it is possible to restate Little's propositions in a way which involves only comparisons of distributions with a given real income.

12. His chapters 6 and 7 and appendix.

13. T. Scitovsky, "A Note on Welfare Propositions in Economics," *Rev. Econ. Stud.,* Vol. 9 (Nov., 1941), pp. 77–88.

to move from *A* to *B* and then from *B* to *A* again. He therefore introduces the "Scitovsky criterion," which is the nonfulfillment of the Kaldor-Hicks criterion for movement in the opposite direction, from *B* to *A*. That is, the Scitovsky criterion is said to be satisfied if there is no redistribution of the goods in situation *A* which will make everyone better off than in situation *B*.

We thus have three conditions which are relevant for deciding whether or not to change from *A* to *B*: the Kaldor-Hicks criterion, the Scitovsky criterion, and the relative desirability of the income distribution in the two situations. Each criterion may or may not be fulfilled, and all eight combinations are possible.[14] For each case Little (p. 103) indicates what action should be taken.

"All possible combinations of answers may be set out in a table thus:

Table I

Case No.	1	2	3	4	5	6	7	8
Criteria								
Kaldor-Hicks criterion satisfied?	Yes	Yes	Yes	Yes	No	No	No	No
Scitovsky criterion satisfied?	Yes	Yes	No	No	No	No	Yes	Yes
Any redistribution good?	Yes	No	Yes	No	No	Yes	No	Yes
Deductions								
Should the change be made?	Yes	?	No	No	No	No	No	Yes
Should redistribution without the change be made?	No	No	Yes	No	No	Yes	No	No

Of these logical possibilities, numbers 1, 4, 5, 6, and 7 seem to be obvious, and do not require discussion. Number 2 is clearly doubtful, but it should seldom remain doubtful because it follows from our argument that, if compensation is not regarded as unfair, or undesirable in itself, it should be paid in order to turn case 2 into case 1. Cases 3 and 8 are the interesting ones."

---

14. I wish to mention that in a previous work I erred in thinking that in any case either the Kaldor-Hicks criterion was satisfied or the Scitovsky criterion was not; see Arrow, *Social Choice and Individual Values,* p. 43, eq. (6). My colleague T. Scitovsky has pointed out to me that if *A* and *B* are both optimal in the Pareto sense, then the Kaldor-Hicks criterion does not hold in either direction, which implies that the Scitovsky criterion is fulfilled.

The quotation is followed by a discussion of those two cases.

This quotation seems on the face of it to be of extraordinary significance. If we follow Little and grant that the income distribution criterion is meaningful (remember that the comparison is of relative, not absolute, income distributions), then we appear to have a reasonably clear-cut formula for deciding what to do in any concrete situation (provided, of course, the necessary compensations can be calculated). However, Little gives essentially no discussion; I can only justify the table by introducing extremely arbitrary assumptions.

In the first place, the question which the table is designed to answer is none too clear. Most discussions of welfare economics have been put in the form, "Shall we change from A to B?" but usually it has been assumed that the change is not temporal but rather potential. Hence, the two situations being compared should enter symmetrically. Little seems to envisage a choice among three alternatives: changing from A to B, making a redistribution of income at A but not a basic policy change, and leaving the status quo. Now either we assume that we have complete freedom to make lump-sum transfers, in which case the alternative of changing to B and then redistributing income should be included, or we do not make this assumption, in which case we should simply have the two alternatives of changing to B or leaving the status quo. (It may be added that the latter possibility is really the most general case; if we can choose between all possible pairs of situations, then we can decide what redistributions to make by calling a situation obtained by redistribution a new situation. Thus, in the set of alternatives which Little seems to be considering, let A' be a situation obtainable from A by redistribution; if we could choose between any pair of alternatives, then assuming consistency in the choices, we would choose that one of A, A', B which was preferred to both others.) It is immediately clear that if we permit lump-sum transfers in both situations, the comparison between the income distributions at A and at B are irrelevant; what we wish to compare are the best distributions obtainable by lump-sum transfers starting with A with the best distribution obtainable by lump-sum transfers starting with B. If we suppose, as Little seems to, that we can order relative distributions independently of total income, then we could proceed immediately to the best relative distribution in each case; then in one case everyone would be better off than in the other. This is indeed the procedure which Little attributes to Bergson and attacks on the ground that the concept of an "ideal" distribution is too vague to be operational.

Even if we take Little's peculiarly asymmetrical point of view,[15] it is not easy to see how he arrives at his results. First, suppose the Scitovsky criterion is not fulfilled. There is a redistribution of the commodities in A, leading to a new state A', which will make everyone better off than in B. Hence, the change to B should not be made, as in Cases 3–6. However, the question remains whether or not there should be a redistribution from A to some A'; clearly, this should be done if and only if there is some A' which is distributively superior to A. Now, if B is distributively superior to A, Little would argue that it is shown that there is some distribution better than that at A, and hence an A' better than A; this yields Cases 3 and 6. If B is not better than A distributively, however, it is not proven that A is better than any A', as Little seems to assert in Cases 4 and 5. The only justification I can see is that we will certainly not move to B, since we know there is a better alternative; but not knowing whether or not there is an A' better than A (distributively), we will stay put. This procedure is, of course, definitely biased in favor of the status quo.

Little also gives a sufficient condition for a change from A to B, without regard to redistributions of A: *if the Scitovsky criterion is satisfied and the distributional change good, then the change should be made.* The reasoning is as follows. We should be able to find a situation A' by redistribution from A which is distributively equivalent to B and therefore distributively superior to A. Since it has the same (relative) distribution as in B, either everyone is better off than in B or everyone is worse off. The former alternative is excluded since the Scitovsky criterion holds; therefore, everyone is better off in B than in A'. But A' is at the same income level as A and distributively superior to it; therefore, B is better than A. This argument underlies Cases 1 and 8; however, the possibility of an A' (obtained by redistribution from A) being still better than B is not excluded. Perhaps Little would say that since it cannot be inferred from the stated criteria whether or not such an A' exists, we should move to B since we know that to be better. (Actually, we do know that there is an A' better than A; why is B preferred?) Interchanging A and B in the preceding reasoning, we get another principle: if the Kaldor-Hicks criterion is not satisfied and the redistribution is bad, then A is better than B. Hence in Case 7 we know that A is preferred to B, while we do not know if

---

15. Little is not completely consistent; the payment of compensation to turn Case 2 into Case 1 of course occurs after the change is made.

there is any A' preferred to A; therefore, in view of the preference for the status quo, we stay at A. (This principle also applies to Case 5.) In Case 2 we cannot infer anything about the relative desirability of A, B, or an A'; to be consistent, I should think that A would be chosen.

To sum up, Little's table can be justified in a fashion if the following assumptions are made: (1) the choice is among the present situation, an alternative situation, and a redistribution in the present situation (but not one in the alternative situation); (2) only information supplied by the three given criteria can be used (thus, we could not infer that there was a redistribution of A superior to A directly but only if B is distributively superior to A); (3) we can compare the (relative) distributions of two situations with different real incomes; (4) the status quo is preferred unless there is some alternative definitely shown to be better by the information under (2); (5) if both the alternative situation and the redistribution of the present situation are preferred to the present situation, then the former is chosen. I would say that not one of these assumptions is truly acceptable.

Little is aiming at an important issue: how do we compare nonoptimal situations? This corresponds to his implied preference for piecemeal reform, gradually improving matters, over Utopian jumping to an all-over optimum. In principle, the Bergson social welfare function seeks the same goal, since it is an ordering of all possible utility distributions. However, Little quite correctly remarks that, as applied, the social welfare function has been used only to establish the proposition that the maximum state of social welfare is achieved when all the Pareto optimal conditions are met and the distribution of welfare is "ideal." What seems most relevant in comparing nonoptimal situations is the case where no redistributions are permitted; for the reason we do not move to Pareto optima is that our powers of redistribution are limited by practical and political considerations.

For such comparisons we have the theorem of Little's that is italicized above. We do not need actually to make comparisons of distributions at different levels of national income, as Samuelson has remarked.[16] The proof given earlier does not require that A' be "distributively equivalent" to B; all that is needed is that everyone be better off in B than in A'. Hence, Little's theorem may be stated this way: *B is preferred to A if there is a situation A'*

---

16. P. A. Samuelson, "Evaluation of Real National Income," *Oxford Economic Papers,* N.S., Vol. 2 (Jan., 1950), p. 29, n. 2.

obtainable by lump-sum transfers from A such that A' is judged to be better than A, while everyone is better off in B than in A'. This proposition is thoroughly in accord with the Bergson analysis.

Once we have stated the theorem this way, we see that there are other theorems of the same type which, however, cannot be expressed in terms of the three criteria used by Little. For example: *B is preferred to A if there exists a situation B' obtainable by lump-sum transfers from B such that everyone is better off in B' than in A and that B is judged to be better than B'.* (Note that the comparison between *A* and *A'* in the first theorem and between *B* and *B'* in the second is a comparison of different distributions with the same national income, in a sense.) Other theorems could easily be devised involving chains of intermediate situations. The usefulness of such theorems is hard to assess.[17] Apart from the difficulties involved in evaluating the various comparisons in a practical situation, the theorems do not seem to provide the basis for choice in enough cases. In particular, the possibility of moving to a situation with a very much higher real income but undesirable distribution seems to be excluded from a decision.

Little discusses the usual optimum conditions from the viewpoint of his criterion for an improvement in welfare.[18] Since any movement to a Pareto optimum necessarily satisfies the Scitovsky criterion (otherwise there would be some position in which everyone was better off than in the Pareto optimum, contrary to definition), a policy of satisfying the optimum conditions is justified, provided the effect on distribution is favorable.[19] Little then considers in turn each of the various standard conditions (equality of marginal rates of substitution and of transformation, and so on). He has a rather nice discussion of the consequences of putting one set of optimum conditions into effect without the rest. He points out that equalizing the marginal rates of substitution in consumption is an improvement (provided distributional effects are favorable) regardless of the degree of optimality in the production process; but equalizing marginal rates of transformation when the optimum exchange conditions are not fulfilled cannot be so well

---

17. It is to be observed that in these theorems it is not implied that either *A* and *B* is the present situation.

18. His chapters 8 and 9.

19. Little makes the curious error of asserting that when there are external relations in consumption or production, the usual optimal conditions are still necessary, though not sufficient. This is in general false; external relations will usually require unequal (private) marginal rates of substitution to achieve an optimum position.

justified. Little is particularly concerned about the fact that the optimum conditions for allocation between leisure and goods and between different kinds of labor cannot be expected to be fulfilled, the former because the hours of labor cannot be individually adjusted at will, for technological reasons, and because both direct and indirect taxes fall on goods but not leisure; the latter because of transfer costs and also because of the effect of taxes in distorting relative wages. As he points out, the well-known rule that price should equal marginal cost can no longer be derived. From this conclusion and his other critical observations on welfare economics in general, he infers that no rule of this type is of much use, and all that can be said is that prices should bear some reasonable relation to costs.

I feel that the inference goes too far. For the moment suppose we have no difficulty with allocation between different kinds of work, say because laborers are indifferent among jobs and transfer costs are absent; we have only the first problem, that hours of labor must be the same for all to avoid excessive technological costs. Let us suppose that the number of hours fixed is optimal, taking into account preferences and costs. Suppose further for simplicity that labor is the only factor. Then for an optimal allocation of resources the ratio of the marginal physical productivities of labor in any two industries must equal the marginal rate of substitution in consumption. If we sell at fixed prices, then the marginal physical productivities of labor in different industries must be inversely proportional to the prices. If wages are taken as the numéraire, then the conclusion is reached that prices should be proportional to marginal costs. The common ratio of price to marginal cost serves here as a distributive rather than an allocative mechanism. In other words, the efficiency argument for marginal-cost pricing is not altered; we can, however, also reach efficiency in other ways which may be superior distributively. If the ratio of average to marginal cost differs considerably in different industries, there seems no conceivable way of concluding that covering average costs is a reasonable criterion.

The second difficulty, allocation among different types of labor, is more serious. One can only hope it possible to arrange for transfer costs to be borne socially and to have a system of taxes and subsidies on different types of labor to compensate for variations in desirability.

Little then turns to some policy problems,[20] principally the criterion for indivisible investments and the pricing policy for nationalized enterprises.

---

20. His chapters 10 and 11. He also has some interesting remarks on the evaluation of real national income and the gains from foreign trade in chapters 12 and 13.

According to Dupuit and Marshall, an indivisible investment should be made if a perfectly discriminating monopoly can cover costs subsequently. This does not mean that the plant once built should be operated as any type of monopoly, simple or discriminating. Little criticizes consumers' surplus on three grounds: (1) it is based on partial analysis and ignores the existence of substitute and complementary commodities; (2) there is no way of subsequently checking to see if the original criterion was satisfied (since presumably discrimination will not be allowed); (3) if there is a discrepancy between price and marginal cost in other industries, then the entrance of a new plant causes losses of producers' surplus which should be offset against a gain in consumers' surplus. He proposes as an alternative building a plant when a simple monopoly can cover costs, and making this operational by permitting the undertaking to act in that way.

His first and third arguments simply mean that a more complicated formula than that of simple consumers' surplus is called for. There is no analytic difficulty in supplying such formulas; the solution of the first problem was given by Hotelling in 1938.[21] Nor has the fact that the proper formula cannot be represented in two dimensions anything to do with its practicality. Any type of consumers' surplus, simple or generalized, is based on the cost and demand equations of the real world, which must be estimated by hard statistical or other empirical work, whether one commodity is involved or several.

The second argument is no more valid. If we compute consumers' surplus on the basis of an estimated demand curve, we can after the event find out whether or not the observed demand lies on the estimated curve.[22] Or we can work on the basis of questionnaires, polls, and perhaps marketing experiments. Little seems to feel that the market is the only source of data on consumer preferences. To secure an optimal allocation of resources when there are indivisibilities, we must have more direct information than the market can supply, perhaps even properly designed voting.

---

21. H. Hotelling, "The General Welfare in Relation to Problems of Taxation and of Railway and Utility Rates," *Econometrica,* Vol. 6 (July, 1938), pp. 242–69. A formula which answers the third question has recently been given by M. Boiteux, "Le 'Revenu Distruable' et les Pertes Economiques," *Econometrica,* Vol. 19 (Apr., 1951), pp. 112–33, esp. 132.

22. I am indebted for this point to my colleague P. Baran.

3 The Principle of Rationality in Collective Decisions

I spent the period from December 1951 to August 1952 in Europe on a Social Science Research Council fellowship. Since I was so available, at Jacob Marschak's suggestion I was invited to participate in a colloquium in Paris on the foundations of risk bearing. While I was in Paris, François Perroux asked me to give an exposition at the Institut des Sciences Economiques Appliquées of my then-new work on social choice. Clearly, it was advisable to give the talk in French. I prepared it with considerable help from some of the economists at the institute and used the opportunity to improve my handling of the proof. Presented on June 9, 1952, the paper was subsequently published by the institute. I have translated it into English for inclusion in this volume.

I should like to present some considerations on the nature of choices and their formation in the context of a society, stressing as I do so the implications for economic policy. A democratic society must choose among various alternative economic policies that pertain to tax structure, land policy, nationalization of certain industries, antimonopoly policy, and the like. It is assumed that the choices are, in some sense, in accord with the individual preferences of the members of the society and at the same time compatible with technological knowledge and the availability of resources.

Published in French as "Le principe de rationalité dans les décisions collectives," *Economie Appliquée,* 5 (1952):469–484.

A normative theory of these collective choices is, it seems to me, the fundamental subject of what has been called "welfare economics." It must be noted, however, that most of the questions treated by this discipline concern the distribution of goods among individual consumers. I think that these special issues have particular aspects which mask the fundamental problem of collective choice; I should like to treat this fundamental problem in a manner at once general and abstract. Without doubt abstraction, here as elsewhere, has a certain esthetic character: the more general our study and the larger our horizon, the more our artistic taste is satisfied. But it is still more important to show that certain complicated problems are, in their essence, analogous to simple problems that are more transparent. It is superfluous, I think, to furnish examples of this method in economic theory.

I wish, then, to focus our attention on choices and decisions which are essentially collective. In the economic domain every form of collective consumption (parks, armaments, schools, and so on) illustrates the problems I have in mind. Collective decisions must be taken proximately by a social organism and, by their very nature, imply a choice among a set of possibilities that vary in quantity or quality. The economic decision, therefore, has a truly *political* character. Election is a still simpler case. We are in the presence of a social organization which, by the mechanism of the vote, chooses among several possibilities, that is, among several candidates. I speak here of the election of a single candidate among several (such as the election of a President of the United States); the theory of choice applied to the formation of an entire legislature poses other problems which I shall not discuss here.

From a purely logical point of view, all these decision problems belong to the same species. The different individuals who make up the society can have different scales of value and consequently different preferences among the available possibilities. In a democratic society it is expected that the final decision takes some account of the diversity of individual preferences. That is, in any case, the purpose of our usual voting procedures.

The distribution problems of classical welfare economics — for which it is sometimes thought that market mechanisms are adequate to arrive at a collective decision — are analogous in a certain sense. I shall return to this point.

The abstract theory of collective choice can then be reduced to the simplest case, in which the choice is made for a *list* of options or candidates; I shall use this illustration constantly in what follows. But it must be understood that the same principles are applicable to every kind of social choice.

Choices and Preferences

To begin, I should like to summarize the classical question of utility preference and choice. What I shall say is not new; I agree completely with the "ordinal" view of Pareto and Hicks. I wish only to restate the theory in a slightly different language.

The underlying basis of the ordinal theory is, it seems to me, the strict link that is established between preferences and choices that would be made in certain hypothetical conditions. Thus, the phrase "x is preferred to y" means "if x and y were offered, x would be chosen." Pareto's hypothesis is that the relation of preference so defined possesses the usual properties of coherence, such as transitivity: if x is preferred to y and y to z, then x is preferred to z. An operational meaning can be similarly given to the notion of indifference; the phrase "x and y are indifferent to me" means "if I prefer x to z, I also prefer y to z" and, inversely, "every z preferred to x is also preferred to y"; that is, every preference judgment true of x is also true of y. Starting from these definitions, it is easy to show that indifference between x and y implies that x is not preferred to y and conversely. To complete our axiom system, we suppose that alternatives are always comparable, that is, for every pair x and y either I prefer x to y, or I prefer y to x, or x and y are indifferent to me.

The formulation I have just given does not differ essentially from that used by Hicks in his 1949 London lectures.[1] This formulation shows that the theory of consumer demand developed by Samuelson and Little by the method of revealed preferences is not fundamentally different from the traditional method of indifference curves. The last perhaps adds something: preferences can be "revealed" by choices, not only under competition but also under monopsony; a questionnaire about preferences between two alternatives is a limiting case of monopsony.

The principal merit of the ordinal theory is the operational, behavioristic, pragmatic character of its method. In the domain of social choices it implies the abandonment of the traditional formula of Bentham and Edgeworth: social decisions should maximize the sum of individual utilities. At least,

---

1. [Subsequently published as *A Revision of Demand Theory* (Oxford: Clarendon Press, 1956).]

this rule must be regarded as without significance so long as an experimental procedure for measuring the utilities that are to be added is not established. The following quotation shows, moreover, that Bentham himself had serious reservations about the formula: " 'Tis in vain to speak of adding quantities which after the addition will continue to be as distinct as they were before; one man's happiness will never be another man's happiness; the gain of one man is no gain to another; you may as well pretend to add 20 apples to 20 pears." [2]

Permit me to add that the theory of cardinal utility constructed by von Neumann and Morgenstern to explain risk-bearing behavior has no relevance to the present discussion, even if the theory is accepted in its own domain; there is no reason to accept this particular utility scale for social decisions; to do so would amount to determining the distribution of income by the tastes of individuals for gambling. Suppose, for example, that we are dividing one unit of a certain good between two individuals for each of whom the utility function (in the sense of von Neumann and Morgenstern) is represented by x^2. If we use the Bentham-Edgeworth formulation, the distribution into x for one individual, Primus, and $1 - x$ for another individual, Secundus, will have a social utility equal to $x^2 + (1 - x)^2$.

It is easy to verify that the maximum of this function in the range $0 \leq x \leq 1$ is attained at the ends of the interval, either $x = 0$ or $x = 1$. Thus the social optimum is attained by giving everything to one individual. Our intuition, I believe, rejects this solution immediately, especially given the symmetry of the data.[3] Moreover, the utility function constructed by von Neumann and Morgenstern is determined only up to a linear transformation; the sum of utilities will therefore be defined only when a unit meaningful for all individuals is determined. The choice of this unit opens all the difficulties of the aggregation of individual utilities into a single social utility.

In the traditional theory of consumer demand, one starts by supposing that individual preferences can be expressed by indifference curves or

---

2. Cited by W. C. Mitchell, "Bentham's felicific calculus," in *The Backward Art of Spending Money and Other Essays* (New York: McGraw-Hill, 1937), p. 184.

3. In the above discussion I have considered only riskless incomes. It might be asked if the social utility could not be increased by distributing the income according to a chance mechanism, especially in the chosen example where both individuals prefer risk. But because of the linear character of both mathematical expectation and the von Neumann-Morgenstern utility, the social utility of a random distribution is equal to the expectation of the social utility; it can therefore not exceeed the maximum of the social utility for riskless distributions.

surfaces; then the individual chooses the best situation among all those accessible to him and satisfying the budget constraint. Similarly here, we can imagine that the individual begins by establishing a system of preferences, once for all time, among the set of all conceivable candidates; then, for a given election, the individual is informed of the actual candidates, after which he votes for the candidate highest on his original list. Let us imagine that society also has a preliminary list, that is, an "ordering." If we knew the preference ordering of society and the list of candidates for a given election, we could determine automatically the choice society will make. Recall that speaking of choice among candidates is only by way of example; choices among social, political, or economic decisions would be parallel. It could be a question of preference concerning public works, the choice between armaments and social services, among differing foreign policies, and so forth. In a word, the ordering, for an individual, represents his entire social ethic.

The picture doubtless does not represent exactly the usual view of ethics; we no longer speak of "goods" but of "advantages"; in place of absolute good and evil, we speak here of a ranking of what should be *more* or *less* respected. In this view, individuals desire to act as well as possible from the moral point of view within the limits of possible actions. The conception of an ethical code and a compromise among imperfections may appear inelegant to some who prefer to devote themselves completely to the Cult of the Good. Surely Burke was not approving when he wrote, "The age of chivalry is dead; the age of sophists, calculators, and economists is upon us." But I believe that that will not trouble most economists.

I want now to introduce the concept of *rationality*. It seems reasonable to say that the minimum of rationality that one can demand of someone who must make decisions is that his choices be in conformity with an ordering or a scale of preferences endowed with the properties explained above. It is all that I will intend by the word "rational." An individual is rational if his preferences among candidates can be expressed by an ordering; similarly, collective decisions are made rationally if they are determined by an ordering acceptable to the entire society.

The Social Choice Function

It seems to me that one purpose of welfare economics or of any study of the nature of rational collective decisions is to examine the possibility of establishing a social preference scale. In a democratic society we suppose that any such scale is determined by the preference scales or ethical systems of individuals.

Each individual is free to choose his own ordering, so that society must have a rule to construct a social scale based on individual scales. Such a rule will be called a *social choice function*. Strictly speaking, a social choice function is a rule or a procedure such that if each individual supplies his ordering of all possible candidates, a social ordering will be determined. We can imagine a machine in which each person introduces his preference scale for all possible candidates; the machine cranks out a social preference scale for all possible candidates. Ballot boxes and voting machines are in fact social choice functions of a particular kind.

In my book[4] I have employed the expression *social welfare function* to designate what I call here *social choice function.* I. M. D. Little has shown that using the term "social welfare" would make the reader believe that the ordering of social preferences which results from it constitutes a system of ethical judgments held by "society." [5] I fully agree that value judgments can be held only by individuals — and that, consequently, the preference ordering constructed by use of the social choice function (based on individual preferences) is only a means of making social decisions and not at all an expression of some interpersonal ethic. Nevertheless, the social choice function does have a very close formal resemblance to the concept of the social welfare function introduced by Bergson[6] some years ago; both functions define an ordering constructed by aggregation of individual orderings.

One could experiment with different social choice functions and see what they imply. It is interesting in this connection to note that neither Bergson nor Samuelson[7] illustrates the Bergson function by concrete examples — except for the sum of utilities, which appears to be incompatible with their "ordinalist" position. I proceed instead by a path that could be called the

4. *Social Choice and Individual Values,* Cowles Commission Monograph No. 12 (New York: Wiley, 1951).

5. [Little's remarks were contained in a lecture delivered at the Institut des Sciences Economiques Appliquées at about the time this lecture was given. His talk was subsequently published, in the same journal as this article, as "L'avantage collectif," *Economie Appliquée,* 5 (1952):455–468; also as "Social Choice and Individual Values," *Journal of Political Economy,* 60 (1952):422–432.]

6. A. Bergson (Burk), "A reformulation of certain aspects of welfare economics," *Quarterly Journal of Economics,* 52 (1938):310–334.

7. P. A. Samuelson, *Foundations of Economic Analysis* (Cambridge, Mass.: Harvard University Press, 1947), chap. 8.

axiomatic method. It is developed thus: Certain properties which every reasonable social choice function should possess are set forth. The possibility of fulfilling these conditions is then examined. If we are lucky, there will be exactly one social choice function that will satisfy them. If we are less fortunate, there can be several social choice functions satisfying the conditions or axioms. Finally, it will be the height of bad luck if there exists no function fulfilling the desired conditions. What is the nature of these conditions? We can suppose that the individuals hold value judgments on the method of formation of collective decisions; the aggregation of the ethical feelings of individuals is itself an object of ethical judgments. The conditions of which we speak form a set of these value judgments that can be regarded as unanimously acceptable.

Condition 1 is implicit in the preceding discussion: the social choice function should be capable of defining an ordering for the collectivity, whatever the individual preference scales.

Condition 2 bears on the relation between the individual orderings and the collective ordering which results from them: the collective ordering should reflect *positively* the individual welfare judgments. Suppose that for a given set of individual preference scales, society prefers x to y. Suppose then that one individual modifies his ordering by raising x on his list, which remains otherwise unchanged; it is clear that in this case we should require that society still prefer x to y. That is to say, if one candidate is raised in the estimation of someone, the social judgment should not be modified in a way that is unfavorable to that candidate.

The third condition that one should, in my opinion, impose on a social choice function is that the social choice among a set of candidates should depend on the individual preferences for those candidates and *those candidates only*. In other words, the collective choice made from a given set of options should be invariant with respect to changes in the individual preferences concerning options outside the set. It must be remarked that this condition has always been implicitly assumed in voting systems. Suppose, for example, that a community has to choose between the construction of a stadium and that of a museum; it is capable of financing either one, but not both. Suppose further that a university is in any case beyond the means of this community. It seems evident to me that the choice between the museum and the stadium should be independent of the preferences of the members of the community between a museum and a university. The essential argument in favor of this principle is its direct appeal to intuition. Notice that in fact the compensation principle, which is the principal explicit form of collective decision making compatible with the ordinal character of utility, satisfies Condition 3. This suggests that it is generally implicitly assumed. Several secondary considerations which reinforce the defense of this condition can be advanced. If it is abandoned, a choice among a given set of candidates can be made only if each individual possesses a list of preferences containing more candidates than those which are really available. What will be the list of candidates that the individual will be asked to order? There is no natural limit except a vague universe comprising all logically possible candidates. It does not appear correct to make the choice among a very limited set of possibilities depend on all preferences among all "imaginable" possibilities. Beyond the difficulty of defining the universe in which preferences should be ordered, there is an operational problem: preferences between impossible alternatives make virtually no sense, for they correspond to no action that an individual could imagine having to perform.

We have just posed three conditions for a satisfactory social choice function: Condition 1, which can be called the Principle of Collective Rationality, says simply that every imaginable system of preference systems of individuals can be aggregated into a system of social preferences or a collective ordering; Condition 2, the Principle of Positive Association between Individual and Social Values, says that if a possibility is raised in the ranking of one or several individuals, the ranking of all other possibilities remaining unchanged, this possibility will not be degraded in the social ranking; and Condition 3, the Principle of Independence of Irrelevant Alternatives, declares that the social choice among a given set of possibilities does not depend on preferences about possibilities which do not figure in the set.

There certainly exist trivial methods of aggregation which satisfy these three conditions. The first is the establishment of a collective ordering independent of any individual preference. Another consists in distinguishing one individual in the society and requiring that the society prefer one possibility to another whenever that individual does so; in short, a dictatorship. Neither of these methods answers the problem of aggregation in a truly democratic society. But do there exist other methods for constructing a social choice function? The answer is NO. There are no methods, other than the two trivial ones just cited, for combining several individual preference systems and making of them a single preference system for society as a whole, at least if the three proposed conditions must be fulfilled. A sketch of the formal proof will be found in the Technical Appendix; I limit myself here to giving a simple example which illustrates this point.

Suppose it is suggested that the system of majority voting be adopted as a social choice function, that is, that one candidate will be preferred to another if a majority of the electors prefer him to the other candidate. What happens can then be seen from the following example, presented originally in 1882 by an Australian, E. J. Nanson.[8] Assume that there are three candidates, A, B, and C, and three voters, 1, 2, and 3. Voter 1 prefers A to B and B to C; voter 2 prefers B to C and C to A; voter 3 prefers C to A and A to B. Under these conditions a majority, composed of voters 1 and 3, prefer A to B, voters 1 and 2 prefer B to C, and 2 and 3 prefer C to A. Consequently, society prefers A to B, B to C, and C to A, which is in evident contradiction to the principle of collective rationality.

There are naturally an infinity of social choice functions besides majority voting, but it can be shown that every imaginable method violates at least one of the three conditions. Notice in this regard that the compensation principle violates the principle of collective rationality; this violation constitutes precisely the celebrated paradox of Scitovsky.[9] This author has shown that there exist two distributions A and B such that the goods available in B can be redistributed so as to put every individual in a better situation than in A and that a redistribution starting from A can also be found which puts every individual in a better situation than he could enjoy in B. The compensation principle (Kaldor, Hicks) would demand then at the same time that A be changed into B and B into A, which the requirement of collective rationality forbids.

Methods which do not violate the principle of collective rationality can be given, but then they will violate one of the other conditions. For example, all possible candidates can be ranked once and for all by the method of plurality voting, each elector voting for that one of all imaginable candidates that he prefers and the candidates being ranked according to the number of votes

---

8. E. J. Nanson, "Methods of Election," *Transactions and Proceedings of the Royal Society of Victoria,* 19 (1882):197–240. [This is in fact far from the first exposition of this example. The earliest known presentation is that of M. J. A. N. Caritat, Marquis de Condorcet, *Essai sur l'application de l'analyse à la probabilité des décisions rendues à la pluralité des voix* (Paris: Imprimerie Royale, 1785).]

9. T. Scitovsky, "A note on welfare propositions in economics," *Review of Economic Studies,* 9 (1941):77–88.

received. This method satisfies conditions 1 and 2 but not condition 3. If an individual prefers C to A and A to B, his vote does not count for a choice between A and B; but if he changes his mind and prefers A to B and B to C, there is now one more vote for A (in the choice between A and B), although the choice of our individual between A and B has not changed.

One can also furnish a method of collective decision which would satisfy conditions 1 and 3 without fulfilling condition 2. First, let a particular individual be identified, then decide that special preferences will always be opposite to those of that individual: if the individual prefers x to y, society will prefer y to x. If the individual is indifferent, society will be also. It is scarcely necessary to insist on the absurdity of the scheme thus constructed.

Classical Welfare Economics

I have used elections or choice among types of collective consumption as examples of decisions taken by society; what relation do these have to the classical problems of welfare economics, such as rate making in nationalized industries? The benefits and costs of different policies are not collective, at least not in the usual analysis; they belong to individuals. However, I hold that allocation problems are essentially of the same nature as decisions on the subject of collective consumption or political questions. To decide on an economic policy is, in principle, to decide on a distribution of goods and services among the members of the community. The preference fields of individuals and of society that we have discussed here become preferences among distributions. Each individual has his own distributional ethic, and one of the problems of welfare economics is to aggregate these ethical preferences. If this aggregation could be done, we would have a social preference scale among distributions of goods and services; in any given context, we could choose the economic policy which would entail the preferred distribution.

Suppose that a change in electricity tariffs is considered, and assume, for simplicity, that no compensation is envisaged. Thus the sole variable is the schedule of electricity prices; for each possible schedule we can (theoretically) calculate the change which the distribution of goods and services among individuals will undergo. Each individual voter examines the resulting distributions and ranks them in order of preference, balancing the satisfactions that he draws directly from consumption with those, of an ethical order, that he draws from the justice of the distribution. He has then a list that expresses the ordering of those preferences which should determine the final decision.

The same (doubtless theoretical) description of the social choice is applicable to the case where compensation can be made. Suppose for example that income tax rates can be modified at the same time as electricity prices. The domain of possible policies is then much more extensive, for we can consider every combination of a change in the electricity price schedule with a change in tax rates as a possible decision for the state. Traditional welfare economics shows that there are certain of these combinations that will be preferred by *all* the voters, which permits us to eliminate the others without too much discussion. However, there will always remain an irreducible kernel of possibilities among which the choice rests on a combination or aggregation of individual ethical attitudes about distribution.

Unfortunately, the results derived above show that a satisfactory analysis of the construction of social preference scales by aggregation of individual scales cannot yet be given. I can only hope that these results, despite their negative form, will serve as a guide for future research.

An Individual's Distributional Ethics

So far we have been concerned with the aggregation of preference scales of different individuals. Let us ask now how a single individual, Primus, would formulate his own scale of preferences for different distributions. Suppose that Primus assumes, as a fundamental value judgment, that the freedom of choice of each individual must be respected; that is, he evaluates the well-being of every other consumer according to the preference scale of that consumer.

Under these conditions the ranking by Primus of different distributions is indeed a combination of the preference scales of all individuals for the various goods. Each individual possesses, in effect, an ordering for all possible sets of goods; that implies an ordering for various distributions, each one preferring the distribution which gives him the set of goods that he prefers. Primus seeks then to create for himself a new ordering of all possible distributions which represents his ethical viewpoint on the various distributions and which is based on the preferences of the different individuals for various goods.

This combination or aggregation procedure corresponds, it seems to me, to the social welfare function of Bergson, in which social welfare is defined as a function of individual utilities. Probably the author was seeking a definition valid regardless of the individual utility functions; it is a matter of constructing a social preference ordering starting from individual orderings. However, Bergson does not mention conditions which would link changes in the collective ordering to changes in the individual orderings.

It seems to me, then, that the three conditions set above are value judgments which might reasonably be part of the ethics of Primus. Since he seeks an ordering, Condition 1 is evidently necessary. The positive association of individual and social values states one relation between the ethical preferences of Primus and changes in the utility functions of other individuals; the relation proposed appears difficult to contest. Finally, here again independence of irrelevant alternatives appears to me a very reasonable value judgment. If Primus compares two distributions, his decision should not be affected by changes in utility by other individuals which would not affect the disposable set of goods in one or the other of the two distributions being compared.

However, Primus will find, as before, that he cannot construct a preference scale which would express his ethical choices among various distributions and would be in accord with these value judgments, except in one of the two completely trivial manners that I have spoken of. Thus, we find a difficulty in establishing value judgments on distribution, judgments which should be taken by a single individual.

Technical Appendix

I wish now to sketch the proof of the impossibility asserted in the section on the social choice function; there exists no method of aggregation (besides the trivial ones) satisfying the three conditions. I shall add, then, to the three conditions of the text, two new conditions that will serve simply to exclude the trivial methods.

CONDITION 4. *It is impossible that the preferences of society be always in agreement with those of a single individual.*

CONDITION 5. *For every pair of possibilities x and y, there exists at least one system of individual preference orderings which causes x to be preferred to y.*

Condition 4 excludes the case of "dictatorship." Condition 5 excludes the case where the social choice function would impose an ordering a priori, independent of individual preferences.

To begin, a consequence of Conditions 2, 3, and 5 will be noted: if the individuals unanimously prefer x to y, then society prefers x to y. This is the Pareto Principle. Indeed, by Condition 5, there exists one system of individual orderings such that society prefers x to y. Consider in this system the individuals who do not prefer x to y, and for each of them raise x in his preference ordering until x is preferred to y, other preferences remaining unchanged; from Condition 2, in the new state so obtained, society continues to prefer x to y. But Condition 3 requires that the choice between x and y depend only on the individual preferences between the two; it is then established that society prefers x to y as soon as the individuals are unanimous on this point. It will be noted that Conditions 2 and 5 intervene only to establish the Paretian Unanimity Principle; they will no longer be referred to hereafter. This principle could therefore have been substituted for the two conditions.

Let me introduce a new definition. A group of individuals V will be called *decisive*[10] with respect to the superiority of x over y if society prefers x to y whenever all the individuals in V prefer x to y and the others y to x.

I am going to deal with the case of three possibilities: x, y, and z. If a contradiction can be established for three, it is clear that the impossibility remains whatever the number of possibilities among which choice is exercised. The demonstration will comprise two steps:

1. We first need an abbreviated notation. The variables $\alpha, \beta, \gamma, \ldots$ are able to take one of the three values $+1, 0, -1$, which denote respectively preference, indifference, and disfavor. The notation $f(\alpha,\beta; x,y) = \gamma$ indicates the social choice between x and y when the individual we call Primus has an opinion denoted α, other individuals having opinion β. Consider then the hypothesis

(A-1) $f(+1,-1; x,y) = +1.$

This means that society prefers x to y according to the opinion of Primus and against that of all others — that is, Primus by himself is decisive in the choice of x against y.

Suppose that Primus ranks the possibilities in the order x, y, z; for all other individuals y is preferred to x and to z while x has the relation α to z. In this case, according to (A-1), society prefers x to y. As on the other hand there is

---

10. This definition is different from that given in my book (*Social Choice and Individual Values*, p. 52); the modification introduced here permits simplifying the demonstration.

unanimity for preferring y to z, society prefers y to z (Pareto Principle). Condition 1 then requires that society prefer x to z; it follows that $f(+1,\alpha; x,z) = +1$, whatever the value of α.

It can be concluded, then, that

(1) hypothesis (A-1) implies $f(+1,\alpha; x,z) = +1$.

But, by analogous reasoning, it can be established that

(2) hypothesis (A-1) implies $f(+1,\alpha; z,y) = +1$.

On the other hand, by permuting y and z in (1), we obtain

(3) if $f(+1,-1; x,z) = +1$, then $f(+1,\alpha; x,y) = +1$,

and by an analogous operation with (2), we obtain

(4) if $f(+1,-1; x,z) = +1$, then $f(1,\alpha; y,z) = +1$.

Continuing and assembling these results shows that hypothesis (A-1) implies $f(1,\alpha; u,v) = +1$ for every value of α and every pair (u,v) taken from (x,y,z). But this consequence is excluded by Condition 4. Hypothesis (A-1) can therefore not be accepted; that is, no individual can, by himself alone, constitute a decisive group.

2. For every pair of possibilities there are one or several decisive groups (since the Pareto Principle shows that the entire society is decisive). On the other hand, we have just shown that a decisive group contains at least two individuals. Among all the sets which are decisive for any one alternative against any other, take the least numerous (or one of the least numerous)—which will be called V—and divide it into two parts, V_1 which contains only a single individual and V_2 which contains the rest. Let V be decisive for x against y. Call V_3 the set of individuals not in V. Consider now the case where the preference ordering of V_1 is x, y, z; that of the members of V_2, z, x, y; and that of the members of V_3, y, z, x. Since V is decisive for the choice of x against y, and all the members of V prefer x to y, society prefers x to y.

On the other hand, it is impossible that society prefer z to y, for that would require that V_2 be decisive in this matter; this is impossible, since V_2 is contained in V and the last, by construction, has as few members as a decisive group can. Therefore society prefers x to z. But then the single individual V_1 would be decisive, and we have seen that that is impossible.

Thus the stated contradiction is established.

4   Values and Collective Decision Making

As an exercise in clarifying terminology, let us consider what can be said about the values of an imaginary, completely isolated individual. His personal skills and qualities and the physical world available to him jointly delimit a range of actions possible to him. To be precise, I shall so define the concept of action that alternative actions are mutually exclusive. An action, then, means a complete description of all the activities that an individual carries on, and two alternative actions are any two descriptions which differ in any relevant way. For example, an individual may describe his activities by indicating the amount of time he spends on each of the alternative modalities of performance available to him; thus, three hours at farming, three hours at hunting, four hours of violin playing, and so on. A change in any one of these time allocations would represent a change in action. This particular definition is truly a formal choice of language, and does not by itself change the nature of the problem. It simply brings out formally that the basic question of the individual is a choice of actions.

Values, Tastes, and Hypothetical Imperatives

To an economist, and I suppose to most philosophers, a value system would, in these terms, be simply the rule an individual uses to choose which of the

Reprinted from P. Laslett and W. G. Runciman, eds., *Philosophy, Politics and Society,* Third Series (Oxford: Basil Blackwell, 1967), pp. 215–232. Originally presented in slightly different form as "Public and Private Values" at a 1966 symposium on Human Values and Economic Policy at the New York University Institute of Philosophy.

mutually exclusive actions he will undertake. If an individual is facing a given set of alternative actions, he will choose one, and there seems to be little interesting to talk about. However, the problem, at least to the economist, is put in slightly different form. Consider an individual who does not yet know which actions will be available and which will not. Let us term the set of available actions the *environment*. One might ask him what action he *would choose* if offered some particular environment. By repeating this question for many alternative environments we obtain a description of his value system in the sense of a rule giving his hypothetical choice for many or all possible environments.[1]

One might want to reserve the term "values" for a specially elevated or noble set of choices. Perhaps choices in general might be referred to as "tastes." We do not ordinarily think of the preference for additional bread over additional beer as being a value worthy of philosophic inquiry. I believe, though, that the distinction cannot be made logically, and certainly not in dealing with the single isolated individual. If there is any distinction between values and tastes it must lie in the realm of interpersonal relations.

The Assumptions of Ordering

The description of a value system as a correlation between possible environments and the hypothetical choices to be made from them is not in itself a very informative procedure. Economists have been accustomed to adding considerable strength (empirical restrictiveness) by specifying that the value system shall have a particular structure — namely, being derivable from an *ordering*. To define this concept let us first consider environments consisting of just two alternative actions. For such two-member environments we can find the one chosen, in accordance with the individual's value system, and we shall speak of it as having been *preferred* to the other action in the environment. We may have to admit that the individual is equally willing to choose neither of the two actions, in which case we speak of the two actions as being *indifferent*. The assumption of an ordering means that certain

---

1. For technical mathematical reasons one must admit that sometimes more than one action should be regarded as chosen in a given environment, by which is meant the individual does not care which of the chosen actions is in fact adopted in a particular set of circumstances. We must also allow for the fact that there may be no chosen action; as an example, consider an individual with a normal desire for money who can choose any amount of gold less than (but not equal to) one ounce.

consistency assumptions are postulated about the relations of preference and indifference, and it is further assumed that choices from any environment can be described in terms of the ordering, which relates to choices in two-member environments.

The first assumption is that of *connexity* (or connectedness, or completeness, or comparability). It is assumed that for each pair of alternatives, either one is preferred to the other or the two are indifferent. The second assumption is that of *transitivity.* Consider three alternatives, to be designated by *x*, *y*, and *z*. Then if *x* is preferred to *y*, and *y* is preferred to *z*, we assume that *x* is preferred to *z*. We can and must also include in the definition cases where some of the choices are indifferent; for example, if *x* is indifferent to *y*, and *y* is indifferent to *z*, then *x* is indifferent to *z*.

For later use we introduce some symbolic notation to express these ordering relations. Specifically, we denote alternatives by *x*, *y*, . . . Then:

xPy means x is preferred to y,
xIy means x is indifferent to y,
xRy means x is preferred to or indifferent to y.

If we start with the relation *R* (that is, only knowing for which ordered pairs of alternatives *x*, *y* the statement *xRy* holds), then we can define the relations *P* and *I* in terms of *R*:

xIy is defined to be xRy and yRx,
xPy is defined to be xRy and not yRx.

The assumption of connexity can be stated:

For all x and y, xRy or yRx.

(Here and below, "or" does not exclude "and.") The assumption of transitivity can be stated:

For all x, y, and z, if zRy and yRz, then xRz.

Finally, and perhaps most important, it is assumed that the choice from any environment is determined by the ordering in the sense that if there is an alternative which is preferred to every other alternative in the environment, then it is the chosen element. This is an additional assumption not logically implied by the existence of an ordering itself.

In symbols, let *S* be any environment (set of alternatives) and *C(S)* the alternative (or alternatives) chosen from *S*. Then:

C(S) is the set of alternatives x in S for which xRy for all y in S.

It is easy to see that if x^1 and x^2 are both in $C(S)$ (both chosen alternatives in S), then $x^1\ Ix^2$.

Obviously, the assumption of ordering is by no means unreasonable. The notion of connexity carries the idea that choices have to be made whether we will or no. The idea of transitivity clearly corresponds to some strong feeling about the meaning of consistency in our choice. Economists have typically identified the concept of rationality with the notion of choices derivable from an ordering.

It may be worthwhile to dwell on the meaning of these two assumptions a little more, in view of their importance. It is not at all uncommon to find denials of the connexity assumption. Sufficiently remote alternatives are held to be incomparable. But I must say I do not find this line of argument at all convincing. If a choice has to be made, it has to be made. In most practical choice situations there is some *null* alternative, which will be chosen in the absence of what might be termed a positive decision. Thus, if there is dispute about the nature of new legislation, the preexisting legislation remains in force. But this does not mean that no choice is made; it means rather that the system produces as its choice the null alternative. I think what those who emphasize incomparability have in mind is rather that if one is forced to make a choice between alternatives which are difficult to compare, then the choice is not apt to satisfy the assumption of transitivity.

The possibility of regarding inaction as an always available alternative is part of the broader question of whether social choices should be historically conditioned. It is here that the importance of transitivity becomes clear. Transitivity implies that the final choice made from any given environment is independent of the path by which it has been derived. From any environment there will be a given chosen alternative, and in the absence of a deadlock no place for the historically given alternatives to be chosen by default.

Independence of Irrelevant Alternatives

Since the chosen element from any environment is completely defined by knowledge of the preferences between it and any other alternative in the environment, it follows that the choice depends only on the ordering of the elements of that environment. In particular, the choice made does not depend on preferences between alternatives which are not in fact available in the given environment, nor—and this is probably more important—on preferences between elements in the environment and those not in the environment. It is never necessary to compare available alternatives with those which are not available at a given moment in order to arrive at a decision. It is this point which is being made when it is argued that only ordinal measures of utility or preference are relevant to decisions. Any cardinal measure, any attempt to give a numerical representation of utility, depends basically on comparisons involving alternative actions which are not (or at least may not be) available, given the environment prevailing at the moment.

Omitted Considerations

For economy of discussion we pass by many interesting issues. Most important, probably, is the relation between hypothetical choices and real ones. It is implied in the discussion that a preference will in fact be translated into a choice if the opportunity ever comes. But the question may be raised how we can possibly know about hypothetical choices if they are not actually made. This is not merely a problem of finding out about somebody else's values; we may not know our own values until put to the crucial test.

Even the actual preferences may not be regarded as in some sense true values. An observer looking from the outside on our isolated individual may say that his decision was wrong either in the sense that there is some other standard of values to which it does not conform or in the sense that it was made on the grounds of insufficient information or improper calculation. The latter possibility is a real and important one, but I will simply state that I am abstracting from it in the course of the present discussion. The former interpretation I am rejecting. For the single isolated individual there can be no other standard than his own values. He might indeed wish to change them under criticism, but this, I take it, means basically that he has not fully thought through or calculated the consequences of his actions and upon more consideration wishes to modify them.

Interpersonal Nature of Social Action

The fundamental fact which causes the need for discussing public values at all is that every significant action involves the joint participation of many individuals. Even the apparently simplest act of individual decision involves the participation of a whole society.

It is important to note that this observation tells us all nontrivial actions are essentially the property of society as a whole, not of individuals. It is quite customary to think of each individual as being able to undertake actions on his own (for example, decisions of consumption, production, and exchange, moving from place to place, forming and dissolving families). Formally, a social action is then taken to be the resultant of all individual actions. In other words, any social action is thought of as being factored into a sequence of individual actions.

I certainly do not wish to deny that such factoring takes place, but I do wish to emphasize that the partition of a social action into individual components, and the corresponding assignment of individual responsibility, is *not* a datum. Rather, the particular factoring in any given context is itself the result of a social policy and therefore already the outcome of earlier and logically more primitive social values.

In economic transactions the point is clearest when we consider what we call property. Property is clearly a creation of society through its legal structure. The actions of buying and selling through offers of property are only at a superficial level the actions of an individual. They reflect a whole series of social institutions, and with different institutions different people would be having control over any given piece of property. Furthermore, the very notion of control over one's "own" property, as is apparent upon the most casual inspection, itself acquires its meaning through the regulations of society.

These are no idle or excessively nice distinctions. When it comes to racial discrimination, notions of liability, and responsibility for injury to others, or the whole concept of a corporation and its special and complex relations to the world as a whole, economic and social, we know that social values have altered considerably the terms on which property can be used in the marketplace or transmitted to others. Needless to say, the taxation system constitutes one of the strongest examples in which the state, as one aspect of society, makes clear the relative nature of ownership. Nor, in this context, should it be forgotten that the claims of society, as modifying the concept of ownership, are by no means confined to the state. Our particular culture has tended to minimize noncoercive obligations relative to the predominant role they have played elsewhere, but they are far from absent even today. There is certainly a whole complex of obligations implied in the concept of a "good neighbor." The use of one's real property is limited by more than legal conditions. As everyone knows — sometimes painfully — there are obligations of generosity and organized giving appropriate to an individual's income status and social position. In short, we argue that the facts of social life show clearly that there is no universally acceptable division of actions with regard to property into mine and thine.

To be sure, there is another category of actions, those which involve the person himself as opposed to his property. We have a stronger feeling here that there is a natural meaning to speaking of one's own actions as opposed to others. Presumably there is a meaningful sense in which we say that *I* am writing this paper—not anyone else. But of course even here the action is full of social interconnections. I am in a conference arranged by others, using words which are a common part of the culture, expressing ideas which draw upon a wide range of concepts of others, and which embody my education.

To be sure, I am using my own capacities at some point in this process. But how logically do we distinguish between the capacities which somehow define the person, and those which are the result of external actions of a society? I may see well because my vision is intrinsically good or because I have glasses. Is the vision more peculiarly *mine* in one case than in the other? One may concede that there is more of an intrinsic idea of property here in certain personal actions, but I think this whole matter needs deeper exploration than it has received thus far. In any case, there are obviously very strong social obligations on personal behavior and the use of one's personal capacities, just as there are on the use of property.

To conclude, then, we must in a general theory take as our unit a social action, that is, an action involving a large proportion or the entire domain of society. At the most basic axiomatic level, individual actions play little role. The need for a system of public values then becomes evident; actions being collective or interpersonal in nature, so must be the choice among them. A public or social value system is essentially a logical necessity.

The point is obvious enough in the contexts that we tend to regard as specifically political. The individuals in a country cannot have separate foreign policies or separate legal systems. Among economists the matter has been somewhat confused because economic analysis has supplied us with a model of factorization of social actions, that achieved through the price system. The system itself is certainly one of the most remarkable of social institutions and the analysis of its working is, in my judgment, one of the more significant intellectual achievements of mankind. But the factorization implied is a particular one made in a particular way. It is one that has turned out to be highly convenient, particularly from the point of view of economizing on the flow of information in the economic system. But at the fundamental level of discourse we are now engaged in, we cannot regard the price system as a datum. On the contrary, it is to be thought of as one of the instrumentalities, possibly the major one, by which whatever social value system there may be is realized.

Individual Preferences for Social Actions

The individual plays a central role in social choice as the judge of alternative social actions according to his own standards. We presume that each individual has some way of ranking social actions according to his preferences for their consequences. These preferences constitute his value system. They are assumed to reflect already in full measure altruistic or egoistic motivations, as the case may be.

Following the discussion above, we assume that the values are expressed in the form of an ordering. Thus, in effect, individuals are taken to be rational in their attitudes toward social actions.

In symbols, we now let $x, y, \ldots$, represent alternative social actions. Then the ith individual has an ordering among these actions which can be represented by a relation, to be denoted by R_i:

xR_iy *means x is preferred or indifferent to y in the view of individual i.*

As before, we can define P_i (preference in the view of individual i) and I_i (indifference in the view of individual i) in terms of R_i:

xP_iy *is defined to be* xR_iy *and not* yR_ix;
xI_iy *is defined to be* xR_iy *and* yR_ix.

We are face to face with an extremely difficult point. A standard liberal point of view in political philosophy, which also has dominated formal welfare economics, asserts that an individual's preferences are or ought to be (a distinction not usually made clear) concerned only with the effects of social actions on him. But there is no logical way to distinguish a particular class of consequences which pertain to a given individual. If I feel that my satisfaction is reduced by somebody else's poverty (or, for that matter, by somebody else's wealth), then I am injured in precisely the same sense as if my purchasing power were reduced. To parallel the observations of the preceding section, I am in effect arguing here that just as we cannot factor social actions so as to make each component pertain to a given individual, so we cannot factor the consequences of social actions in any meaningful way into separable consequences to individual members of the society. That is, let me make it clear, we cannot do it as a matter of fact. The interdependence of mankind is after all not a novel ethical doctrine. The man who questioned whether he was his brother's keeper was, according to an ancient source, not highly approved of. The general conclusion here is not one that I find myself entirely comfortable with. I do share the general liberal view that every individual should have the opportunity to find his own way to personal development and satisfaction. The question of interference with the actions of others has been raised most acutely in recent years in legal rather than economic contexts, specifically in the English discussion on laws regulating deviant sexual behavior. Homosexual behavior between consenting adults is probably a classic example of an action affecting no one else, and therefore should be exempt from social control. Yet many find themselves shocked and outraged. They would strongly prefer, let us say, the situation to be different. Similarly, I may be disturbed that the Negro is discriminated against and judge accordingly social actions which lead to this result.

One could say that the general principle of restraint in judging the affairs of others is an empirical assumption that people in fact do not care about (or, strictly, have no preferences concerning) matters which would in the usual terminology be regarded as none of their business. But of course empirically we know that this is quite false. The very fact that restrictive legislation is passed or even proposed shows clearly that people are willing to sacrifice effort and time because of the satisfactions to be received from seeing others' patterns of life altered.

The only rational defense of what may be termed a liberal position, or perhaps more precisely a principle of limited social preference, is that it is itself a value judgment. In other words, an individual may have as part of his value structure precisely that he does not think it proper to influence consequences outside a limited realm. This is a perfectly coherent position, but I find it difficult to insist that this judgment is of such overriding importance that it outweighs all other considerations. Personally, my values are such that I am willing to go very far indeed in the direction of respect for the means by which others choose to derive their satisfactions.

At this stage I want to emphasize that value judgments in favor of limited social preference, just as other value judgments emphasizing social solidarity, must be counted as part of the value systems which individuals use in the judgment of alternative social actions.

The problem of social choice is that of aggregating the multiplicity of individual preference scales about alternative social actions.

Welfare Judgments and Constitutions

Classical utilitarianism specifies that alternative social actions be judged in terms of their consequences for people. In the present terminology I take this to mean that they are to be judged in terms of individual preference scales. This by itself does not supply a sufficient basis for action in view of the multiplicity and divergence of individual preference scales. It is therefore at least implicit in classical utilitarianism that there is a second level at which the individual judgments are themselves evaluated, and this point has been given explicit recognition in a celebrated paper of Abram Bergson.[2] Let us call this second-order evaluation a *welfare judgment;* it is an evaluation of the consequences to all individuals based on their evaluations. If in each individual evaluation two social actions are indifferent, then the welfare judgment between the two must also be one of indifference.

The process of formation of welfare judgments is logically equivalent to a social decision process or *constitution.* Specifically, a constitution is a rule which associates to each possible set of individual orderings a social choice function, that is, a rule for selecting a preferred action out of every possible environment. That a welfare judgment is a constitution indeed follows immediately from the assumption that a welfare judgment can be formed, given any set of individual preference systems for social actions. The classification of welfare judgments as constitutions is at this stage a tautology, but what makes it more than that is a specification of reasonable conditions to be imposed on constitutions, and it is here that any dispute must lie.

Social Decision Processes and the Notion of Social Welfare

While I have just argued that a welfare judgment is necessarily a constitution or process of social decision, the converse need not be true, at least not without further clarification of the meaning of "welfare judgment." A welfare judgment requires that some one person be judge; a rule for arriving at social decisions may be agreed upon for reasons of convenience and

---

2. "A Reformulation of Certain Aspects of Welfare Economics," *Quarterly Journal of Economics,* 52 (1938), 310–34; reprinted in A. Bergson, *Essays in Normative Economics* (Cambridge, Mass.: Harvard University Press, 1966), 1–49.

necessity without its outcomes being treated as evaluations by anyone in particular.[3] Indeed, I would go further and argue that the appropriate standpoint for analyzing social decision processes is precisely that they not be welfare judgments of any particular individuals. This seems contrary to Bergson's point of view.[4] In my view, the location of welfare judgments in any individual, while logically possible, does not appear to be very interesting. "Social welfare" is related to social policy in any sensible interpretation; the welfare judgments of any single individual are unconnected with action and therefore sterile. Bergson has recognized that there may be this alternative interpretation of the concept of social welfare; I quote the passage at length since it displays the issue so well:

> I have been assuming that the concern of welfare economics is to counsel individual citizens generally. If a public official is counselled, it is on the same basis as any other citizen. In every instance reference is made to some ethical values which are appropriate for the counselling of the individual in question. In all this I believe I am only expressing the intent of welfare writings generally; or if this is not the intent, I think it should be. But some may be inclined nevertheless to a different conception, which allows still another interpretation of Arrow's theorem. *According to this view, the problem is to counsel not citizens generally but public officials.* Furthermore, the values to be taken as data are not those which would guide the official if he were a private citizen. The official is envisaged instead as more or less neutral ethically. His one aim in life is to implement the values of other citizens as given by some rule of collective decision making. [Emphasis added.][5]

My interpretation of the social choice problem agrees fully with that given by Bergson beginning with the italicized statement, although, as can be seen, this is not the view that he himself endorses.

The fundamental problem of public value formation, then, is the construction of constitutions. In general, of course, there is no difficulty in construct-

---

3. This point has been well stressed by I. M. D. Little, "Social Choice and Individual Values," *Journal of Political Economy,* 60 (1952), 422–32.

4. A. Bergson, "On the Concept of Social Welfare," *Quarterly Journal of Economics,* 68 (1954), 233–52, reprinted in *Essays in Normative Economics,* 27–49, esp. pp. 35–6.

5. Ibid., pp. 37–8.

ing a rule if one is content with arbitrary rules. The problem becomes meaningful if reasonable conditions are suggested, which every constitution should obey.[6]

Some Conditions on Constitutions

I suggest here four conditions which seem very reasonable to impose on any constitution. More can undoubtedly be suggested but unfortunately, as we shall see below, these four more than suffice.

Recall that a constitution is a rule which assigns to any set of individual preference orderings a rule for making society's choices among alternative social actions in any possible environment. Thus, for a given set of individual orderings the result of the process is a particular value system; that is, a rule for making selections out of all possible environments. The first condition may be termed that of

• *Collective Rationality:* For any given set of orderings, the social choice function is derivable from an ordering.

In other words, the social choice system has the same structure as that which we have already assumed for individual value systems. The next condition is one that has been little disputed and is advanced by almost every writer in the economic literature.

• *Pareto Principle:* If alternative x is preferred to alternative y by every single individual according to his ordering, then the social ordering also ranks x above y.

Notice that we can use the term "social ordering" in view of the previous condition of Collective Rationality. The next condition is perhaps the most important as well as the most controversial. For my own part, I am less tempted to regard it as ultimately satisfactory than I formerly did, but it has strong pragmatic justification.

• *Independence of Irrelevant Alternatives:* The social choice made from any environment depends only on the orderings of individuals with respect to the alternatives in that environment.

To take an extreme case, suppose that individuals are informed that there are a certain number of social actions available. They are not even aware that there are other conceivable social actions. They develop their own

---

6. The analysis that follows is based on my book *Social Choice and Individual Values* (New York, London, and Sydney: Wiley: 1st ed. 1951; 2nd ed. 1963).

preference systems for the alternatives contained in this particular environment, and then the constitution generates a choice. Later they are told that in fact there were alternatives which were logically possible but were not in fact available. For example, a city is taking a poll of individual preferences on alternative methods of transportation (rapid transit, automobile, bus). Someone suggests that in evaluating these preferences they also ought to ask individual preferences for instantaneous transportation by dissolving the individual into molecules in a ray gun and re-forming him elsewhere in the city as desired. There is no pretense that this method is in any way an available alternative. The assumption of Independence of Irrelevant Alternatives is that such preferences have no bearing on the choice to be made.

It is of course obvious that ordinary political decision-making methods satisfy this condition. When choosing among candidates for an elected office, all that is asked are the preferences among the actual candidates, not also preferences among other individuals who are not candidates and who are not available for office.

Finally, we enunciate probably the least controversial of all the conditions.

• *Nondictatorship:* There is no individual whose preferences are automatically society's preferences independent of the preferences of all other individuals.

There is a difference worth noting between the first two conditions and the last two. The assumptions of Collective Rationality and the Pareto Principle are statements which apply to any fixed set of individual orderings. They do not involve comparisons between social orderings based on different sets of individual orderings. On the contrary, the conditions of Independence of Irrelevant Alternatives and of Nondictatorship are assertions about the responsiveness of the social ordering to variations in individual orderings.

Impossibility Theorem

The conditions of Collective Rationality and of Independence of Irrelevant Alternatives taken together imply that in a generalized sense all methods of social choice are of the type of voting. If we consider environments composed of two alternatives alone, then the condition of Independence of Irrelevant Alternatives tells us that the choice is determined solely by the preferences of the members of the community between those two alternatives, and no other preferences are involved. Define a set of individuals to be *decisive* for alternative x over alternative y if the constitution prescribes that *x* is chosen over *y* whenever all individuals in the set prefer *x* to *y* and all others prefer *y* to *x*. Then the rule for choosing from any two-member environment has the form of specifying which sets of individuals are decisive for *x* and *y* and which for *y* over *x*. The majority voting principle, for example, states simply that any set containing a majority of the voters is decisive for any alternative over any other.

Then if the social value system is generated by a social ordering, all social preferences are determined by the choices made for two-member environments, and hence by pairwise votes (thus systems like plurality voting are excluded).

Now it has been known for a long time that the system of majority voting can give rise to paradoxical consequences. Consider the following example. There are three alternatives, *x*, *y*, and *z*, among which choice is to be made. One-third of the voters prefer *x* to *y* and *y* to *z*, one-third prefer *y* to *z* and *z* to *x*, and one-third prefer *z* to *x* and *x* to *y*. Then *x* will be preferred to *y* by a majority, *y* to *z* by a majority, and *z* to *x* by a majority.[7]

One might be tempted to suppose that the paradox of voting is an imperfection in the particular system of majority voting, and that more ingenious methods could avoid it. Unfortunately this is not so. The following general theorem may be stated and is proved below.

There can be no constitution simultaneously satisfying the conditions of Collective Rationality, the Pareto Principle, the Independence of Irrelevant Alternatives, and Nondictatorship.

This conclusion is quite embarrassing, and it forces us to examine the conditions which have been stated as reasonable. It is hard to imagine anyone quarreling with either the Pareto Principle or the condition of Nondictatorship. The principle of Collective Rationality may indeed be

---

7. This paradox seems to have been first observed by the Marquis de Condorcet, *Essai sur l'application de l'analyse à la probabilité des décisions rendues à la pluralité des voix* (Paris, 1785). That a rational voting scheme requires knowledge of all preferences among the candidates and not only the first choice was already argued even earlier by Jean-Charles de Borda, "Mémoire sur les élections au scrutin," *Mémoires de l'Académie Royale des Sciences,* 1781, 657–65. For a modern analysis of Condorcet's work on voting, see G.-G. Granger, *La Mathématique Social du Marquis de Condorcet* (Paris: Presses Universitaires de France, 1956, esp. pp. 94–129). For an English translation of Borda's work see A. de Grazia, "Mathematical Derivation of an Election System," *Isis,* 44 (1953), 42–51. For a general history of the theory of social choice, see D. Black, *The Theory of Committees and Elections* (Cambridge: Cambridge University Press, 1958), pt. 2.

questioned. One might be prepared to allow that the choice from a given environment be dependent on the history of previous choices made in earlier environments, but I think many would find that situation unsatisfactory. There remains, therefore, only the Independence of Irrelevant Alternatives, which will be examined in greater detail below.

Proof of the Impossibility Theorem

We assume the existence of a social choice mechanism satisfying the conditions of Collective Rationality, the Pareto Principle, the Independence of Irrelevant Alternatives, and Nondictatorship, and show that the assumption leads to a contradiction. Since the condition of Collective Rationality requires that social choice be derivable from an ordering, we can speak of social preference and social indifference. In particular, as defined above, a set of individuals V is *decisive* for x against y if x is socially preferred to y whenever all individuals in V prefer x to y and all others prefer y to x.[8]

The proof falls into two parts. It is first shown that if an individual is decisive for some pair of alternatives, then he is a dictator, contrary to the condition of Nondictatorship. Hence, no individual is decisive for any pair of alternatives, and the Impossibility Theorem itself then follows easily with the aid of the Pareto Principle.

We first distinguish one individual, called I, and introduce the following notations for statements about the constitution:

(4-1) $x\overline{D}y$ means that x is socially preferred to y whenever individual I prefers x to y, regardless of the orderings of other individuals;

(4-2) xDy means that x is socially preferred to y if individual I prefers x to y and all other individuals prefer y to x.

Notice that this notation is legitimate only because of the assumption of Independence of Irrelevant Alternatives. Note too that the statement $x\overline{D}y$ implies xDy, and that xDy is the same as the assertion that I is a decisive set for x against y.

Suppose then that xDy holds for some x and y. We will first suppose that there are only three alternatives altogether. Let the third alternative be z.

---

8. The following proof is quoted, with minor alterations, from Arrow, *Social Choice and Individual Values,* pp. 98–100.

Suppose I orders the alternatives x, y, z in descending order, whereas all other individuals prefer y to both x and z but may have any preferences between the last two. Then I prefers x to y, whereas all others prefer y to x; from (4-2) this means that xPy. All individuals prefer y to z; by the Pareto Principle, yPz. Then, by transitivity, xPz; but then this holds whenever xP_iz, regardless of the orderings of other individuals between x and z. In symbols,

(4-3) xDy implies $x\bar{D}z$.

Again suppose xDy, but now suppose that I orders the alternatives z, x, y, whereas all other individuals prefer both z and y to x. By a similar argument, xPy and zPx, so that xPy.

(4-4) xDy implies $z\bar{D}y$.

Interchanging y and z in (4-4) yields

(4-5) xDz implies $y\bar{D}z$.

Replacing x by y, y by z, and z by x in (4-3) yields

(4-6) yDz implies $y\bar{D}x$.

Since $x\bar{D}z$ implies xDz, and $y\bar{D}z$ implies yDz, we can, by chaining the implications (4-3), (4-5), and (4-6), deduce

(4-7) xDy implies $y\bar{D}x$.

If we interchange x and y in (4-3), (4-4), and (4-7), we arrive at the respective implications

> yDx implies $y\bar{D}z$,
>
> yDx implies $z\bar{D}x$,
>
> yDx implies $x\bar{D}y$,

and these can each be chained with the implication (4-7) to yield

(4-8) xDy implies $y\bar{D}z$, $z\bar{D}x$, and $x\bar{D}y$.

Implications (4-3), (4-4), (4-7), and (4-8) together can be summarized as saying

(4-9)   If xDy, then $u\bar{D}v$ are for every ordered pair u, v from the three alternatives x, y, and z;

that is, individual I is a dictator for the three alternatives.

We can extend this result to any number of alternatives by an argument due to Blau.[9] Suppose aDb holds, and let x and y be any pair of alternatives. If x and y are the same as a and b, either in the same or in the reverse order, we add a third alternative c to a and b; then we can apply (4-9) to the triple a, b, c and deduce $x\bar{D}y$ by letting $u = x$, $v = y$. If exactly one of x and y is distinct from a and b, add it to a and b to form a triple to which (4-9) is again applicable. Finally, if both x and y are distinct from a and b, two steps are needed. First, add x to a and b, and deduce from (4-9) that $a\bar{D}x$ and therefore aDx. Then, again applying (4-9) to the triple a, x, y, we find that $x\bar{D}y$. Thus, aDb for some a and b implies that $x\bar{D}y$ for all x and y—in other words, individual I is a dictator. From the condition of Nondictatorship it can be concluded that

(4-10) xDy cannot hold for any individual I and any pair x, y.

The remainder of the proof is now an appropriate adaptation of the paradox of voting. By the Pareto Principle, there is at least one decisive set for any ordered pair x,y, namely, the set of all individuals. Among all sets of individuals which are decisive for some pairwise choice, pick one such that no other is smaller; by (4-10) it must contain at least two individuals. Let V be the chosen set and let the ordered pair for which it is decisive be x,y. Divide V into two parts, V_1, which contains only a single individual, and V_2, which contains all the rest. Let V_3 be the set of individuals not in V.

Consider now the case where the preference order of V_1 is x,y,z, that of all members of V_2 is z,x,y, and that of all members of V_3 is y,z,x. Since V is decisive for x against y, all members of V prefer x to y while all others have the opposite preference xPy. On the other hand, it is impossible that society prefers z to y, since that would require that V_2 be decisive on this issue; this is impossible, since V_2 has fewer members than V—which, by construction, has as few members as a decisive set can have. Hence, yRz, and since xPy, society must prefer x to z. But then the single member of V_1 would be decisive, and we have shown that to be impossible.

Thus the contradiction is established.

The Independence of Irrelevant Alternatives and Interpersonal Comparisons of Intensity

Modern economic theory has insisted on the ordinal concept of utility; that is, only orderings can be observed, and therefore no measurement of utility

---

9. J. H. Blau, "The Existence of Social Welfare Functions," *Econometrica,* 25 (1957), 310.

independent of these orderings has any significance. In the field of consumer's demand theory the ordinalist position turned out to create no problems; cardinal utility had no explanatory power above and beyond ordinal. Leibniz' Principle of the Identity of Indiscernibles demanded then the excision of cardinal utility from our thought patterns. Bergson's formulation of the social welfare function carried out the same principle in the analysis of social welfare. Social choices were to depend only on individual orderings; hence, welfare judgments were based only on interpersonally observable behavior.

The condition of Independence of Irrelevant Alternatives extends the requirement of observability one step farther. Given the set of alternatives available for society to choose among, it could be expected that ideally one could observe all preferences among the available alternatives, but there would be no way to observe preferences among alternatives not feasible for society.

I now feel, however, that the austerity imposed by this condition is stricter than desirable. In many situations we do have information on preferences for nonfeasible alternatives. It can certainly be argued that when available this information should be used in social choice. Unfortunately, it is clear, as I have already suggested, that social decision processes which are independent of irrelevant alternatives have strong practical advantages, and it remains to be seen whether a satisfactory social decision procedure can really be based on other information.

The potential usefulness of irrelevant alternatives is that they may permit empirically meaningful interpersonal comparisons. The information which might enable us to assert that one individual prefers alternative x to alternative y more strongly than a second individual prefers y to x must be based on comparisons by the two individuals of the two alternatives, not only with respect to each other but also to other alternatives.

Let me conclude by suggesting one type of use of irrelevant alternatives, which may be termed "extended sympathy." We do seem prepared to make comparisons of the form *Action x is better (or worse) for me than action y is for you.* This is probably in fact the standard way in which people make judgments about appropriate income distributions; if I am richer than you, I may find it easy to make the judgment that it is better for you to have the marginal dollar than for me.

How is this consistent with our general point of view that all value judgments are at least hypothetical choices among alternative actions? Interpersonal comparisons of the extended sympathy type can be put in operational form. The judgment takes the form *It is better (in my judgment) to be myself under action x than to be you under action y.*

In this form the characteristics that define an individual are included in the comparison. In effect, these characteristics are put on a par with the items usually regarded as constituting an individual's wealth. The possession of tools is ordinarily regarded as part of the social state which is being evaluated; why not the possession of the skills to use those tools, and the intelligence which lies behind those skills? Individuals, in appraising each other's states of well-being, not only consider material possessions but also find themselves "desiring this man's scope and that man's art."[10] The principle of extended sympathy as a basis for interpersonal comparisons seems basic to many of the welfare judgments made in ordinary practice. It remains to be seen whether an adequate theory of social choice can be derived from this and other acceptable principles.

---

10. The moral implications of the position that many attributes of the individual are similar in nature to external possessions have been discussed by V. C. Walsh, *Scarcity and Evil* (Englewood Cliffs, N.J.: Prentice-Hall, 1961).

5   The Place of Moral Obligation in Preference Systems

Professor Brandt's paper raises a number of very interesting issues, but I wish to concentrate here on only one, the place of moral obligation in the preference systems of individuals [Brandt, 1967, pp. 26–28].

I should make it thoroughly clear that the preference systems of individuals that I regard as basic raw material for the formulation of social choice refer to what Brandt calls "personal welfare," *not* moral principle. In the typical economic situation, it is true, issues of moral principle in the ordinary sense are not faced in any very explicit form (though they probably play a much larger role, even in narrowly economic circumstances, than is usually considered). We rather think of a set of individuals, each with his own personal preference scales, who have to make a collective decision of some kind. Suppose that they surmount all the difficulties of collective decision making and come to an agreement. In general, this agreement will not be the best possible decision for any single individual, according to his own personal preference scale. Each one carries out his part of the agreement, not because he wants to undertake this obligation for its own sake, but because it is part of an agreement, the net result of which is beneficial to him as compared with the alternative of no agreement—though not as compared with the best state he could achieve if he were a perfect dictator.

Reprinted by permission of New York University Press from *Human Values and Economic Policy,* edited by Sidney Hook, pp. 117–119. Copyright © 1967 by New York University. This is a comment on Richard Brandt's paper in the same volume.

To illustrate, consider two individuals living in a valley to which there is presently no road. Assume that the road brings each of them great benefits, but neither enjoys the labor of building it. Obviously, from the point of view of either one the optimal situation is to have the other man build the road. Nevertheless, they may agree to share the labor of building a road because the alternative of failing to agree is worse for both of them; each one would rather have the road and do half the labor than not have the road at all. If one observes their behavior, he might be tempted to say that they have not followed out their personal preferences in that they would have preferred not to work on the road. But in fact, considering the whole agreement, they are behaving in a preferred way, that is, preferred to the actually possible alternatives, not to unattainable alternatives.

Thus, behavior in accordance with an agreement is compatible with judgment based on personal preference scales, but might not appear to be so if the analysis is not complete enough. I now come to the key point: I interpret moral obligation as the carrying out of agreements which may, however, be implicit. A society in which everyone immediately executed his aggressive impulses would be untenable. Therefore, there is an agreement that I will refrain from aggressive actions, which in themselves give me satisfaction, in return for your not taking aggressive action against me. However, conscious agreements to achieve these ends are much too costly in terms of information and bargaining. As societies have evolved they have found it economical to make these agreements at an unconscious, implicit level. Internalized feelings of guilt and right are essentially unconscious equivalents of agreements that represent social decisions.

In the light of changes in circumstances and the development of knowledge, it may indeed be important to rethink these past agreements. Many aspects of conventional morality are being altered, partly consciously, partly unconsciously. What may be thought of as moral obligations to obey the law or to help the poor have come under increasing reexamination; in other words, a new decision based on the synthesis of individual preferences under an altered environment is being formed.

In regard to Brandt's question, then, my answer would be the following: strictly speaking, the preference scales that I deal with are those relating to personal welfare only. The range of moral obligations is part of the social decision to be arrived at by the collective decision-making machinery. In practice, of course, we do not continually make decisions about everything, so that in any concrete instance some parts of a collective agreement, and in particular some moral principles, are left unexamined and taken as data while other matters are under discussion. But this is a matter of economy of thought and action, not of long-run immutable principles.

Reference

Brandt, R. B. Personal values and the justification of institutions. In S. Hook, ed., *Human Values and Economic Policy.* New York: New York University Press, 1967, pp. 22–40.

6   Tullock and an
       Existence Theorem

Gordon Tullock's latest book[1] is a continuation of the now-flourishing tradition which seeks to explain the political process in terms of the rational behavior of its participants, the voters and the politicians. What is sought is a theory analogous to that which has dominated economics, in which the observed behavior of all is found as an equilibrium in which each participant is maximizing some suitably defined criterion, given institutional and technological constraints and the behavior of others. This tradition has had several sources: (1) an intermittent interest in evaluating alternative voting systems, the natural criteria being measures of resemblance between individual preference scales and the social outcome of the voting process; the key names are Borda and Condorcet in the eighteenth century, Nanson and Dodgson (Lewis Carroll) in the nineteenth; (2) the interest of the marginal-utility theorists in demonstrating that their tools were applicable to wider areas of human behavior than the purely economic (Wicksteed, Marshall, and, in modern times, Becker serve as examples); (3) closely related, the economic theory of bargaining, especially in the form developed by Edgeworth, clearly invites extension to the political and social

---

1. G. Tullock, *Toward a Mathematics of Politics* (Ann Arbor: University of Michigan Press, 1967).

Reprinted from *Public Choice*, 6 (1969):105–112.

spheres, a step taken by Hotelling and Zeuthen and, in very great generality, by von Neumann and Morgenstern and many of the subsequent game theorists (Nash, Shapley, Shubik, Aumann, Harsanyi, and Maschler, among others); and (4) the interest of public-finance theorists in finding a public demand analogous to private demand (Wicksell, Lindahl, Bowen, and, more recently, Musgrave and Samuelson). Duncan Black's work of the 1940s synthesized several of these intellectual streams and began the continuous tradition which has been further developed by many writers, among whom Downs, Riker, Buchanan, Olson, and Tullock are especially to be mentioned.

Tullock's book is, as the author notes in his preface, not the development of a single theme, but a series of essays on distinct aspects of a rational theory of politics. The title is misleading; there are no developments of any mathematical complexity. The mode of analysis is that of literary economic theory, the logical development being conveyed in words rather than symbols. Though empirical references are frequent, they are casual in nature, not systematic attempts at refutation of precisely stated hypotheses.

After an introductory chapter which discusses the nature of preferences and changes in them, the book falls into four main parts. In chapters 2 to 4 the implications of majority voting for the behavior of political parties (assumed to maximize votes) are explored. In chapters 5 and 6 there is some study of the implications of single-peaked preferences for monopolistic competition and, in particular, for the production of information. Chapters 7 to 9 analyze the production and consumption of information in the political sphere, with emphasis on persuasion by true or false information. Finally, chapter 10 is an essay on proportional representation, the chief novelty of which is an ingenious proposal by the author that every elected representative cast as many votes in the legislature as he received in the election.

Chapter 3 presents what I feel is the major analytic contribution of the book — an argument that, under certain plausible hypotheses, the Condorcet voting paradox (the intransitivity of majority voting) will not arise. In view of the importance of this result I want to present a general formulation of Tullock's proposition and some comments on its applicability. My comments on the remainder of the book will therefore be brief.

The basic model throughout the book is that of a multidimensional space of social issues over which each individual has a preference ordering. In chapter 2 a geometric analysis of the two-dimensional case is carried through with great care. This chapter is a superb piece of pedagogy. As a result of careful examination of a number of examples, it is concluded that when the number of choosers greatly exceeds the dimensionality of the issue space, then the set of Pareto-optimal points is apt to be a fairly large proportion of the total space; the interesting question then is the choice within the Pareto region, and a voting rule which tends to pick out some average point is desirable. If, on the other hand, the dimensionality of the issue space is large compared with the number of choosers, the Pareto region is relatively small; simply attaining a point in it becomes important, so that the rule of unanimity is powerful. The former case Tullock identifies with the domain of politics, the latter with that of economics (the market).

Chapter 4 attempts to extend the Hotelling-Downs model of competition among parties to two-dimensional issue spaces: a number of examples are given, suggesting that the tendency to a median is frequently still valid.

Chapter 5, on monopolistic competition, is mainly devoted to an argument that the monopolistically competitive equilibrium may be close to optimal. The author here suffers from a lack of reference to the literature: even Chamberlin's later editions made this point, and in any case no rigorous analysis or even formulation of the notion of a monopolistically competitive equilibrium has yet been made. Chapter 6 has a number of interesting comments on the incentive for the provision of different kinds of information (here, principally editorial opinion) in response to demand, but no strong generalizations appear.

Chapters 7 to 9 expand on a theme introduced into the literature by Anthony Downs; since the effect of any individual vote is so very small, it does not pay a voter to acquire information unless his stake in the issue is enormously greater than the cost of information. The resulting rational ignorance in the political field in turn creates incentives to political parties· and other strongly motivated groups to engage in persuasive activities by dissemination of information, selected or even false. Tullock's discussion is discursive; a number of provocative points are made which do not lend themselves to easy summary.

Let me return to chapter 3. To quote:

A phantom has stalked the classrooms and seminars of economics and political science for nearly fifteen years. This phantom, Arrow's General Impossibility Theorem, has been generally interpreted as proving that no sensible method of aggregating preferences exists. The purpose of this essay is to exorcise the phantom, not by disproving the theorem in its strict mathematical form, but by showing that it is insubstantial. I shall show that when a rather simple and probable type of interdependence is assumed among the preference functions of the choosing individuals, the problem becomes trivial if the number of voters is large. Since most cases which require aggregation of preferences involve large numbers of people, "Arrow problems" will seldom be of much importance.

What Tullock does, in effect, is to give an example, considered to be typical of real-world situations, where there is one point in the social issue space which is preferred by a majority to all others. He assumes (1) that the number of voters is large, so large that we may consider them to constitute a continuum, (2) that the indifference curves of each individual in the space of social issues are circles concentric about a global optimum (as seen by the individual), and (3) that the global optima of the different voters are uniformly distributed over the issue space, taken to be a rectangle. From (2), an individual will prefer point A to point B if and only if his global optimum is closer to A than to B. If we draw the perpendicular of the line joining the two points and thus divide the rectangle into two regions, then those individuals whose global optima are in the region containing A are precisely those who prefer A to B. In view of (3), then, a majority prefer A to B if the area of the region containing A exceeds that of the region containing B.

It is then easy to infer that A is preferred to B if and only if it is closer to the center of the rectangle. Since the relation "closer to the center" is certainly transitive, it follows that majority decision yields a true ordering under these circumstances. In particular, the center of the rectangle is preferred to any other alternative.

The question needs to be raised, does this example generalize in any meaningful way? It so happens that a generalization can be found by making use of an unpublished paper by Sonnenschein.[2] Sonnenschein's interest was in a seemingly remote problem: was it possible to get the usual results in the theory of consumer's demand without assuming the transitivity of the preference relation? His answer was, in effect, that it was, provided another hypothesis was adopted, that the set of alternatives preferred to a given alternative is always convex.

Sonnenschein's result immediately suggests application to (weak) majority choice, a relation which is connected but not necessarily transitive. For

---

2. H. F. Sonnenschein, "Demand Functions without Transitive Preferences, with Applications to the Theory of Competitive Equilibrium" [in J. Chipman, L. Hurwicz, M. K. Richter, and H. F. Sonnenschein, eds., *Preferences, Utility, and Demand* (New York: Harcourt-Brace-Jovanovich, 1971), pp. 215–223].

any pair of alternatives x,y, let $N(x,y)$ be the number of individuals who prefer x to y. Then let xMy be the statement $N(x,y) \geq N(y,x)$ and $x\overline{M}y$ the statement that $N(x,y) > N(y,x)$. The question then is, given a set of alternatives, say S, under what conditions does there exist an alternative chosen by majority decision, that is, an alternative x in S such that xMy for all y in S? An answer is provided by the following.

THEOREM. *Suppose that, for each alternative x^0, the set of alternatives x for which xMx^0 is closed and the set of alternatives for which $x\overline{M}x^0$ is convex. Then for any compact (closed and bounded) convex set of alternatives S, there is (at least) one alternative x in S such that xMy for all y in S.*

Although the proof is simply a transcription of that in Sonnenschein's paper, it may be worth extracting the essential points from the consumer's demand context. The proof is based on the following two mathematical lemmas valid for finite dimensional Euclidean spaces.

LEMMA 1. *Let S be a compact set and F a family of closed subsets of S such that every finite collection of sets in F has an element in common. Then there is an element common to all the sets in F.*

LEMMA 2. *For each $i = 1, \ldots , m$, let a_i be a point and S_i a closed set. Suppose that for any subset L of the indices $1, \ldots , m$, any convex combination of the a_i's ($i \in L$) belongs to at least one S_i with $i \in L$. Then there is a convex combination of the a_i's ($i = 1, \ldots , m$) which belongs to all of the S_i's ($i = 1, \ldots , m$).*

Lemma 1 is a standard proposition in real analysis. Lemma 2 is a slight generalization of the well-known Knaster-Kuratowski-Mazurkiewicz lemma in topology, a proposition closely related to Brouwer's Fixed Point Theorem.

Proof of Theorem. Consider any given compact convex set of alternatives, S; for any y in S, let $S(y)$ be the set of alternatives x in S for which xMy. By hypothesis, the set of all alternatives x for which xMy is a closed set, and therefore the set of alternatives for which both x in S and xMy is also a closed set, since S is closed.

Let $a_i(i = 1, \ldots , m)$ be any m elements of S, and let L be any subset of the indices $1, \ldots , m$. Let y be a convex combination of the points $a_i(i \in L)$; it is first shown that $y \in S(a_i)$ for some $i \in L$. For suppose not; then, from the definition, it must be that yMa_i is false for all i in L, that is, $a_i\overline{M}y$ for all i in L. But y is a convex combination of the points a_i; by hypothesis, the set of alternatives $x\overline{M}y$ is convex, so that $y\overline{M}y$, an obvious contradiction. Hence, any convex combination of the points $a_i (i \in L)$ belongs to at least one $S(a_i)$ with $i \in L$. From Lemma 2, it then follows immediately that there is at least one point common to all the sets $S(a_i)$, $i = 1, \ldots, m$.

Let F be the family of all sets $S(y)$ as y varies over S. It has just been shown that any finite collection of sets in F has an element in common. By Lemma 1 there is a point x which is common to all the sets $S(y)$. That is, xMy for all y in S; since $x \in S(y)$, it certainly belongs to S, by definition. Q.E.D.

The hypotheses of the theorem are obviously fulfilled in Tullock's example.

Several remarks are in order to help clarify the meaning of this theorem.

Remark 1. The conclusion of the theorem is something weaker than transitivity; it asserts the existence of a preferred point (more strictly a noninferior point) in any *convex* set. This is an important restriction, since all cases of increasing return are ruled out of consideration, and these are, after all, a major portion of the scope of public decision making. It is not absolutely clear that this restriction is in fact necessary. In Tullock's example transitivity held, so that there would exist a noninferior point (according to the majority decision criterion) from any compact set of alternatives. I would conjecture that the conclusion of the theorem cannot be improved on without further hypotheses, but I have no example to prove this.

Remark 2. The hypothesis of convexity of the majority preference sets is, in some rough sense, a hypothesis of similarity of attitudes, but its exact meaning is obscure. It would be useful to find sufficient conditions for the convexity of majority preference sets, conditions which might be stronger but which are more transparent. One condition can be given which is transparent but perhaps not yet sufficiently so: for any fixed x_0, the function $N(x,x_0) - N(x_0,x)$ is quasi-concave. First, note that this condition means that the set of x's for which $N(x,x_0) - N(x_0,x) > c$ is convex for any c and, in particular, for $c = 0$, which defines the majority preference set. To understand the meaning of this condition, take any straight line in the space of alternatives. For any x on the line, we can ask each voter if he prefers x to the given alternative, x_0; the statement that the function, $N(x,x_0) - N(x_0,x)$, is quasi-concave amounts to saying that the number of voters who answer "yes" to the above question increases to a maximum as we move along the line and then decreases (or the number may increase all the way or decrease all the way). This does appear to me to convey an idea of similarity of preferences without imposing absolute identity.

Remark 3. Perhaps the deepest motivation for study of the theory of social choice, at least for the economist, is the hope of saying something useful about the evaluation of income distributions. It should be made clear that the theorem of this review note does not directly help at all in the resolution of this problem. Suppose a number of individuals with completely egoistic preferences use the method of majority decision to divide up a fixed total of a single commodity. Then, as has been remarked many times, there is no allocation which will command a majority against any other. For the allocation which gives zero to all is inferior, by unanimous vote, to one which gives a positive amount to each chosen sufficiently small to be feasible. For any allocation which gives some individual, say 1, a positive amount, there is another, which gives 1 nothing and divides up his share in the first allocation among all the others; the second is preferred to the first by all but one individual. It can easily be shown in this case that the majority preference sets are not convex.

In this case of unrestricted income distribution the dimensionality of the issue space is the same as the number of individuals. Thus, as Tullock argues, political resolution of distributional issues is apt to be possible solely if only a few parameters of the income distribution are under consideration, not the whole distribution. Why this restriction of the scope of choice should occur is not easy to explain on simple economic grounds. On the other hand, the restriction does conform to the long-standing view of writers on ethics, among whom Kant is perhaps most conspicuous, that decisions on distribution ought to be made as if by an impartial observer, who considers then only the mean, a measure of inequality, and perhaps one or two further parameters characterizing the income distribution, but not specifically who gets what. If voters acted like Kantian judges, they might still differ, but the chances of coming to an agreement by majority decision would be much greater than if voters consulted egoistic values only. Does this suggest that ethics may have survival value for political systems, and therefore descriptive as well as prescriptive significance?

7   A Utilitarian Approach to the Concept of Equality in Public Expenditures

J. S. Coleman[1] and doubtless many others have stressed the distinction between equality of output and equality of input in evaluating public expenditures, particularly those devoted to individual benefit, as in the case of education or health. The point is that the benefit derived by an individual from a given volume of government expenditures depends upon other characteristics of that individual. Hence, the dictum that the government ought to treat its citizens equally becomes ambiguous; equality of expenditures on different individuals does not produce equality of benefit to them.

I suggest here a reconsideration of the whole concept of equality in this domain by reverting to the utilitarian concepts of Bentham, as applied more precisely to the economic realm by F. Y. Edgeworth.[2] That is, instead of discussing equality per se, we seek to derive the concept from a maximiza-

---

1. J. S. Coleman, "The Concept of Equality of Educational Opportunity," *Harvard Educational Review,* 38 (1968), 14–22.

2. F. Y. Edgeworth, *Mathematical Psychics* (London: C. Kegan & Paul, 1881), pp. 56–82, and "The Pure Theory of Taxation," in *Papers Relating to Political Economy,* vol. 2 (London: Macmillan, 1925), pp. 100–122. The latter was originally published in *The Economic Journal,* 7 (1897), 46–70, 226–38, 550–71.

Reprinted from *Quarterly Journal of Economics,* 85 (1971):409–415. Reprinted by permission of John Wiley & Sons, Inc.

tion of the sum of individual utilities.[3] In the utilitarian discussion of income distribution, equality of income is derived from the maximization conditions if it is further assumed that individuals have the same utility functions, each with diminishing marginal utility. The utilitarian approach is not currently fashionable, partly for the very good reason that interpersonally comparable utilities are hard to define; nevertheless, no simple substitute has yet appeared, and I think it will be useful to pursue this line of study for whatever clarification it will bring.

I assume that when we speak of seeking to equalize government expenditures, or, more especially, expenditures in some particular field, we want to study that problem in some isolation from the general problem of income distribution. In other words, we seek to equalize, for example, educational expenditures — or, in utilitarian terms, to maximize the benefit from a given volume of such expenditures, but we do not consider these expenditures as a compensation for other income qualities. Therefore, it is assumed that there is for each individual a function relating the volume of expenditures to the utility derived from them. These utilities are taken to be interpersonally comparable, and the total volume of expenditures is to be allocated among individuals so as to maximize the sum of these utilities. The utility function for any given individual, however, depends not only on the expenditures on him but also on some personal characteristics. For simplicity, we term the latter "ability." Since individuals of identical ability are identical from the government's point of view, an allocation policy consists in determining expenditures as a function of ability.

Formal Statement of the Model and the Analysis of Input Equality

Let x = ability of a given individual, y = expenditures on a given individual, and $U(x,y)$ = utility derived by the individual.

In this context we understand ability to mean capacity to benefit from the expenditures in question, so that, necessarily,

(7-1) $U_x > 0;$

---

3. This analysis corresponds to the interpretation of tax equity as equal marginal sacrifice, thereby permitting the same condition to meet both efficiency and equity criteria. Other views of tax equity in terms of equal or proportional sacrifice (Pigou) or maximization of minimum ability (Rawls) may also be considered with regard to expenditure analysis. See A. C. Pigou, *A Study in Public Finance* (London: Macmillan, 1951), pt. 2, and J. Rawls, "Distributive Justice," in P. Laslett and W. G. Runciman, eds., *Philosophy, Politics, and Society*, Third Series (Oxford: Basil Blackwell, 1967), pp. 58–82.

we also assume that expenditures are always productive of some benefit, that is,

(7-2) $U_y > 0$.

Then an optimal policy (from the utilitarian viewpoint) satisfies the condition

(7-3) $U_y = $ constant over individuals.

We will assume that suitable concavity conditions are satisfied.

(7-4) $U_{yy} < 0$.

Relation (7-3) determines y as a function of x, and this is the optimal allocation policy. The constant is determined by the budget level. The expenditures y are the inputs into the individuals' production of benefits; therefore we define

DEFINITION 1. *The policy $y(x)$ is input equal if $dy/dx = 0$.*

More generally, we may want to define

DEFINITION 2. *The policy $y(x)$ is input progressive·if $dy/dx < 0$ and input regressive if $dy/dx > 0$.*

These terms correspond to usual usage with regard to taxation, except that we are dealing with "ability to receive" rather than "ability to pay." If we start from an initial situation of input equality, then by (7-1) higher utility is associated with higher ability. Hence, a shift toward an input-regressive policy is a reallocation of resources in favor of the better off.

From (7-3), at the optimal policy, U_y is constant over individuals and therefore independent of x. If we differentiate (7-3) totally with respect to x, we find

(7-5) $U_{xy} + U_{yy}(dy/dx) = 0$.

In view of (7-4) and Definitions 1 and 2 (D-1 and D-2), we can state

PROPOSITION 1. *The optimal policy is input progressive, input equal, or input regressive as $U_{xy} < 0, = 0,$ or > 0.*

Thus, the optimal policy is input progressive if the utility increase attributable to a given volume of government expenditures is less for individuals of higher ability.

The conditions for input equality will be analyzed more closely. Suppose we have a policy which is input equal throughout, and further suppose that the optimal policy would remain input equal even if the budget level were to change. Then it must be that U_{xy} is identically equal to zero, at least in some region of (x,y)-space. As is well known, this is equivalent to the assertion that the utility function can be written as the sum of a function of x and a function of y.

DEFINITION 3. *A function $f(x,y)$ is additively separable if it can be written $f(x,y) = g(x) + h(y)$.*

An additively separable function is one that can be calculated on a suitably constructed slide rule.

PROPOSITION 2. *The optimal policy is input equal for all budgets if and only if the utility function $U(x,y)$ is additively separable.*

Output Equality

In this model the output of the system is the utility itself, $U(x,y)$, with $y = y(x)$, or $U[x,y(x)]$.

DEFINITION 4. *The policy $y(x)$ is output equal if $dU[x,y(x)]/dx = 0$, output progressive if $dU/dx < 0$, and output regressive if $dU/dx > 0$.*

By straightforward differentiation,

(7-6) $dU/dx = U_x + U_y(dy/dx).$

Suppose $dy/dx \geq 0$. Then, since $U_x > 0$, $U_y > 0$, by Exp. (7-1) and (7-2) it must be that $dU/dx > 0$.

PROPOSITION 3. *If a policy is input equal or input regressive, it is necessarily output regressive. If a policy is output equal or output progressive, it is necessarily input progressive.*

(The two sentences of this proposition make the same assertion in different words.)

Multiply both sides of (7-6) by U_{yy} and substitute from (7-5).

(7-7) $U_{yy}(dU/dx) = U_x U_{yy} - U_y U_{xy}.$

For analysis of output equality it turns out to be useful to express expenditures as a function of ability and of the utility achieved. That is, we define $V(x,u)$ as the value of y for which $U(x,y) = u$, so that the relation

(7-8) $U[x, V(x,u)] = u$

is an identity. Differentiate Eq. (7-8) partially, first with respect to x and then with respect to u:

(7-9) $U_x + U_y V_x = 0,$

(7-10) $U_y V_u = 1.$

Now differentiate Eq. (7-10) partially with respect to x, holding u constant. Notice that U_y is a function of x both directly and through $y = V(x,u)$, so that

$$\partial U_y / \partial x = U_{xy} + U_{yy} V_x$$

and therefore

$$(U_{xy} + U_{yy} V_x) V_u + U_y V_{ux} = 0.$$

Multiply through by U_y^2. Note that $U_y V_u = 1$, by (7-10), so that $U_y^2 V_u = U_y$, and $U_y^2 V_u V_x = U_y V_x = -U_x$, by Eq. (7-9).

$$U_y U_{xy} - U_{yy} U_x + U_y^3 V_{ux} = 0,$$

or, from (7-7),

$$U_y^3 V_{ux} = U_{yy}(dU/dx).$$

Since $U_y > 0$ and $U_{yy} < 0$, it follows that dU/dx has a sign opposite to that of V_{ux}.

PROPOSITION 4. *The optimal policy is output progressive if and only if the following condition holds: when initial expenditures have been so adjusted to ability that all individuals have the same utility, then the cost of achieving a given increment of utility is higher for individuals of higher ability. The conditions for output equality and output regressivity are obtained by substituting the words "equal" and "less," respectively, for "higher" in the preceding sentence.*

The condition for output equality for all budgets is that V_{ux} be identically zero and therefore that V be additively separable. From (7-1), (7-2), (7-9), and (7-10),

(7-11) $V_x < 0,$ $V_u > 0,$

so that $V(x,u)$ can be written as the difference between an increasing function of utility and an increasing function of ability.

PROPOSITION 5. *The optimal policy is output equal for all budgets if and only if the expenditures needed to achieve a given utility level for a given ability can be expressed as the difference between a function of utility and a function of ability, both functions being increasing in their respective arguments.*

The Case of Objectively Measurable Outputs

In many situations the benefits derived from government expenditures are measured in some objective way, not merely in terms of utility. Thus, educational accomplishments may be measured in terms of various test scores, manpower training in terms of increased wages and employment opportunities, or health benefits in terms of longevity and decreased morbidity. It is natural in those circumstances to consider the utility as a function of the measured output, and the output in turn as a function of the two "inputs," ability and expenditures. Let z = measured output, $U(z)$ = utility, $z = f(x,y)$; the last may be thought of as a production function.

The utility derived from a given ability, x, and expenditures, y, is then given by $U[f(x,y)]$, which plays the role taken by $U(x,y)$ in the preceding discussion. All the earlier propositions remain valid, of course; indeed, the model of this section is simply a special case. However, some further conclusions can be drawn if special assumptions are made about the production relation.

DEFINITION 5. *The production relation, $z = f(x,y)$, will be termed additively separable if there exist monotonic functions, $H(z)$, $F(x)$, and $G(y)$, such that $H(z) = F(x) + G(y)$ whenever $z = f(x,y)$.*

The statement that the production *relation* is additively separable is considerably weaker than the statement that the production *function* is additively separable; the latter would require that $z = F(x) + G(y)$. Additive separability is a frequently made hypothesis in the study of production functions; CES production functions, in particular Cobb-Douglas functions, imply additively separable production relations.

In the special case where $H(z)$ happens to be the same as $U(z)$, the derived utility function $U[f(x,y)]$ is additively separable and, by Proposition 2, the optimal policy exhibits input equality. In general, we have, by differentiation of the production relation in additively separated form,

$$(7\text{-}12) \qquad H'f_x = F'(x), \qquad H'f_y = G'(y).$$

Let U_x and U_y be the partial derivatives of $U[f(x,y)]$. Then, with the aid of (7-12),

$$U_x = U'(z)f_x = [U'(z)/H'(z)]F'(x).$$

Differentiate this with respect to y, holding x constant.

$$U_{xy} = F'(x)[d(U'/H')/dz]f_y = (F'G'/H')d(U'/H')/dz.$$

We may obviously suppose that F, G, and H are all increasing functions, and therefore that F', G', and H' are all positive. Then the sign of U_{xy} is the same as that of $d(U'/H')/dz$. In view of Proposition 1, we have

PROPOSITION 6. *If the production relation is additively separable, the optimal policy is input progressive, equal, or regressive as U'/H' is a decreasing, constant, or increasing function of z.*

We can give a similar characterization of output equality for the case of additively separable production. Define $z(u)$ as the solution of the equation $U(z) = u$. Then the function $V(x,u)$, defined above, satisfies the following relation identically in x and u:

$$H[z(u)] = F(x) + G[V(x,u)].$$

Differentiate partially with respect to x, and then differentiate the resulting equation partially with respect to u:

$$0 = F'(x) + G'(y)V_x,$$

$$G''(y)V_xV_u + G'(y)V_{ux} = 0.$$

From (7-11) and the fact that $G' > 0$, it follows directly that V_{ux} has the same sign as G''. Proposition 4 then implies

PROPOSITION 7. *If the production relation is additively separable, then the optimal policy is output progressive, equal, or regressive as $G''(y)$ is positive, zero, or negative.*

In Propositions 6 and 7, the special cases of input or output equality reduce to those already noted in Propositions 2 and 5.

Comments

Obviously not much in the way of policy implications should be drawn from such a simplified model. However, some tentative observations may be ventured.

1. In the case of education and many other contexts, we ordinarily assume that ability is correlated with the securing of benefits from government expenditures at the margin as well as in total; hence, Proposition 4 seems to suggest that the utilitarian criterion leads to output regressivity, which is certainly the policy currently in use, at least in the field of education. In the field of health, however, ability means essentially "state of health"; expenditures will be less productive of increased utility for a healthier individual, so we would expect output progressivity and a fortiori input progressivity to be the norm. On the other hand, Proposition 6 makes it somewhat plausible that there should be input progressivity, particularly if U' is decreasing at all rapidly.

2. The relevance of the analysis of objectively measurable outputs depends on the possibility of appropriate econometric investigations into the relevant production functions. It does suggest caution in using functional forms (linearity, for instance), which imply the nature of the optimal policy even before knowing the results of empirical study.

3. The case for equality may be made on other than utilitarian grounds; thus Rawls[4] has argued for maximizing the minimum utility, rather than the sum of utilities, as an ethical criterion, and this criterion would tend toward output equality and therefore strong input progressivity.

---

4. "Distributive Justice."

8 Some Ordinalist-Utilitarian Notes on Rawls's Theory of Justice

Rawls's major work [*A Theory of Justice* (Cambridge, Mass: Belknap Press, Harvard University Press, 1971)] has been widely and correctly acclaimed as the most searching investigation of the notion of justice in modern times. It combines a genuine and fruitful originality of viewpoint with an extraordinary systematic evaluation of foundations, implications for action, and connections with other aspects of moral choice. The specific postulates for justice that Rawls enunciates are quite novel, and yet, once stated, they clearly have a strong claim on our attention as at least plausible candidates for the foundations of a theory of justice. The arguments for accepting these postulates are part of the contractarian tradition, but have been developed in many new and interesting ways. The implications of these postulates for specific aspects of the institutions of liberty, particularly civil liberty, and for the operations of the economic order are spelled out in considerable and thoughtful detail. (As an economist accustomed to much elementary misunderstanding of the nature of an economy on the part of philosophers and social scientists, I must express my gratitude for the sophistication and knowledge which Rawls displays here.) Finally, the relations between justice of social institutions and the notion of morally right behavior on the part of individuals is analyzed at considerable and intelligent length.

It will become clear in what follows that I have a number of questions and

Reprinted from *Journal of Philosophy*, 70 (1973): 245–263.

objections to Rawls's theory. Indeed, it is not surprising that no theory of justice can be so compelling as to forestall some objections; indeed, that very fact is disturbing to the quest for the concept of justice, as I shall briefly note toward the end of this chapter. These questions are a tribute to the breadth and fruitfulness of Rawls's work.

My critical stance is derived from a particular tradition of thought: that of welfare economics. In the prescription of economic policy, questions of distributive justice inevitably arise. (Not *all* such questions arise, only some; in particular, justice in the allocation of freedoms rather than goods is not part of the formal analysis of welfare economics, though some economists have made strong informal and unanalyzed commitments to some aspects of freedom.) The implicit ethical basis of economic policy judgment is some version of utilitarianism. At the same time, descriptive economics has relied heavily on a utilitarian psychology in explaining the choices made by consumers and other economic agents. The basic theorem of welfare economics — that under certain conditions the competitive economic system yields an outcome that is optimal or efficient (in a sense which requires careful definition) — depends on the identification of the utility structures that motivate the choices made by economic agents with the utility structures used in judging the optimality of the outcome of the competitive system. As a result, the utility concepts which, in one form or another, underlie welfare judgments in economics as well as elsewhere (according to Rawls's and many other theories of justice) have been subjected to an intensive scrutiny by economists. There has been more emphasis on their operational meaning, but perhaps less on their specific content; philosophers have been more prone to analyze what individuals should want, where economists have been content to identify "should" with "is" for the individual (not for society).

I do not mean that all economists or even those who have concerned themselves with welfare judgments will agree with the following remarks, but I do want to suggest the background from which these concerns originated.

I begin by highlighting the basic assumptions of Rawls's theory and stress those aspects which especially intersect my interests. I shall be brief, since by now the theory is doubtless reasonably familiar to the reader. Next, I raise some specific questions about different aspects of the theory, in particular, the logic by which Rawls proceeds from the general point of view of the theory (the "original position," the "difference principle" in its general form) to more specific implications, such as the priority of liberty and the maximin principle for distribution of goods. In the central section of this chapter I raise a number of the epistemological issues that seem to me to be crucial in the development of most kinds of ethical theory and in particular Rawls's: How do we know other people's welfare enough to apply a principle of justice? What knowledge is assumed to be possessed by those in Rawls's original position when they agree to a set of principles? I continue by stating more explicitly what may be termed an *ordinalist* (epistemologically modest) version of utilitarianism and argue that, in these terms, Rawls's position does not differ sharply. I briefly discuss the role of majority and other kinds of voting in a theory of justice, especially in light of the earlier discussion. Next, I turn to a different line, an examination of the implication of Rawls's theory for economic policy. In the final section some of the preceding discussions are applied and extended to raise some questions about the possibility of any theory of justice; the criterion of universalizability may be impossible to achieve when people are really different, particularly when different life experiences mean that they can never have the same information.

Some Basic Aspects of Rawls's Theory

The central part of Rawls's theory is a statement of fundamental propositions about the nature of a just society, what may be thought of as a system of axioms. On the one side, it is sought to justify these axioms as deriving from a contract made among rational potential members of society; on the other side, the implications of these axioms for the determination of social institutions are drawn.

The axioms themselves can be thought of as divided into two parts: one is a general statement of the notion of justice, the second a more detailed elaboration of more specific forms.

The general point of view is a strongly affirmed egalitarianism, to be departed from only when it is in the interest of all to do so. "All social values—liberty and opportunity, income and wealth, and the bases of self-respect—are to be distributed equally unless unequal distribution of any, or all, of these values is to everyone's advantage" (p. 62; parenthetical page references hereafter are to Rawls's book). This *generalized difference principle,* as Rawls terms it, is no tautology. In particular, it implies that even natural advantages, superiorities of intelligence or strength, do not in themselves create any claims to greater rewards. The principles of justice are "an agreement to regard the distribution of natural talents as a common asset and to share in the benefits of this distribution" (101).

Personally, I share fully this value judgment; and, indeed, it is implied by almost all attempts at full formalization of welfare economics.[1] But a contradictory proposition — that an individual is entitled to what he creates — is widely and unreflectively held; when teaching elementary economics, I have had considerable difficulty in persuading the students that this *productivity principle* is not completely self-evident.

It may be worth stressing that the assumption of what may be termed *asset egalitarianism* (that all the assets of society, including personal skills, are available as a common pool for whatever distribution justice calls for) is so much taken for granted that it is hardly argued for. All the alternatives to his principles of justice that Rawls considers imply asset egalitarianism (though some of them are very inegalitarian in result, since more goods are to be assigned to those most capable of using them). The productivity principle is not even considered. It must be said, on the other hand, that asset egalitarianism is certainly an implication of the "original position" contract. (The practical implications of asset egalitarianism are, however, severely modified in the direction of the productivity principle by incentive considerations.)

But Rawls's theory is a much more specific statement of the concept of justice. This consists in two parts. First, among the goods distributed by the social order, liberty has a priority over others; no amount of material goods is considered to compensate for a loss of liberty. Second, among goods of a given priority class, inequalities should be permitted only if they increase the lot of the least well off. The first principle will be referred to as the *priority of liberty,* the second as the *maximin* principle (*max*imizing the welfare at its *min*imum level; Rawls himself refers to this as the *difference principle*).

Rawls argues for these two principles as being those which would be agreed to by rational individuals in a hypothetical *original position,* where they have full general knowledge of the world, but do not know which individual they will be. The idea of this "veil of ignorance" is that principles of justice must be universalizable; they must be such as to command assent by anyone who does not take account of his individual circumstances. If it is assumed that rational individuals under these circumstances have some degree of aversion to uncertainty, then they will find it desirable to enter into an insurance agreement, that the more successful will share with the less,

---

1. See A. Bergson, *Essays in Normative Economics* (Cambridge, Mass.: Harvard, 1966), chap. 1; P. A. Samuelson, *The Foundations of Economic Analysis* (Cambridge, Mass.: Harvard, 1947), pp. 230–248; or F. Y. Edgeworth, *Mathematical Psychics* (London: Kegan Paul, 1881), pp. 56–82.

though not so much as to make them both worse off. Thus, the original-position argument does lead to a generalized view of justice. Rawls then further argues that his more specific principles (priority of liberty and the maximin principle) also follow from the original-position argument, at least in the sense of being preferable to other principles advanced in the philosophical literature, such as classical utilitarianism.

Two final remarks on the general nature of Rawls's system: (1) The principles of justice are intended to apply to the choice of social institutions, not to the actual allocative decisions of society separately. (2) The principles are supposed to characterize an ideal state of justice. If the ideal state is not achieved, they do not in themselves supply any basis for deciding that one nonideal state is more or less just than another. "Questions of strategy are not to be confused with those of justice . . . The force of opposing attitudes has no bearing on the question of right but only on the feasibility of arrangements of liberty" (231). It is intended of course that a characterization of ideal or optimal states of justice is a first step in a complete ordering of alternative institutional arrangements as more or less just.

The Derivation of Rawls's Specific Rules

From the viewpoint of the logical structure of the theory, a central question is the extent to which the assumption of the original position really implies the highly specific forms of Rawls's two rules. Let me take the priority of liberty first. This is given a central place in the presentation, and at a number of points the fact that the theory puts such emphasis on liberty is used to distinguish it favorably from utilitarianism; the latter, it is argued, might easily lead to sacrificing the liberty of a few for the benefit of many. "Each person possesses an inviolability founded on justice that even the welfare of society as a whole cannot override. For this reason justice denies that the loss of freedom for some is made right by a greater good shared by others" (3–4).

Despite its importance, the definitive argument for the priority of liberty is postponed to very late in the book (541–548). The key argument is that the priority of liberty is desired by every individual. In technical terms, each individual has a *lexicographical* (or "lexical," in Rawls's simplification) ordering of goods of all kinds, with liberty coming first; of any two possible states, an individual will always prefer that with the most liberty, regardless of other goods (such as income), and will choose according to income only among states with equal liberty. "The supposition is that . . . the persons . . . will not exchange a lesser liberty for an improvement in their economic well-being, at least not once a certain level of wealth has been attained . . . As the conditions of civilization improve, the marginal significance for our good of further economic and social advantages diminishes relative to the interests of liberty" (542).

The argument is clearly an empirical judgment, and the reader can decide for himself how much weight it will bear. I want to bring out another aspect, the relation to utilitarianism. If in fact each individual assigns priority to liberty in the lexicographical sense, then the most classical sum-of-utilities criterion will do the same for social choice; the rule will be for society to maximize the sum of individuals' liberties and then, among those states which accomplish this, choose that which maximizes the sum of satisfactions from other goods.

Let me now turn to the maximin rule (this is to be applied separately to liberty and to the nonpriority goods). The justification appears most explicitly on pages 155–158; it is mainly an argument for maximin as against the sum-of-utilities criterion. It should first be noted that the original-position assumption had also been put forth by the economists W. S. Vickrey[2] and J. C. Harsanyi[3]; but they used it to supply a contractarian foundation to a form of utilitarianism (discussed at considerable length by Rawls, 161–175). They started from the position, that of F. P. Ramsey, and J. von Neumann and O. Morgenstern, that choice under risky conditions can be described as the maximization of expected utility. In the original position each individual may with equal probability be any member of the society. If there are n members of the society and if the ith member will have utility u_i under some given allocation decision, then the value of that allocation to any individual is $\Sigma u_i(1/n)$, since $1/n$ is the probability of being individual i. Thus, in choosing among alternative allocations of goods, each individual in

---

2. "Measuring Marginal Utility by Reactions to Risk," *Econometrica,* 13 (1945): 319–333, p. 329; "Utility, Strategy, and Social Decision Rules," *Quarterly Journal of Economics, 74* (1960): 507–535.

Vickrey's 1945 statement has been overlooked by all subsequent writers—not surprisingly, since it received relatively little emphasis in a paper overtly devoted to a seemingly different subject. I read the paper before I was concerned with the theory of social choice; the implications for that theory were so easy to overlook that they did not occur to me at all when they would have been relevant.

3. "Cardinal Utility in Welfare Economics and the Theory of Risk-taking," *Journal of Political Economy,* 61 (1953): 434–5; "Cardinal Welfare, Individualistic Ethics, and Interpersonal Comparisons of Utility," ibid., 63 (1955): 309–321.

the original position will want to maximize this expectation, or, what is the same thing for a given population, maximize the sum of utilities.

Rawls, however, starting from the same premises, derives the statement that society should maximize min u_i. The argument seems to have two parts: first, that in an original position, where the quality of an entire life is at stake, it is reasonable to have a high degree of aversion to risk, and being concerned with the worst possible outcome is an extreme form of risk aversion; and, second, that the probabilities are in fact ill defined and should not be employed in such a calculation. The first point raises some questions about the meaning of the utilities and does not do justice to the fact that, at least in Vickrey and Harsanyi, the utilities are already so measured as to reflect risk aversion (see some further discussion below). The second point is a version of a recurrent and unresolved controversy in the theory of behavior under uncertainty; are all uncertainties expressible by probabilities? The view that they are has a long history and has been given an axiomatic justification by Ramsey[4] and by L. J. Savage.[5] The contrary view has been upheld by F. H. Knight[6] and by many writers who have held to an objective view of probability; the maximin theory of rational decision making under uncertainty was set forth by A. Wald[7] specifically in the latter context. Among economists, G. L. S. Shackle[8] has been a noted advocate of a more general theory which includes maximin as a special case. L. Hurwicz and I[9] have given a set of axioms which imply that choice will be based on some function of the maximum and the minimum utility.

It has, however, long been remarked that the maximin theory has some implications that seem hardly acceptable. It implies that any benefit, no matter how small, to the worst-off member of society will outweigh any loss to a better-off individual, provided it does not reduce the second below the level of the first. Thus, there can easily exist medical procedures which serve

---

4. "Truth and Probability," in *The Foundations of Mathematics and Other Logical Essays* (London: K. Paul, Trench, Trubner, 1931), pp. 156–198.

5. *The Foundations of Statistics* (New York: Wiley, 1954).

6. *Risk, Uncertainty, and Profit* (New York: Houghton Mifflin, 1921).

7. "Contributions to the Theory of Statistical Estimation and Testing Hypotheses," *Annals of Mathematical Statistics,* 10 (1939): 299–326.

8. *Expectations in Economics* (Cambridge: University Press, 1949) and subsequent works.

9. "An Optimality Criterion for Decision-making under Ignorance," in C. F. Carter and J. L. Ford, eds., *Uncertainty and Expectation in Economics* (Oxford: Basil Blackwell, 1972), pp. 1–11.

to keep people barely alive but with little satisfaction, and which are yet so expensive as to reduce the rest of the population to poverty. A maximin principle would apparently imply that such procedures be adopted.

Rawls considers this argument, but rejects it on the ground that it will not occur in practice. He fairly consistently assumes that the actual society has the property he calls *close-knittedness:* "As we raise the expectations of the more advantaged the situation of the worst off is continuously improved . . . For the greater expectations of the more favored presumably cover the costs of training and encourage better performance" (158). It is hard to analyze this argument fairly in short compass. On the face of it, it seems clearly false; there is nothing easier than to point out changes that benefit the well-off at the expense of the poor, including the least advantaged, for example, simultaneous reduction of the income tax for high brackets and of welfare payments. Rawls holds that one must consider his principles in their totality — in particular, a strongly expressed demand for open access to all positions. But even with perfect equality of opportunity, there will presumably remain inequalities due to biological and cultural inheritance (Rawls nowhere advocates abolition of the family) and chance events, and once inequalities do exist, the harmony of interests seems to be less than all-pervasive. In any case, the assumption of close-knittedness undermines all the distinctions that Rawls is so careful to make. For if it holds, there is no difference in policy implication between the maximin principle and the sum of utilities; if all satisfactions go up together, the conflict between the individual and the society disappears.

Epistemological Issues in the Theory of Justice

Many theories of justice, including both Rawls's and utilitarianism, imply that the social institutions or their creators have access to some kinds of knowledge. This raises the question whether they can in fact or even in principle have such knowledge. In this section two epistemological questions are raised, though there are others: (1) How can interpersonal comparisons of satisfaction be made? and (2) What knowledge is available in the original position?

1. The problem of interpersonal comparison of utilities seems to bother economists more than philosophers. As already indicated, utility or satisfaction or any other similar concept appears in economic theory as an explanation of individual behavior, for example, of a consumer. Specifically, it is

hypothesized that the individual chooses his consumption so as to maximize his utility, subject to the constraints imposed by his budget. But for this purpose a quantitatively measurable utility is a superfluous concept. All that is needed is an ordering, that is, a statement for each pair of consumption patterns as to which is preferred. Any numerical function over the possible consumption patterns having the property that it assigns larger numbers to preferred bundles could be thought of as a utility function. Clearly, then, any monotonic transformation of a utility function is also a utility function.

To turn the matter around, it might be asked, how can we have any evidence about the magnitude of utility? The only evidence on an individual's utility function is supplied by his observable behavior, specifically the choices he makes in the course of maximizing the function. But such choices are defined by the preference ordering and must therefore be the same for all utility functions compatible with that ordering. Hence there is no quantitative meaning of utility for an individual. (This *ordinalist* position was introduced into economics by V. Pareto and I. Fisher and has become fairly orthodox in the last thirty [now forty] years.)

If the utility of an individual is not measurable, then a fortiori the comparison of utilities of different individuals is not meaningful. In particular, the sum-of-utilities criterion becomes indefensible as it stands. Rawls's maximin criterion also implies interpersonal comparison, for we must pick out the least advantaged individual, and that requires statements of the form "Individual *A* is worse off than individual *B*." Unlike the sum-of-utilities approach, however, it does not require that the units in which different individuals' utilities are measured be comparable, only that we be able to rank different individuals according to some scale of satisfaction. However, we do not have any underlying numerical magnitude to use for this purpose, and the question still remains, what is the operational meaning of the interpersonal comparison?

If one is to take the sum-of-utilities criterion seriously, then it would have to be considered possible for individuals to have different utility functions; in particular, they might derive different amounts of satisfaction from the same increments to their wealth. Then the utilitarian would have to agree that the sum of utilities would be increased by shifting wealth to the more sensitive individuals. This does not occur in Rawls's theory, but something parallel to it does. Consider an individual who is incapable of deriving much pleasure from anything, whether because of psychological or physical limitations. He may well be the worst-off individual and therefore be the touchstone of distribution policy, even though he derives little satisfaction from the additional income.

In the usual applications of the sum-of-utilities approach, the problem of differing utilities is dodged by assuming it away; it is postulated that everyone has the same utility function. This avoids not only what may be thought of as the injustice of distributing income in favor of the more sensitive, but also the problem of ascertaining in detail what the utility functions are, a task which might be thought impossible, as argued above, or at least very difficult in practice, if the ordinalist position is not accepted. Rawls criticizes this utilitarian evasion, though cautiously; he does not wish to reject interpersonal comparisons (90–91). But in fact he winds up with a somewhat similar approach. He introduces the interesting concept of *primary goods,* those goods which are needed whatever an individual's preference relation ("rational plan of life," in Rawls's terms) is. These might be liberties, opportunities, and income and wealth. Then, even though individuals might have very different uses for these primary goods, we need consider only some simple index of them for purposes of interpersonal comparison. The fact that one individual was satisfied with water and soy flour, while another was desperate without prephylloxera clarets and plovers' eggs, would have no bearing on the interpersonal comparison; if they had the same income, they would be equally well off.

If this comparison appears facetious, consider the hemophiliac who needs about $4,000 worth per annum of coagulant therapy to arrive at a state of security from bleeding at all comparable to that of the normal person. Does equal income mean equality? If not, then, to be consistent, Rawls would have to add health to the list of primary goods; but then there is a trade-off between health and wealth which involves all the conceptual problems of differing utility functions.

The restriction to some list of primary goods is probably essential. I have but two comments: (a) so long as there is more than one primary good, there is an index-number problem in commensurating the different goods, which is in principle as difficult as the problem of interpersonal comparability with which we started; (b) if we could resolve the problem of interpersonal comparability in Rawls's system by reducing everything in effect to a single primary good, we could do the same in the sum-of-utilities approach. To the last statement, however, there is a qualification: the maximin criterion requires only interpersonal ordinality, whereas the classical view requires interpersonally comparable units; to that extent, the Rawls system is epistemologically less demanding.

2. Let us turn from the epistemological problems of the current decision maker for society to those in the original position. Individuals are supposed

to know the laws of the physical and the social worlds, but not to know who they are or will be. But empirical knowledge is after all uncertain, and even in the original position individuals may disagree about the facts and laws of the universe. For example, Rawls argues for religious toleration on the grounds that one does not know what religion one will have, and therefore one wants society to tolerate all religions. Operationally, a Catholic would have to recognize that in the original position he would not know he would be a Catholic and would therefore have to tolerate Protestants or Jews or whatever, since he might well have been one. But suppose he replies that in fact Catholicism is the true religion, that it is part of the knowledge which all sensible people are supposed to have in the original position, and that he insists on it for the salvation of all mankind. How could this be refuted?

Indeed, just this sort of argument is raised by writers like Marcuse, not to mention any totalitarian state and, within wider limits, any state. Only those who correctly understand the laws of society should be allowed to express their political opinions. I feel I know that Marxism (or laissez-faire) is the truth; therefore, in the original position, I would have supported suppressing other positions. Even Rawls permits suppression of those who do not believe in freedom.

I hope it is not necessary to say that I am in favor of very wide toleration. But I am not convinced that the original position is a sufficient basis for this argument, for it transfers the problem to the area of factual disagreement.

There is another kind of knowledge problem in the original position: that about social preferences. Rawls assumes that individuals are egoistic, their social preferences being derived from the veil of ignorance. But why should there not be views of benevolence (or envy) even in the original position? All that is required is that they not refer to named individuals. But if these are admitted, then there can be disagreement over the degree of benevolence or malevolence, and the happy assumption that there are no disagreements in the original position disappears.

Some Remarks on Utilitarianism

It will already have been seen that my attitude toward utilitarianism is ambivalent. On the one hand, I find it difficult to ascribe operational meaning to the utilities to be added. On the other hand, I have suggested that the practical differences between the maximin and the sum-of-utilities criteria are not great, and indeed that the maximin principle would lead to unacceptable consequences if the world were such that the two principles really differed.

I want now to take up several different points raised by Rawls and try to defend utilitarianism against them.

First, let me extend a little the discussion of the Vickrey-Harsanyi position, which Rawls calls *average utilitarianism.* In part, this discussion continues the epistemological considerations of the last section. As Ramsey and von Neumann and Morgenstern have shown, if one considers choice among risky alternatives, there is a sense in which a quantitative utility can be given meaning. Specifically, if choice among probability distributions satisfies certain apparently natural rationality conditions, then it can be shown that there is a utility function (unique up to a positive linear transformation) on the outcomes such that probability distributions of outcomes are ordered in accordance with the mathematical expectation of the utility of the outcome.

By itself, this theorem does not establish any welfare implications for this utility function; after all, the choice among probability distributions of outcomes could equally well be described by any monotonic transformation of the expected utility. When I first wrote on this matter,[10] I therefore denied the welfare relevance of expected-utility theory. But the Vickrey-Harsanyi argument puts matters in a different perspective: if an individual assumes he may with equal probability be any member of society, then indeed he evaluates any policy by his expected utility, *where the utility function is specifically that defined by the von Neumann-Morgenstern theorem.* Rawls therefore errs when he argues that average utilitarianism assumes risk neutrality (165); on the contrary, the degree of risk aversion of the individuals is already incorporated in the utility function.

This point may be given further strength by noting that the maximin criterion, far from being opposed to average utilitarianism, can be regarded as a limiting case of it. For let U be any utility function, in the sense of a function that represents preferences without uncertainty. Then, for any $a > 0$, $-U^{-a}$ is an increasing function of U and so is also a utility function. Any member of this family could be the von Neumann-Morgenstern utility function, that is, that utility function for which it is true that the individual seeks to maximize expected utility. It is easy to see that the larger the value of a, the higher the degree of risk aversion. Then, according to Vickrey, the value of a policy to an individual with a random stake in society would be

$$V = \Sigma(-U_i)^{-a} = -\Sigma U_i^{-a}.$$

10. *Social Choice and Individual Values* (New York: Wiley, 1951), 1st ed., pp. 9–10.

But a social-welfare function is only an index of choice and can itself be subject to monotonic transformation; hence, another criterion that would yield the same choice is

$$W = (-V)^{-1/a} = (\Sigma U_i^{-a})^{-1/a}.$$

It can, however, easily be proved that, as a approaches infinity, representing increasing degrees of risk aversion, W approaches min U_i.

I do not wish to argue that average utilitarianism meets all the problems that can be raised. Rawls very properly points out that each individual may have a different utility function, so that although each wishes to maximize a sum of utilities, each individual has a different utility function in his maximand (173); in addition, the use of equiprobability in this case is certainly not beyond cavil.

A second of Rawls's objections to utilitarianism is that it may require that some individuals sacrifice for the benefit of others, so that other men appear to be means, not only ends (181, 183). But I do not understand this argument at all. A maximin principle certainly seems to imply that the better-off should sacrifice for the less well-off, if that will in fact help. The talents of the more able are, in Rawls's system (and in my value judgments), to be used on behalf of the less able; is this not using some people as means?

A third criticism of classical utilitarianism is that it makes an illegitimate analogy between individuals and society. "The classical view results, then, in impersonality, in the conflation of all desires into one system of desire" (188). Yet it would appear to me a purely formal requirement of any theory of justice that it act as such a conflation. A theory of justice is presumably an ordering of alternative social states and therefore is formally analogous to the individual's ordering of alternative social states. Further, Rawls and Bentham and I would certainly all agree that justice should reflect individual satisfactions; hence the social choice made in accordance with any of these theories of justice is "a conflation of all desires." No doubt perfectionist theories or those based on religious considerations would not be so characterized; but Rawls is not defending *them*.

A Remark on Voting

The expression and aggregation of individual preferences through voting does not have a high place in Rawls's system: "There is nothing to the view, then, that what the majority wills is right" (356). The legislators or voters are thought of as experts in justice and are not to vote in self-interest. The assumption seems to be simply that the workings of justice will not always be clear and that a pooling of opinions is worthwhile; a majority makes more sense from this point of view than a minority.

Clearly, there is something to Rawls's position, which, as he notes, he shares with many political philosophers. A political system in which there is no other-regardingness will not function at all. Further, Rawls is right in saying that the analogy with the market is imperfect. In the market he agrees that selfish behavior is socially correct, but holds that the political process can never lead to perfect justice if based on self-seeking behavior. I would argue that the analogy, though imperfect, is not completely wrong either. Political competition does serve some of the same functions in its sphere as economic competition. Further, the expression of one's own interests in voting seems to me an essential part of the information process needed for voting. Unless voters express their interests, how is anyone going to know if the ends of justice are in fact being carried out? "If I am not for myself, then who is for me?" said Hillel, though he continued in more Rawlsian terms, "and if I am not for others, then who am I?"

To put the matter more emotionally, I would hold that the notion of voting according to one's own beliefs and then submitting to the will of the majority represents a recognition of the essential autonomy and freedom of others. It recognizes that justice is a pooling of irreducibly different individuals, not the carrying out of policies already known in advance.

Economic Implications of Rawls's Principles

Rawls's views have implications most directly for the redistribution of income, both among contemporaries and across generations. The maximin rule would seem on the face of it to lead to radical equalization of income. Indeed, so would the sum-of-utilities rule, if it is assumed that all individuals have the same utility function which displays decreasing marginal satisfactions from additional increments of income. Rawls, however, holds that the close-knittedness of members of the society means that perfect equality of income is not to the advantage of the least well-off, but that typically they will benefit by an increase in income to some higher up on the income scale.

Rawls is rather brief on why one might expect this kind of relation, but economists have laid considerable stress on the *incentive* effects of taxation. Assume that each individual can produce a certain amount per hour worked, but that this productivity varies from individual to individual. In the absence of taxation, the least productive individual will be the worst off.

Therefore, a Rawlsian (or even an old-fashioned utilitarian) may advocate a tax on the income of the more able to be paid out to the less able. This is, in fact, essentially the widespread proposal for a negative income tax. However, since the effort to produce may in itself detract from satisfaction, an income tax will lead individuals to reduce the number of hours they work and therefore the amount they produce. If the tax rate on the more able is high enough, the amount of work will go down so much that the amount collected in taxes for redistribution to the worst off will actually decrease. It is at this stage that the economy becomes close-knit.

The conflict between incentive and equity occurs in a utilitarian framework and was already noted by Edgeworth (who was really very conservative and was glad to escape from the rigorous egalitarianism to which his utilitarianism led). The mathematical problem of choosing a tax schedule to maximize the sum of utilities, taking account of the adverse incentive effects, is a very difficult one; it was broached by Vickrey in his 1945 paper and analyzed by J. A. Mirrlees,[11] R. C. Fair,[12] and E. Sheshinski,[13] among others. More recently, the tax implications of the Rawls criterion have been analyzed along similar lines in papers by Atkinson, Phelps, and Sheshinski. The practical implications of this research are as yet dubious, primarily because too little is known about the magnitude of the incentive effects, particularly in the upper brackets.

As I have indicated, Rawls is inexplicit about the incentive effects and so does not give clear guidance to the determination of tax rates. On pages 277–279 he argues for progressive income and inheritance taxes to achieve justice, but there is no indication how the rates should be chosen. Clearly, the philosophy of justice is under no obligation to tell us what the rates should be in a numerical sense; but it is supposed to define the rule that translates any given set of facts into a tax schedule. The maximin rule would, on the face of it, lead to perfect equalization, that is, 100-percent taxation above a certain level, with corresponding subsidies below it. As far as I can see, it is only the incentive question that prevents us from carrying this policy out.

---

11. "An Exploration in the Theory of Optimal Income Taxation," *Review of Economic Studies,* 38 (1971): 175–208.

12. "The Optimal Distribution of Income," *Quarterly Journal of Economics,* 85 (1971): 551–579.

13. "The Optimum Linear Income Tax," *Review of Economic Studies,* 39 (1972): 297–302.

The incentive question raises another issue with regard to the obligation of an individual to perform justice. (Rawls has much to say on the notion of duties and obligations on individuals, though I have slighted that discussion in this review.) If each individual revealed his productivity (the amount he could produce per unit of time), it would be possible to achieve a perfect reconciliation of justice and incentives; namely, tax each individual according to his ability, not according to his actual output. Then he could not escape taxes by working less, and so the tax system would have no adverse incentive effects. Practical economists would reject this solution, because it would be taken for granted that no individual would be truthful if the consequences of truth telling were so painful. But Rawls, like most social philosophers, takes it for granted that individuals are supposed to act justly, at least in certain contexts. For example, as legislators or voters, it is an obligation or duty to judge according to the principles of justice, not according to self-interest. If, then, an individual is supposed to assess his own potential for earning income, is there an obligation to be truthful?

One of the most difficult questions in allocative justice is the distribution of wealth over generations. To what extent is one generation obligated to save, so as to increase the welfare of the next generation? The traditional economic problem has been the general act of investment in productive land, machines, and buildings which produce goods in the future; more recently, we have become especially concerned with preservation of undisturbed environments and natural resources. The most straightforward utilitarian answer is that the utilities of future generations enter equally with those of the present. Since the present generation is a very small part of the total number of individuals over a horizon easily measurable in thousands of years, the policy conclusion would be that virtually everything should be saved and very little consumed, a conclusion which seems offensive to common sense. The most usual formulation has been to assert a criterion of maximizing a sum of *discounted* utilities, in which the utilities of future generations are given successively smaller weights. The implications of such policies seem to be more in accordance with common sense and practice, but the foundations of such a criterion seem arbitrary.

Rawls argues that the maximin criterion, properly interpreted, can be applied to the determination of a just rate of savings (284–292). In the original position, individuals do not know which generation they belong to and should therefore judge a just rate on that basis. That is, they agree to leave a fixed fraction of their income to the next generation in return for receiving an equal fraction of the previous generation's income. There are two difficulties with this argument: (1) Why should they agree on a *fraction* rather than some more complicated rule—for example, an increasing fraction as wealth increases? (2) More serious, it would appear that the maximin rule would most likely lead to zero as the agreed-on savings rate; for the first generation would lose under any positive savings rate, whereas the welfare of all future generations would increase. This point is reinforced strongly if one adds the empirical fact of technological progress, so that even in the absence of savings the successive generations are getting better off. Then a maximin policy would call for improving the lot of the earlier generations, which can only be done by negative saving (running down existing capital equipment) if at all possible. (To be precise, the above argument is valid only in the absence of population growth. If population is growing, then zero saving would mean less capital per person and therefore a falling income per capita. Hence, a maximin rule in the absence of techno-logical progress would call for positive saving; it can easily be shown that the rule would be that the rate of savings equals the rate of population growth multiplied by the capital-output ratio.)

Rawls, however, modifies the motivations in the original position at this point in the argument. "The parties are regarded as representing family lines, say, with ties of sentiment between successive generations" (292). This is a major departure from the egoistic assumptions held up to this point about behavior and choice in the original position. It should be noted that so long as fathers think more highly of themselves than of their sons, or even more highly of their sons than of subsequent generations, the effect of this modification is very much the same as that of discounting future utilities. Although my guess is that any justification for provision for the future will run somewhat along these lines, it cannot be said that the solution fully escapes all difficulties. (1) It introduces an element of altruism into the original position; if we introduce family sentiments, why not others (nation, tribal)? And why not elements of envy? (2) One might like a theory of justice in which the role of the family was derived rather than primitive. In a reexamination of social institutions, why should the family remain above scrutiny, its role being locked into the original assumptions? (3) Anyway, the family argument for saving has an implication that should be displayed and possibly questioned. Presumably the burden of saving should fall only on those with children and perhaps in proportion to the number of children. Since education and public construction are essentially forms of saving, taxes to support them should fall only on those with children. In the original position this is just the sort of contract that would be arrived at if the concern for the future were based solely on family ties.

A Critical Note on the Possibility of Justice

Rawls's work is based on the hypothesis that there is a meaningful universal concept of justice. If there is, it surely must, as he says, be universalizable in some sense, that is, based on principles that are symmetric among the particular accidents that distinguish one individual's position from another. But as I look around at the many conflicts that plague our humanity, I find many for which I can imagine no argument of a symmetric nature which would convince both sides.

One problem is that any actual individual must necessarily have limited information about the world, and different individuals have different information. Hence, they cannot possibly argue themselves back into an original position with common information, even if they succeed in "forgetting" who they are. Indeed, one of the most brilliant passages in Rawls's book is that on what he calls "social union" (520–530). He argues that no human life is enough to encounter more than a small fraction of the experiences needed for completeness, so that individuals have a natural complementarity with one another (a more mundane version of this idea is Adam Smith's stress on the importance of the division of labor). The social nature of man springs from this variegation of experience. But precisely the same differentiations imply differing and incompletely communicable life experiences and therewith the possible impossibility of agreeing on the just action in any concrete situation.

Indeed, the thrust of Rawls's work, particularly in its latter passages, is highly harmonistic; the principles of justice are stable, according to Rawls, because the moral education they induce reinforces them. But if the specific application of the principles is judged to be different according to different life experiences (and of course different genetic experiences), even as between parent and child, then the needed concordance of views may evaporate.

To put the matter somewhat differently, many sociologists would hold that in a world of limited information, conflict unresolved by appeal to commonly accepted principles may have a positive value; it is the means by which information about others is conveyed. In its own sphere, this is the role assigned to competition by economists; if everyone attempted to act justly at every moment in his economic life, it might be difficult ever to find out what the true interests of anyone were.

To the extent that individuals are really individual, each an autonomous end in himself, to that extent they must be somewhat mysterious and inaccessible to one another. There cannot be any rule that is completely acceptable to all. There must be, or so it now seems to me, the possibility of unadjudicable conflict, which may show itself logically as paradoxes in the process of social decision making.

9   Formal Theories of Social Welfare

The purpose of a theory of social welfare, or social choice as it is sometimes revealingly termed, is to provide a normative rationale for making social decisions when the individual members of the society have varying opinions about or interests in the alternatives available. Any kind of decision, social or individual, can be regarded as the interaction of the preferences or desires of the decision maker with the range of alternative decisions actually available to him, to be termed the *opportunity set.* The latter may vary from time to time because of changes in the wealth or technology of the community. The usual formalism of social welfare theory, derived from economic theory, is that preferences (or tastes or values) are first expressed for all logically possible alternatives. Then the most preferred is chosen from any given opportunity set.

As will be seen, there is serious and unresolved dispute about the strength of the statements which it is appropriate to make about preferences. One common demand is that preferences form an *ordering* of the alternatives. In terms of formal logic, a preference relation between pairs of alternatives is said to be *transitive* if whenever alternative A is preferred to alternative B and alternative B to alternative C, then A is preferred to C; and it is said to be *connected* if, for any two distinct alternatives, either A is preferred to B or B to A. An ordering of the alternatives is a preference relation which is both

Reprinted from *Dictionary of the History of Ideas,* Philip P. Wiener, editor, vol. 4, pp. 276–284, with the permission of Charles Scribner's Sons. Copyright © 1973 Charles Scribner's Sons.

transitive and connected; and it will be seen that this definition corresponds to an everyday use of the term "ordering."

(In the economic literature, it has proved essential to consider the possibility of indifference as well as preference between pairs of alternative social decisions. For the purposes of this discussion, however, we assume the absence of indifference, to simplify the exposition.)

Still a stronger demand is that preferences be measurable, that there exist a numerical representation which correctly reflects preference (the more preferred of two alternatives always has a higher number associated with it). Such a numerical representation is usually termed a *utility function.* In the terminology used by mathematical psychologists, a utility function may constitute an *interval scale,* that is, statements of the form "the preference for A over B is so many times the preference for C over D" are regarded as meaningful. In that case, the utility function is arbitrary as to the location of its zero point and its unit of measurement, but otherwise uniquely defined. A still stronger requirement is that the utility function constitute a *ratio scale,* that is, statements of the form "the utility (or value) of A is so many times as great as that of B." Such statements imply a natural zero; the utility function is unique up to a unit of measurement. If it is assumed that no meaning can be given to quantitative comparisons of preference but only to the ordering of alternatives, it is customary to speak of *ordinal* utility or preferences; if, on the contrary, utility is considered to constitute an interval or ratio scale, the term *cardinal* utility or preferences is used.

The need for a theory of social welfare arises from the need in the real world for social decisions. It is simply a fact, as Hobbes pointed out, that there are a great many decisions which by their nature must be made collectively and without which all members of the society would be much worse off—decisions on legal systems, police, or certain economic activities best conducted collectively (such as highways, education, and the kind of insurance represented by public assistance to disadvantaged groups).

A formal theory of social welfare, then, has the following form. Given a representation of the preferences of the individual members of the society in ordinal or cardinal form, a preference system is formed by aggregating them in some reasonable manner for society as a whole. Given the social preference system, and given a particular opportunity set of alternatives, the choice which society should make is that alternative highest on the social preference system.

Individual Choice and Values

The historical development of the notion of social welfare cannot be easily understood without reference to the gradual evolution of a formal analysis of individual choice, which I briefly summarize. Three characteristics of this history, shared with the history of the concept of social welfare, are striking: (1) the form of the basic problems was established during the eighteenth century and displays the characteristic rationalism and optimism of the Enlightenment; (2) the analysis retained its general form but underwent systematic transformation under the impact of twentieth-century epistemological currents; and (3) there are strong historical links with the development of the theory of probability and its applications, links which are not easy to explain on purely logical grounds.

The first work to discuss individual choice systematically is that of Daniel Bernoulli in 1738. He was concerned with explaining phenomena of which insurance was typical — that individuals would engage in bets whose actuarial value was negative. Bernoulli's solution was that what guided the individual's decisions to accept or reject bets was not the money outcomes themselves but their "moral values," as he termed them. In later terminology, the individual attached utilities to different amounts of money and accepted an uncertainty if and only if it increased the expected value of the utility. He also postulated that, in general, utility increased by lesser and lesser amounts as the quantity of money increased, an assumption now known as *diminishing marginal utility.* Then the individual would shy away from bets which were actuarially favorable if they increased uncertainty in money terms (in particular, if they involved a very small probability of very high returns) and would accept insurance policies if they reduced monetary uncertainty, for the high returns offered in the one case had relatively little additional utility, while the low returns avoided in the second case implied large losses of utility. Bernoulli thus required a cardinal utility (in this case, an interval scale) for his explanation of human behavior under uncertainty.

The idea that the drive of an individual to increase some measure of satisfaction explained his behavior was widespread, though rather vague, in the eighteenth century; Galiani, Condillac, and Turgot argued that in some measure the prices of commodities reflected the utilities they presented to individuals, for individuals were willing to pay more for those objects which provided them more satisfaction. This particular doctrine, indeed, ran into a difficulty that Adam Smith noted, that water was surely more useful than diamonds but commanded a much lower price. Nevertheless, the doctrine that the increase of utility or happiness is the complete explanation of individual behavior was most emphasized by Jeremy Bentham in writings extending from 1776 to his death in 1832. Even more important, Bentham introduced the doctrine of the parallelism between the descriptive and the normative interpretations of utility: not only does an individual seek happiness, but he ought to do so, and society ought to help him to this end. "Nature has placed mankind under the governance of two sovereign masters, *pain* and *pleasure*. It is for them alone to point out what we ought to do, as well as to determine what we shall do . . . By the principle of utility is meant that principle which approves or disapproves of every action whatsoever, according to the tendency which it appears to have to augment or diminish the happiness of the party whose interest is in question" (Bentham, 1780; 1961). Bentham took it for granted that utility was a measurable magnitude; he further elaborated in various ways the factors which determine utility, such as nearness in time and certainty, but at no point is there a clearly defined procedure for measuring utility, such as would be demanded by modern scientific philosophy. The one suggestion he made was that sufficiently small increments in wealth were not perceptible; therefore, a natural unit for measuring utility was the *minimum sensibile*—or just noticeable difference, as psychophysicists were later to term it.

Although Bentham's notions were widely influential, especially among English economists (as well as being violently repudiated by the romantic thinkers of the early nineteenth century), a further elaboration was not achieved until about 1870, when Bentham's simple hedonistic psychology proved to be of surprising use in economic analysis. Smith's water-diamond paradox was at last resolved; while water as a whole was more valuable than diamonds, the relevant comparison was between an additional increment of water and an additional increment of diamonds, and since water was so much more abundant, it was not surprising that the incremental or *marginal* utility of water was much lower. (Actually, Bentham had already shown Smith's error but did not directly relate utilities to prices in any form; in any case, Bentham's contribution was not recognized.) This basic point was grasped simultaneously by Stanley Jevons in England, Léon Walras in France, and Carl Menger in Austria, between 1871 and 1874; they had in fact been anticipated by Hermann-Heinrich Gossen in Germany in 1854.

The further technical developments of the theory of individual choice in economic contexts are not of interest here, but the power of the utility concept led among other things to an analysis of its meaning. In his doctoral dissertation in 1892, *Mathematical Investigations in the Theory of Value and Prices,* the American economist Irving Fisher observed that the assumption of the measurability of utility in fact was inessential to economic theory. This point was developed independently and taken much further by Vilfredo Pareto, from 1896 on. At any moment, given the prices of various goods and his income, an individual has available to him all bundles of goods the cost of which does not exceed his income. The "marginal utility" theory stated that he chooses among those bundles the one with the highest utility. But all that was necessary for the theoretical explanation was that the individual have an ordering of different bundles; then the individual is presumed to select that bundle among those available which is highest on his ordering. Thus only ordinal preferences matter; two utility functions which implied the same ordinal preference comparisons would predict the same choice of commodity bundles at given prices and income. But this meant in turn that no set of observations on the individual's purchasing behavior could distinguish one of these utility functions from another. In fact, more generally, no observation of the individual's choices from any set of bundles could make this distinction. Later the neopositivist and operational epistemology, so characteristic of this century, would insist that there was no meaning to distinguishing one utility function from another. It was the ordering itself that was meaningful, and all utility functions which implied it were equally valid or invalid.

The ordinalist position, defined above, only began to spread widely in the 1930s and became orthodox, ironically enough, at a moment when the foundations for a more sophisticated theory of cardinal utility had already been laid. The general approach is to make some additional hypotheses about the kind of choices an individual will or ought to make. Then it is demonstrated that there is a way of assigning numerical utilities to different possible bundles of goods or other alternative decisions such that the utilities assigned reflect the ordering (higher utility to preferred alternatives) and that the function assigning utilities to alternatives has some especially simple form. More particularly, it is assumed that the different commodities can be divided into classes in such a way that the preferences for commodities in one class are independent of the amounts of the commodities in the other classes. Then there is a way of assigning utilities to bundles of commodities within each class and defining the utility of the entire bundle as the sum of the utilities over classes. Such a definition of utility can easily be shown to be an interval scale. This process by which utilities are simultaneously assigned within classes and in total so as to satisfy an additivity property has become known as *conjoint measurement.*

A particular case of conjoint measurement is of special significance. An ordinalist position undermined Bernoulli's theory of choice in risky situations; if cardinal utility had no meaning, there was no way of taking its mathematical expectation. In the case of risk bearing, it was very natural to make an appropriate independence assumption, and it was possible so to choose a utility function that an individual's behavior in accepting or rejecting risks could be described by saying that he was choosing the higher expected utility. The philosopher Frank Ramsey made this observation in a paper published posthumously in 1931, in the collection called *The Foundations of Mathematics and Other Essays* (p. 156), but it made no impact; the point was rediscovered by John von Neumann and Oskar Morgenstern, as part of their great work on the theory of games, in 1944. The cardinalist position in this case was rehabilitated, but it has changed its meaning. It is no longer a measure inherently associated with an outcome; instead, the utility function is precisely that which measures the individual's willingness to take risks.

The Social Welfare Function

Bentham's Utilitarianism

To Bentham the utility of each individual was an objectively meaningful magnitude; from the point of view of the community, one man's utility is the same as another's and therefore it is the sum of the utilities of all individuals which ought to determine social policy. Bentham argued strongly that the actual measurement of another's utility is apt to be very difficult, and therefore it is best to let each individual decide as much as possible for himself. In symbols, if $U_1, \ldots, U_n$ are the utilities of the n individuals in the society, each being affected by a social decision, the decision should be made so as to make the sum $U_1 + U_2 + \ldots + U_n$ as large as possible. An expression of this form, which defines a utility for social choices as a function of the utilities of individuals, is usually termed a *social welfare function*. Bentham's conclusion is really clearly enough stated, but there are substantial gaps in the underlying argument. The addition of utilities assumes an objective or at least interpersonally valid common unit; but no argument is given for the existence of one, and no procedure for determining it — except possibly the view that the just-noticeable difference is such a unit. Even if the existence and meaningfulness of such a unit is established, it is logically arbitrary to add the utilities instead of combining them in some other way. The argument that all individuals should appear alike in a social judgment leads only to the conclusion that the social welfare function should be a symmetric function of individual utilities, not that it should be a sum.

The Bentham criterion was defended later by John Stuart Mill, but his arguments bear mostly on the propriety and meaning of basing social welfare judgments on individual preferences and not at all on the commensurability of different individuals' utilities or on the form of social welfare function. Mill, like Henry Sidgwick and others, considered the primary use of Bentham's doctrines to be applicability to the legal system of criminal justice; since the conclusions arrived at were qualitative, not quantitative, in nature, vagueness on questions of measurability went unnoticed.

After the spread of marginal utility theory, the economist F. Y. Edgeworth expounded the notion of utility much more systematically than Bentham had done, with little originality in the foundations, though with a great deal of depth in applications. In particular, he applied the sum-of-utilities criterion to the choice of taxation schemes. The implication is one of radical egalitarianism, as indeed Bentham had already perceived. If, as is usually assumed, the marginal utility of money is decreasing, if all individuals have the same utility function for money, and if a fixed sum of money is to be distributed, then the sum of utilities is maximized when money income is distributed equally. (Here "money" may be thought of as standing for all types of desired goods.) Then the only argument against complete equality of income is that any procedure to accomplish it would in addition reduce total income, which is the amount to be divided. The argument can be also put this way; resources should be taken from the rich and given to the poor, not because they are poorer per se but because they place a higher value on a given quantity of goods. If it were possible to differentiate between equally wealthy individuals on the basis of their sensitivities to income increments, it would be proper to give more to the more sensitive.

Apart from Edgeworth, there was little interest in applying the sum-of-utilities criterion to economic or any other policy. Very possibly, the radically egalitarian implications were too unpalatable, as they clearly were to Edgeworth. Subsequent work on "welfare economics," as the theory of economic policy is usually known, tended to be very obscure on fundamentals (although very edifying in other ways).

Ordinalist Views of the Social Welfare Function

Pareto's rejection of cardinal utility rendered meaningless a sum-of-utilities criterion. If utility for an individual was not even measurable, one could hardly proceed to adding utilities for different individuals. Pareto recognized this problem.

First of all, he introduced a necessary condition for social optimality, which has come to be known as *Pareto optimality:* a social decision is Pareto-optimal if there is no alternative decision which could have made everybody at least as well off and at least one person better off. In this definition, each individual is expressing a preference for one social alternative against another, but no measurement of preference intensity is required. Pareto optimality is thus a purely ordinal concept.

It is, however, a weak condition. It is possible to compare two alternative social decisions only if there is essential unanimity. To put the matter another way, among any given set of alternatives there will usually be many which would satisfy the definition. A manifestly unjust allocation, with vast wealth for a few and poverty for many, will nevertheless be Pareto-optimal if there is no way of improving the lot of the many without injuring the few in some measure. Pareto himself was very clear on this point.

Pareto optimality is nevertheless a very useful concept in clearing away a whole realm of possible decisions which are not compatible with any reasonable definition of social welfare. It might be argued that every application of utilitarianism in practice, such as to the legal system, has in fact used only the concept of Pareto optimality. In welfare economics, similarly, it has turned out to be useful in characterizing sharply the types of institutional arrangements which lead to efficient solutions, making it possible to isolate the debate on distributive problems which it cannot solve.

Pareto later (1913) went further. He suggested that each individual in his judgments about social decisions considers the effects on others as well as on himself. The exposition is a bit obscure, but it appears to coincide with that developed later and independently by the economist Abram Bergson (1938). Each individual has his own evaluation of a social state, which is a function of the utilities of all individuals: $W_i(U_1, \ldots, U_n)$. Since the evaluation is done by a single individual, this function has only ordinal significance. The U_i's themselves may be thought of as an arbitrary numerical scaling of the individuals' preferences; they also have only ordinal significance, but this creates no conceptual problem, since the choice of the social welfare function W_i for the ith individual already takes account of the particular numerical representation of individuals' ordinal utilities.

Interpersonal comparisons of utility are indeed made, but they are ethical judgments by an observer, not factual judgments.

Pareto (but not Bergson) went one step further. The "government" will form the social welfare function which will guide it in its choices by a parallel amalgamation of the social welfare functions of the individuals, that is, a function $V(W_1, \ldots, W_n)$. Pareto's concept of a social welfare function remained unknown, though the concept of Pareto optimality became widely known and influential beginning with the 1930s, as is clear in Bergson's work. The latter became very influential and is accepted as a major landmark; but in fact it has had little application.

Bergson accepted fully the ordinalist viewpoint, so that the ethical judgments are always those of a single individual. This approach, however, loses an important feature of most thinking about social welfare, namely, its impartiality among individuals, as stressed by Bentham and given classic, if insufficiently precise, expression in the categorical imperative of Kant. In Bergson's theory, any individual's social welfare function may be what he wishes, and it is in no way excluded that his own utility plays a disproportionate role. Pareto, by his second-level social welfare function for the government, implicitly recognized the need for social welfare judgments not tied to particular individuals. Still, the ordinalist position seems to imply that all preferences are acts of individuals, so that in fact Pareto had no basis for the second level of judgment.

Conjoint Measurement and Additive Social Welfare Functions

In the field of social choice, as in that of individual choice, the methods of conjoint measurement have led to cardinal utilities which are consistent with the general operational spirit of ordinalism.

William S. Vickrey, in 1945, suggested that the von Neumann-Morgenstern theory of utility for risk bearing was applicable to the Bergson social welfare function. The criterion of impartiality was interpreted to mean that the ethical judge should consider himself equally likely to have any position in society. He then would prefer one decision to another if the expected utility of the first were higher. The utility function used was his von Neumann-Morgenstern utility function—that utility function which explains his behavior in risk bearing. Since all positions are assumed to be equally likely, the expected utility is the same as the average utility of all individuals. In turn, making the average utility as large as possible is equivalent to maximizing the sum of utilities, so that Vickrey's very ingenious argument is a resuscitation, in a way, of Benthamite utilitarianism.

Though Vickrey's criterion is impartial with respect to individuals' positions, it is not impartial with respect to their tastes; the maker of the social welfare judgment is implicitly ascribing his own tastes to others. Furthermore, it has the somewhat peculiar property that social choices among decisions where they may be no uncertainty are governed by attitudes toward risk bearing.

Fleming, in 1952, took another direction, which has not been followed up but is worthy of note. Suppose that an ethical judge is capable of making social welfare judgments for part of the society independently of the remainder. More precisely, suppose that for any social decision which changes the utilities of some individuals but not of others, the judge can specify his preferences without knowing the utility level of those unaffected by the decision. Then it can be shown that there are cardinal utility functions for the individuals and a cardinal social welfare function, such that $W = U_1 + \ldots + U_n$. Although W and $U_1, \ldots, U_n$ are interval scales, the units of measurement must be common. Again there is additivity of utility, but note now that the measurements for individual utility and for social welfare are implied by the social welfare preferences and do not serve as independent bases for them.

Harsanyi, in 1955, in effect synthesized the points of view of Vickrey and of Fleming. His argument was that each individual has a von Neumann-Morgenstern utility function expressing his attitude toward risk, and society, if it is rational, must also have a von Neumann-Morgenstern utility function. It is then easy to demonstrate that society's utility function must be a weighted sum of the individuals' utilities, that is, that $W = a_1 U_1 + \ldots + a_n U_n$. Since each individual utility is an interval scale, we can choose the units so that all the coefficients a_i are 1. This result differs from Vickrey's in that the utility function of the ith individual is used to evaluate his position, rather than the utility function of the judge.

Distantly related to these analyses is the revival, by W. E. Armstrong and by Leo Goodman and Harry Markowitz, of Bentham's use of the just-noticeable difference as an interpersonally valid unit of utility. It has proved remarkably difficult to formulate theories of this type without logical contradiction or at least paradoxical implications.

So far all these results have led to a sum-of-utilities form, though with varying interpretations. As remarked earlier, the notion of impartiality requires symmetry, but not necessarily additivity. John Rawls in 1958 proposed an alternative form for the social welfare criterion, to maximize the *minimum* utility in the society. This formulation presupposes an ordinal interpersonal comparison of utilities. Rawls shares with Vickrey and Harsanyi a hypothetical concept of an original position in which no individual knows who he is going to be in the society whose principles are being formulated. However, he does not regard this ignorance as being adequately formulated by equal probabilities of different positions; in view of the permanence of the (hypothetical) choice being made, he argues that a more conservative criterion, such as maximizing the minimum, is more appropriate than maximizing the expected value.

Social Welfare and Voting

The Theory of Elections in the Eighteenth and Nineteenth Centuries

In a collective context, voting provides the most obvious way by which individual preferences are aggregated into a social choice. In a voting context, the ordinalist-cardinalist controversy becomes irrelevant, for voting is intrinsically an ordinal comparison and no more. (Indeed, the failure of voting to represent intensities of preference is frequently a major charge against it.) The theory of elections thus forcibly faced the problems raised by ordinalism long before it had been formulated in economic thought.

The theoretical analysis of social welfare judgments based on voting first appeared in the form of an examination of the merits of alternative election systems in a paper of Jean-Charles de Borda, first read to the French Academy of Sciences in 1770 and published in 1784 (a translation by Alfred de Grazia is in *Isis,* 44 [1953]:42 – 51). Borda first demonstrated by example that when there are more than two candidates, the method of plurality voting can easily lead to choice of a candidate who is opposed by a large majority. He then proposed another method of voting, one which has been subsequently named the rank-order method (or, sometimes, the method of marks). Let each voter rank all the candidates, giving rank one to the most preferred, rank two to the second, and so forth. Then assign to each candidate a score equal to the sum of the ranks assigned to him by all the voters and choose the candidate for which the sum of ranks is lowest.

Borda's procedure is ordinal, but the arguments advanced for it were in effect cardinal. He held that, for example, the candidate placed second by an individual was known to be located in preference between the first- and third-place candidates; in the absence of any further information, it was reasonable to argue that the preference for the second-place candidate was located halfway between those of the other two. This established an interval scale for each individual. Borda further asserted that the principle of equality of the voters implied that the assignments of ranks by different individuals should count equally.

Borda thus raised most of the issues which have occupied subsequent analysis: (1) the basing of social choice on the entire orderings of all individuals of the available candidates, not merely the first choices; (2) the measurability of individual utilities; and (3) the interpersonal comparability of preference (Borda made interpersonal comparability an ethical judgment of equality, not an empirical judgment).

In 1785 Condorcet published a book on the theory of elections, which raised important new issues. He seems to have been somewhat aware of Borda's work, but had not seen any written version of it when he wrote. Condorcet's aim was to use the theory of probability to provide a basis for social choice, and his program takes up most of the work, though this aspect has had little subsequent influence. Although he purports to apply the theory of probability to the theory of elections, in fact the latter is developed in a different way.

The most important criterion which Condorcet laid down is that if there were one candidate who would get a majority against any other in a two-candidate race, he should be elected. The argument might be put this way. Let us agree that in a two-candidate race majority voting is the correct method. Now suppose, in an election with three candidates, A, B, and C, that C, for example, is not chosen. Then, so it is argued, it is reasonable to ask that the result of the three-candidate race be the same as if C never had been a candidate. To put it another way, it is regarded as undesirable that if A is chosen over B and C, and the voters are then told that in fact C was not even eligible, the election should fall to B. The Condorcet criterion is in the fullest ordinalist spirit; it is consistent with the view that the choice from any set of alternatives should use no information about voters' preferences for candidates not available. Condorcet himself noticed an objection: if an individual judges A preferred to B and B to C, there is some vague sense in which his preference for A over C is stronger than his preference for A over B. As we have seen, this was the starting point for Borda's defense of the rank-order method.

In fact, Condorcet used his criterion to examine Borda's rank-order method. He showed that it did not necessarily lead to choosing the pairwise majority candidate. Moreover, no modification of the rank-order method which allowed for nonuniform ranks would satisfy the Condorcet criterion.

Condorcet's second major achievement was to show that his criterion had the possibility of paradoxical consequences. It was perfectly possible that with three candidates, A be preferred to B by a majority, B to C by a majority, and C to A by a majority. An example is if one-third of the voters prefer A to B and B to C, one-third prefer B to C and C to A, and one-third prefer C to A and A to B. This possibility has become known in the literature as the "paradox of voting," or the Condorcet effect. This paradox of voting, in generalized form, and the possibility of its elimination, have become the main themes of recent literature.

In the terminology introduced at the beginning of this chapter, (pairwise) majority voting defines a relation which is connected (there must be a majority for one or the other of two alternatives, if the number of voters is odd) but need not be transitive.

Condorcet has a proposal for dealing with a case of intransitivity, at least when there are three candidates. Of the three statements of majority preference, disregard the one with the smallest majority; if this is the statement, C preferred to A by a majority, then the choice is A, being preferred to B and "almost preferred" to C. Condorcet extends this proposal to cases with more than three candidates, but no one has been able to understand the extension.

Like Bernoulli's work (1738; translated 1954) on the expected-utility criterion for choice under uncertainty, the papers of Borda and Condorcet had few significant direct successors. (Laplace, however, gave a more rigorous version of Borda's probabilistic argument for the rank-order method.) Indeed, the value of their work only came to be appreciated when others came to the problem independently, 160 years later. Since Condorcet's work made use of the theory of probability, it, like Bernoulli's, was recorded in various histories of the theory of probability during the nineteenth century; in the thorough and widely read history of Todhunter (1865), Borda's and Condorcet's theories of elections were included with the probabilistic theory.

The only significant published nineteenth-century work on the theory of elections that is known today is that of the English mathematician E. J. Nanson, published in 1882 in Australia, in *Transactions and Proceedings of the Royal Society of Victoria,* 19 (1882):197–240. Nanson makes no reference to Condorcet, but it is hard to believe that his work is independent. He notes the paradox of voting, in a manner which suggests that he regarded it as well known, and accepts fully the Condorcet criterion. His work consists primarily in showing that each of several voting methods that have been proposed fail to satisfy the Condorcet criterion, in that one could find a system of preference orderings for individuals such that there exists a candidate who would get a majority against any other but still would not be chosen. Nanson proposes a method which will satisfy the criterion: rank all candidates according to the rank-order method. Then eliminate all candidates for which the sum of ranks is above the average. With the remaining candidates form the rank orders again, considering only those candidates, and repeat the process until one candidate is selected.

Among the methods considered and found wanting by Nanson was preferential voting, an adaptation of the Hare system of proportional representation to the election of a single candidate. In 1926 George Hallett, a leading American advocate of proportional representation, suggested a modification which met the Condorcet criterion. He developed a procedure (the details need not be repeated here) which, starting with the orderings of all the candidates by all the voters, picked out a candidate, A, and a set of candidates $B_1, \ldots, B_r$, such that A is preferred by a majority to each of $B_1, \ldots, B_r$. Then the B_i's are eliminated from further consideration; the orderings of only the remaining candidates are used, and the process is repeated. It may be added that Hallett was fully aware of the work of both Condorcet and Nanson and referred to both of them.

Duncan Black has called attention to some contributions of C. L. Dodgson (Lewis Carroll), printed but not published, particularly one of 1876. Dodgson accepted the Condorcet criterion and observed the possibility of paradox of voting; he used the criterion, as Nanson did a few years later, to criticize certain voting methods. By implication rather than directly, he suggested an ingenious solution for the cases of paradox: choose that candidate who would have a majority over all others if the original preference scales of the voters were altered in a way which involved the least possible number of interchanges of preferences. (When there are three candidates, this proposal coincides with Nanson's.)

Dodgson raised one more conceptually interesting point, that of the possibility of "no election." Yet his discussion is inconsistent. At one point he contends that if the paradox occurs, there should be "no election"; however, a little further on, he argues that if "no election" is a possibility, then it should be entered among the list of candidates and treated symmetrically with them. In the context of elections themselves, the possibility is uninteresting; but if we think of legislative proposals, "no election" means the preservation of the status quo. Dodgson is noting that legislative choice processes do not take all the alternatives on a par but give a special privileged status to one.

Dodgson made no reference to predecessors; however, his pamphlets were designed to influence the conduct of Oxford elections, and scholarly foot-noting would have been inappropriate. Whether or not he read Todhunter's passages on Borda and Condorcet cannot now be determined. Of course, no subsequent work was influenced by him.

Current Analysis of Social Welfare Based on Rankings

After a long but exiguous history, the general theory of elections suddenly became a lively subject of research beginning with the papers of Black published in 1948 and 1949 and my own 1951 monograph. Since then there has been an uninterrupted spate of discussion. It is perhaps not easy to see exactly why the interest has changed so markedly. Neither Black nor I were aware at the time we first wrote of any of the preceding literature, though it is hard to exclude the possibility that some of this knowledge was in a vague sense common property. I have noted (*Social Choice and Individual Values,* p. 93) that when I first hit upon the paradox of voting, I felt sure that it was known, though I was unable to recall any source.

Both Black and I are economists, and some historical tendencies in economics, in addition to the general theory of marginal utility, played their role. (1) A number of marginal utility theorists, such as Marshall and Wicksteed, had tried to demonstrate that their theories were, as Bentham had originally held, applicable in fields wider than the purely economic. (2) In particular, economists in the field of public finance were forced to recognize that public expenditures, which are plainly a form of economic activity, were in principle regulated by voters. A voter who was also a taxpayer could usefully be thought of as making a choice between public and private goods; the actual outcome would depend upon the voting process. Problems of this type were studied by Knut Wicksell in 1896, Erik Lindahl in 1919, and Howard Bowen in 1943. These works tend in a general way to a combined theory of political-economic choice. (3) Other economists, partic-ularly Harold Hotelling in 1929 and Joseph Schumpeter in his 1942 book *Socialism, Capitalism, and Democracy,* had suggested models of the politi-cal process analogous to that of the economic system, with voters taking the place of consumers and politicians that of entrepreneurs. (4) Marginal utility theorists such as Edgeworth in 1881, and the Austrians Carl Menger and Eugen von Böhm-Bawerk about the same time, had been concerned with problems of bargaining, where one buyer meets one seller, rather than the more usual competitive assumptions of many buyers and sellers. The development of game theory by von Neumann and Morgenstern was intended to meet this problem, but the formulation took on such general proportions that it suggested the possibility of a very general theory of social behavior based on the foundation of individual behavior as governed by utility functions. (5) The ideas of Pareto and Bergson were now widespread and raised demands for clarification.

Most of these topics could be interpreted both descriptively and normatively, and some of this duality has persisted in the current literature. There are two main themes, associated with the names of Black and Arrow, respectively: (1) demonstration that if the preference scales of individuals are not arbitrary but satisfy certain hypotheses, then majority voting is transitive; (2) formulation of sets of reasonable conditions for aggregating individual preferences through a kind of generalized voting and examining the consequences; if the set of conditions is strong enough, there can be no system of voting consistent with all of them.

Suppose that all the alternative decisions can be imagined arrayed in such a way that each individual's preferences are single-peaked — that is, of any two alternatives to the left of the most preferred (by an individual), he prefers the one nearest to it, and similarly with two alternatives to the right. This would be the case if the "Left-Right" ordering of political parties were a valid empirical description. Black demonstrated that if preferences are single-peaked then no paradox of voting can arise. Put another way, the relation "alternative A preferred by a majority to alternative B" is an ordering and in particular is transitive.

Later work, particularly that of Amartya Sen and Gordon Tullock, has developed generalizations of the single-peaked preference condition in different directions. The conditions are too technical for brief presentation, but, like single-peakedness, they imply certain types of similarity among the preference scales of all individuals.

I stated formally a set of apparently reasonable criteria for social choice and demonstrated that they were mutually inconsistent. The study arose as an attempt to give operational content to Bergson's concept of a social welfare function. The conditions on the social decision procedure follow: (1) for any possible set of individual preference orderings, there should be defined a social preference ordering (connected and transitive) which governs social choices; (2) if everybody prefers alternative A to alternative B, then society must have the same preference (Pareto optimality); (3) the social choice made from any set of available alternatives should depend only on the orderings of individuals with respect to those alternatives; (4) the social decision procedure should not be dictatorial, in the sense that there is one whose preferences prevail regardless of the preferences of all others.

Condition (3) in effect restricts social decision procedures (or social welfare criteria) to generalized forms of voting; only preferences among the available candidates are used in deciding an election. The inconsistency of these conditions is in fact a generalized form of the paradox of voting. No system of voting, no matter how complicated, can avoid a form of the paradox. As in the original Condorcet case of simple majority voting, all that is meant by the paradox is that it could arise for certain sets of individual preference orderings. If individual preference orderings were restricted to a set for which the conditions of Black, Sen, or Tullock hold, then majority voting and many other methods would satisfy conditions (2) to (4).

The evaluation of the Arrow paradox has led to considerable controversy, still persisting.

In one version of my system, condition (2) was replaced by another which, loosely speaking, stated that a change of individuals' preferences in favor of a particular alternative A would raise its social preference, if possible. The existence of the paradox is not altered by this substitution. Recent work by Kenneth May, and later Yasusuke Murakami, has showed that this condition, together with condition (3), has powerful implications for the nature of the social decision process. Specifically, it followed that the choice from any pair of alternatives is made by a sequence of majority votes, where outcomes of the vote at one step can enter as a vote at a later step. Some individuals may vote more than once, and some votes may be prescribed in advance. If, however, it is assumed in addition that all individuals should enter symmetrically into the procedure and also that the voting rule should be the same for all pairs of alternatives, then the only possible voting rule is pairwise majority decision, the Condorcet criterion.

Bibliographic Note

For histories of the theory of individual choice in economics see E. Kauder, *A History of Marginal Utility Theory* (Princeton, 1965), and G. J. Stigler, "The Development of Utility Theory," *Journal of Political Economy,* 58 (1950), 307–27, 373–96. Bernoulli's paper originally appeared in *Commentarii Academiae Scientiarum Imperiales Petropolitanae,* 5 (1738), 175–92. It has been translated into English in *Econometrica,* 12 (1954), 23–36. The quotation from J. Bentham appears in his *Introduction to the Principles of Morals and Legislation,* reprinted in *The Utilitarians* (Garden City, N.Y., 1961), p. 17. For a survey of the theory of conjoint measurement, see P. C. Fishburn, "A Note on Recent Developments in Additive

Utility Theories for Multiple-Factor Situations," *Operations Research,* 14 (1966), 1143–48.

No adequate secondary sources exist for most of the section on the social welfare function. See Bentham's work just cited; W. Stark, ed. *Jeremy Bentham's Economic Writings* (London, 1954); M. P. Mack, *Jeremy Bentham: An Odyssey of Ideas, 1748–1792* (New York, 1963); F. Y. Edgeworth, *Mathematical Psychics* (London, 1881), and idem, "The Pure Theory of Taxation," in *Papers Relating to Political Economy* (London, 1925), II, 102; V. Pareto, *The Mind and Society* (New York, 1935), 4, 1459–74; A. Bergson, *Essays in Normative Economics* (Cambridge, Mass., 1966), pt. 1; W. S. Vickrey, "Measuring Marginal Utility by Reaction to Risk," *Econometrica,* 13 (1945), 319–33, and idem, "Utility, Strategy, and Decision Rules," *Quarterly Journal of Economics,* 74 (1960), 507–35; J. M. Fleming, "A Cardinal Concept of Welfare," *Quarterly Journal of Economics,* 64 (1952), 366–84; J. Harsanyi, "Cardinal Welfare, Individualistic Ethics, and Interpersonal Comparisons of Utility," *Journal of Political Economy,* 56 (1953), 309–21; W. E. Armstrong, "Utility and the Theory of Welfare," *Oxford Economic Papers, New Series,* 3 (1951), 259–71; L. Goodman and H. Markowitz, "Social Welfare Functions Based on Individual Rankings," *American Journal of Sociology,* 58 (1952), 257–62; J. Rothenberg, *The Measurement of Social Welfare* (Englewood Cliffs, N.J., 1961); and J. Rawls, "Distributive Justice," in P. Laslett and W. G. Runciman, eds. *Philosophy, Politics, and Society, Third Series* (Oxford, 1967), pp. 58–82.

For the discussion of social welfare and voting see C. G. Hoag and G. Hallett, *Proportional Representation* (New York, 1926), for the work of Hallett, Hare, and others on proportional representation and preferential voting. See also J. Rothenberg, *The Measurement of Social Welfare;* K. J. Arrow, *Social Choice and Individual Values,* 2nd ed. (New York, 1963); D. Black, *The Theory of Committees and Elections* (Cambridge, 1958); I. Todhunter, *A History of the Mathematical Theory of Probability from the Time of Pascal to that of Laplace* (Cambridge and London, 1865); A. K. Sen, "A Possibility Theorem on Majority Decisions," *Econometrica,* 34 (1966), 491–99; G. Tullock, *Toward a Mathematics of Politics* (Ann Arbor, 1967), chap. 3; and Y. Murakami, *Logic and Social Choice* (London and New York, 1968). The work of Condorcet is discussed by Black, pp. 159–80; see also G. G. Granger, *La mathématique sociale du Marquis de Condorcet* (Paris, 1956), esp. pp. 94–129. Condorcet's study was entitled *Essai sur l'application de l'analyse à la probabilité des décisions rendues à la pluralité des voix* (Paris, 1785). For Laplace's work on elections, see Black, pp. 180–83.

10 Rawls's Principle of Just Saving

The problem of justice in the distribution of resources is of course basic. At no time in the history of economic thinking has there been a thoroughly agreed-upon criterion, but among the more philosophic circles of economists a utilitarian criterion has been more or less accepted. That is, we assume there exists for each individual i an interpersonally meaningful cardinal utility functon, $U_i(c_i)$, where c_i is the consumption of the ith individual. Then a just or optimal distribution is one which maximizes $\Sigma_i U_i(c_i)$, where the variables c_i are constrained by technology, initial resources, and informational and other difficulties in transferring goods among individuals.

Rawls (1971) has proposed an alternative criterion for just allocation. He imagines all the individuals in the society getting together in an "original position," where each knows the possible resource allocations but no one knows which member of the society he is going to be. They must decide on a criterion function for the distribution of goods. Then, he argues, they will find it rational to agree not on the sum-of-utilities criterion but on the rule of maximizing the welfare of the least well-off member of the society (since this might be any one of them). That is, they maximize $\min_i U_i(c_i)$, subject to the same constraints on the variables c_i. I ignore here the richness of Rawls's discussion, some other constraints he imposes on the allocation of resources (particularly setting an infinitely higher value on liberty than on goods), and

Reprinted from *Swedish Journal of Economics,* 75 (1973):323–335.

the validity of Rawls's reasoning from the original position to the maximin criterion.[1] (See Chapter 8 for remarks on some of these matters.)

One important aspect of justice is the intertemporal. What is a just allocation of goods among individuals of different generations? The intertemporal problem of justice differs from the contemporary problem fundamentally only in one empirical point: namely, that resources are productive, so that a transfer from an earlier to a later generation means, in general, that the later generation receives more (measured in commodity units) than the earlier generation gave up. In this case our egalitarian presuppositions are somewhat upset; clearly, if we have any regard at all for future generations (as justice demands) and if the gain from waiting is sufficiently great, then we will want to sacrifice some for the benefit of future individuals even if they are, to begin with, somewhat better off than we are. We will not do this indefinitely; this is usually formalized by assuming that they and we have diminishing marginal utility, so that at some point the gain in commodity terms ceases to be a gain in utility terms.

I shall introduce a very simple model of production to illustrate this point, and then analyze the implications of Rawls's criterion of justice in this context. Assume there is but one good. Within each generation all individuals are alike, so that we may assume that there is only one. This also implies a stationary population; the adjustment to growing populations is easy and merely distracts attention from our analysis of the meaning of justice. The one good can either be consumed or used as capital which bears a return. Let K_t be the accumulated capital at the beginning of time period t. At that moment part of the stock, c_t, is consumed and the remainder, $K_t - c_t$, is used in production. Each unit so used yields α units at the beginning of the next time period, so that

$$(10\text{-}1) \qquad K_{t+1} = \alpha(K_t - c_t).$$

Unless otherwise specified, it will be understood that the economy is in fact productive, so that one unit invested yields more than one unit of output, that is,

$$(10\text{-}2) \qquad \alpha > 1.$$

The individual at time t derives satisfaction from the consumption, c_t; it is assumed that the amount of satisfaction or *felicity* from any given con-

---

sumption is the same for all t—in other words, there is a function $U(c)$ such that the analogue of the sum-of-utilities criterion is the maximization of $\Sigma_{t=0}U(c_t)$, where the variables c_t are subject to the constraint (10-1) and the obvious conditions

(10-3) $\qquad K_t \geq 0$ for all t; K_0 given.

However, it is reasonable to require that the future look the same from any initial time point. This implies that the sum-of-felicities maximand must have the special form

$$(10\text{-}4) \qquad \sum_{t=0} \beta^t U(c_t)$$

for some fixed β and some function $U(c)$. Here β is the *subjective discount rate*. The value $U(c_t)$ might be interpreted as the *immediate* satisfaction derived from consumption c_t.

A straightforward transposition of the Rawls maximin criterion to the intertemporal context might seem to be to maximize

$$(10\text{-}5) \qquad \min_t\ U(c_t)$$

subject to the constraints (10-1) and (10-3). This interpretation has been used by Solow (1974), although he recognizes that it is not the one advocated by Rawls. It is pretty obvious (and will follow from some results below) that the maximization of (10-5) would lead to zero savings in every generation, for there is no way to compensate the first generation for any saving they may do, and they would be worse off than any of their successors.

Rawls's own discussion (1971, sec. 44) is by no means clear. However, the one way in which he meets the point just raised is by arguing that "since it is assumed that a generation cares for its immediate descendants, as fathers, say, care for their sons, a just savings principle, or more accurately, certain limits on such principles, would be acknowledged" (p. 288).

I will take up this sentence as the basis for a Rawlsian analysis of intertemporal justice.[2] It appears to me that in fact the assumption made uniquely defines a just savings principle, not merely "limits on such principles," and this savings principle so defined has much the same problems with it as the zero savings associated with the maximization of $\min_t\ U(c_t)$.

---

2. Rawls has informed me that he did not intend to supply any form of the maximin principle to intergenerational justice. But the logic which derives the maximin principle from the "original position" seems to me to be equally applicable to intergenerational comparisons.

Specifically, while savings may under some circumstances take place, they will always be followed by dissavings.

Following the sentence just quoted, it will be assumed that the utility derived by an individual of generation t is a function, $W(c_t, c_{t+1})$, of its consumption and that of the succeeding generation. Then the *Rawls criterion* becomes

(10-6)   maximize $\min_t W(c_t, c_{t+1})$.

For simplicity, it will be assumed, in agreement with Dasgupta (1974, assumption A.2.2) that W is additively separable in its two arguments, that the felicity ascribed by individual t to individual $t + 1$ is the same as that ascribed by individual $t + 1$ to himself, that this felicity function is the same for all t, and finally that the felicity of the future generation may be discounted in the utility of the present generation. In symbols,

(10-7) $W(c_t, c_{t+1}) = U(c_t) + \beta U(c_{t+1})$.

As usual, it is assumed that

(10-8) $U(c)$ is increasing, differentiable, and concave.

Finally, it is not excluded that $\beta = 1$ in (10-7); each generation might care for its heirs as much as it does for itself. I do, however, exclude the possibility $\beta > 1$.

Feasibility Conditions

Recall some simple restatements of the feasibility conditions (10-1) and (10-3). First, for any t and u, $u \geq t$, we can express capital at time u in terms of capital at time t and consumptions at times $t, t + 1, \ldots, u - 1$:

(10-9) $K_u = \alpha^{u-t} \left(K_t - \sum_{v=t}^{u-1} \alpha^{t-v} c_v \right)$.

This holds trivially for $u = t$, and the general case follows from (10-1) by an easy induction on u, for

$$K_{u+1} = \alpha K_u - \alpha c_u = \alpha K_u - \alpha^{u+1-t} \alpha^{t-u} c_u;$$

if we substitute for K_u from (10-9) we deduce (10-9) with u replaced by $u + 1$.

If in (10-9) we replace t by 0 and u by t, we see immediately that the condition (10-3), that capital never be negative, can be stated

$$\sum_{v=0}^{t-1} \alpha^{-v} c_v \le K_0, \qquad \text{for all } t.$$

But since each term of the left-hand sum is nonnegative, this requirement in turn implies and is implied by the familiar condition

(10-10) $\displaystyle\sum_{v=0}^{\infty} \alpha^{-v} c_v \le K_0.$

There is one consumption level, $\bar{c}$, such that capital will be maintained intact, that is, there is no saving. From (10-1), with $t = 0$ and $K_1 = K_0$, we see that $K_0 = \alpha(K_0 - \bar{c})$, or

(10-11) $\displaystyle \bar{c} = \left(\frac{\alpha - 1}{\alpha}\right) K_0.$

Clearly, at time period 1, since $K_1 = K_0$, the consumption of $\bar{c}$ will cause $K_2 = K_1 = K_0$ and so forth, so that the constant consumption, $\bar{c}$, will indeed cause K_t to remain constant at the initial level K_0.

Starting from any given program, consider any alternative, say $\{c_t'\}$, such that

(10-12) $\displaystyle\sum_{v=t}^{u-1} \alpha^{t-v} c_v' = \sum_{v=t}^{u-1} \alpha^{t-v} c_v.$

Then from Eq. (10-9), if $K_t = K_t'$, it must be true that $K_u = K_u'$. Variations satisfying Eq. (10-12) leave the opportunities beginning at time u undisturbed. If, in particular, $u = t + 2$, we can say:

if $K_t = K_t'$ and $c_t' + \alpha^{-1} c_{t+1}' = c_t + \alpha^{-1} c_{t+1}$,

(10-13)   then $K_{t+2} = K_{t+2}'.$

I shall refer to variations satisfying (10-13) as *balanced* variations.

By the same argument, an unbalanced variation will cause an increase or decrease in the capital stock. In the latter case, if it is repeated indefinitely, the feasibility condition (10-3), that capital stock be nonnegative, may ultimately be violated. In the following lemma I consider variations from the constant-capital level of consumption.

LEMMA 1. *Suppose $\alpha > 1$, and define $\bar{c}$ by (10-11). If, for some $\delta > 0$, $c_{2t} + \alpha^{-1} c_{2t+1} \ge \bar{c}(1 + \alpha^{-1}) + \delta$ for all t, then the program $\{c_t\}$ is infeasible.*

Proof. For any program, replace u by $2t + 2$ and t by $2t$ in Eq. (10-9).

(10-14) $K_{2t+2} = \alpha^2[K_{2t} - (c_{2t} + \alpha^{-1}c_{2t+1})]$.

In particular, if $c_t = \bar{c}$ for all t, Eq. (10-14) holds with $K_{2t+2} = K_{2t} = K_0$.

(10-15) $K_0 = \alpha^2[K_0 - \bar{c}(1 + \alpha^{-1})]$.

Let

(10-16) $c_{2t} + \alpha^{-1}c_{2t+1} - \bar{c}(1 + \alpha^{-1}) = h_t$.

Subtract (10-15) from (10-14) and use definition (10-16):

(10-17) $K_{2t+2} - K_0 = \alpha^2[(K_{2t} - K_0) - h_t]$.

Define $x_t = \alpha^{-2t}(K_{2t} - K_0)$. Multiply through in (10-17) by α^{-2t-2}:

$$x_{t+1} = x_t - \alpha^{-2t}h_t.$$

Since $x_0 = 0$,

$$x_t = -\sum_{u=0}^{t-1} \alpha^{-2u}h_u.$$

Suppose that

(10-18) $\displaystyle\limsup_{t\to\infty} \sum_{u=0}^{t-1} \alpha^{-2u}h_u > 0$.

Then for some $\varepsilon > 0$, $x_t < -\varepsilon$ for arbitrarily large values of t. Since $\alpha^{-2t}K_0 < \varepsilon$ for all t sufficiently large, $x_t < -\alpha^{-2t}K_0$ for some t. But from the definition of x_t, this implies that $K_{2t} < 0$, and therefore the program $\{c_t\}$ must be infeasible.

Under the hypothesis of the lemma, $h_u \geq \delta$ for all u, and therefore (10-18) certainly holds.

COROLLARY TO LEMMA 1. *The maximum feasible constant level of consumption is* $\bar{c}$, *as defined by Eq. (10-11).*

Proof. If $\tilde{c} > \bar{c}$, then $\tilde{c}(1 + \alpha^{-1}) > \bar{c}(1 + \alpha^{-1})$; hence, by Lemma 1, the constant consumption level $\tilde{c}$ would be infeasible.

Lemma 1 can be generalized easily to cover consumption patterns for time intervals greater in length than 2.

LEMMA 2. *Suppose* $\alpha > 1$ *and define* $\bar{c}$ *by (10-11). If for some* $\delta > 0$, $\sum_{v=mt}^{m(t+1)-1} \alpha^{mt-v}c_v \geq \bar{c}\ \sum_{v=mt}^{m(t+1)-1} \alpha^{mt-v} + \delta$ *for all* t, *then the program* $\{c_t\}$ *is infeasible.*

Proof. Corresponding to Eq. (10-14), we note that

$$K_{m(t+1)} = \alpha^m \left(K_{mt} - \sum_{v=mt}^{m(t+1)-1} \alpha^{mt-v} c_v \right).$$

The rest of the argument is completely parallel.

Just for formal completeness, we examine the case where the economy is not productive in goods, that is, where $\alpha \leq 1$.

LEMMA 3. *If $\alpha \leq 1$, then for any feasible consumption program $\{c_t\}$, $\sum_{t=0}^{\infty} c_t$ converges and therefore $c_t \rightarrow 0$ as $t \rightarrow +\infty$.*

Proof. For feasibility, we must have $K_{t+1} \geq 0$ and therefore, from (10-3), $K_t \geq c_t$. Hence,

$$K_{t+1} = \alpha(K_t - c_t) \leq K_t - c_t \quad \text{and} \quad K_t \leq K_0 - \sum_{u=0}^{t-1} c_u.$$

The condition, $K_t \geq 0$ for all t, then implies the lemma.

Just Savings in a Utility-Productive Economy

We shall say that an economy is *utility productive* if, given any feasible consumption program in which consumption is the same for two successive periods t and $t + 1$, individual t would prefer a balanced variation which increases c_{t+1} and decreases c_t. In other words, the economy is sufficiently productive, α sufficiently bigger than 1, that the individual would prefer to shift consumption to the next generation even though he may to some extent discount the felicity gains.

LEMMA 4. *An economy is utility productive if and only if $\alpha\beta > 1$.*

Proof. Start with a program where the consumptions at times t and $t + 1$ are both c. Suppose that individual t prefers c_t, c_{t+1}, a balanced variation of c, c, with $c_{t+1} > c$. In other words,

(10-19)　　$U(c_t) + \beta U(c_{t+1}) > U(c) + \beta U(c)$

(10-20)　　$c_t + \alpha^{-1} c_{t+1} = c(1 + \alpha^{-1}) \quad \text{or} \quad (c_t - c) + \alpha^{-1}(c_{t+1} - c) = 0.$

Since $U(c_t) + \beta U(c_{t+1})$ is concave in its two variables, from (10-8), (10-19) can hold only if the derivative of W at (c, c) in the direction of (c_t, c_{t+1}) is positive:

$$U'(c)(c_t - c) + \beta U'(c)(c_{t+1} - c) > 0,$$

or, dividing through by $U'(c) > 0$,

(10-21) $(c_t - c) + \beta(c_{t+1} - c) > 0.$

But (10-20) and (10-21) hold simultaneously, with $c_{t+1} - c > 0$, if and only if $\alpha\beta > 1$.

We now note that for any productive economy, whether or not utility productive, the just savings policy must necessarily forbid any extended growth in welfare. The just savings policy will not necessarily require a constant utility level as defined by (10-7), but any generation which has a higher utility level must be preceded and followed by generations whose utility level is the minimum. Since more precise results will be obtained later, we give here only an informal sketch of a proof, though one that could be made rigorous.

THEOREM 1. *Suppose $\alpha > 1$. Then if $\{c_t\}$ is a program which maximizes min_t $W(c_t, c_{t+1})$, as defined by (10-7), over all feasible programs, it must be that (a) $W(c_0, c_1) = min_t W(c_t, c_{t+1})$ and (b) if $(Wc_u, c_{u+1}) > min_t W(c_t, c_{t+1})$, then $W(c_v, c_{v+1}) = min_t W(c_t, c_{t+1})$ for $v = u - 1$ and $v = u + 1$.*

Proof. Reduce c_0 slightly and increase c_t for $t > 0$ by the income from the additional capital invested. If $W(c_0, c_1)$ were greater than the minimum, the latter would be increased if we make the reduction sufficiently small so that $W(c_0, c_1)$ does not become the new minimum.

Suppose $W(c_u, c_{u+1})$ and $W(c_{u+1}, c_{u+2})$ are both above the minimum. As before, reduce c_{u+1} slightly and increase all subsequent c_t's. This will increase $W(c_t, c_{t+1})$ for all $t > u + 1$. The change will reduce both $W(c_u, c_{u+1})$ and $W(c_{u+1}, c_{u+2})$, but for a sufficiently small change they will still be above the original minimum. Now increase c_t for $t \leq u$ by a small amount. This will reduce K_{u+1} proportionately. If c_{u+1} is then reduced by an equal amount, K_{u+2} will be unchanged; the subsequent c_t's remain feasible. Clearly, $W(c_t, c_{t+1})$ is increased for all $t < u$. Again, $W(c_u, c_{u+1})$ may be and $W(c_{u+1}, c_{u+2})$ is reduced, but with a sufficiently small change, they still remain above the original minimum. Hence, $W(c_t, c_{t+1})$ is above the original minimum for every t, which contradicts the assumption that the original program was a just savings rule in the sense of Rawls.

With the general flavor of the solutions now displayed, we give an exact characterization of the optimal policy.

THEOREM 2. *Suppose $\alpha\beta > 1$ and $\beta \leq 1$. Then the feasible consumption program which maximizes min_t $W(c_t, c_{t+1})$ can be characterized as follows. Choose c_0^*, c_1^* to maximize $W(c_0, c_1)$ subject to the constraint $c_0 + \alpha^{-1}c_1 = \bar{c}(1 + \alpha^{-1})$; then at the optimum $c_t = c_0^*$ for even t, $c_t = c_1^*$ for odd t. For this policy the following properties hold: $c_0^* < c_1^*$; $W(c_t, c_{t+1}) = min_t W(c_t, c_{t+1})$ for t even; $W(c_t, c_{t+1}) \geq min_t W(c_t, c_{t+1})$ for t odd, with the equality holding if and only if $\beta = 1$.*

Proof. From the definition of utility productivity and Lemma 4, $c_0^* < c_1^*$. By construction of the program, $W(c_t, c_{t+1})$ is the same for all even t. Now let t be odd; then $c_t = c_1^*$ and $c_{t+1} = c_0^*$. We know that $U(c_1^*) > U(c_0^*)$. Multiply both sides of this inequality by $1 - \beta \geq 0$, and transpose:

$$U(c_0^*) + \beta U(c_1^*) \leq U(c_1^*) + \beta U(c_0^*) = W(c_t, c_{t+1}).$$

The inequality is strict if $\beta < 1$. The left-hand side, however, is the common value of $W(c_t, c_{t+1})$ for all even t. Hence, the minimum is indeed achieved at every even t.

Now consider any program $\{c_t'\}$ for which $min_t W(c_t', c_{t+1}') > min_t W(c_t, c_{t+1})$. In particular, then, it must be true that for some $\varepsilon > 0$,

$$W(c_t', c_{t+1}') \geq W(c_t, c_{t+1}) + \varepsilon \quad \text{for all even } t.$$

But by construction of the policy $\{c_t\}$ the right-hand side maximized W subject to the constraint $c_t + \alpha^{-1}c_{t+1} = \bar{c}(1 + \alpha^{-1})$. Let b be the minimum value of $c_0 + \alpha^{-1}c_1$ subject to the condition

$$W(c_0, c_1) \geq W(c_0^*, c_1^*) + \varepsilon.$$

Then clearly, $b > c_0^* + \alpha^{-1}c_1^*$, and, by definition of a minimum,

$$c_t' + \alpha^{-1}c_{t+1}' \geq b = (c_0^* + \alpha^{-1}c_1^*) + \delta = \bar{c}(1 + \alpha^{-1}) + \delta, \qquad \delta > 0.$$

If we replace t by $2t$ in this inequality, we see from Lemma 1 that the program $\{c_t'\}$ is infeasible, so that the policy $\{c_t\}$ is optimal.

It is at least questionable that the sawtooth pattern corresponds to any intuitive idea of justice.

An Extension of Concern to Further Generations: Approach to Utilitarianism

Suppose that an individual is concerned not merely with the subsequent generation but with generations still further into the future, say m after his own. Then we might wish to generalize (10-7) to read

$$(10\text{-}22) \quad W_t = W(c_t, \ldots, c_{t+m}) = \sum_{i=0}^{m} \beta_i U(c_{t+i}),$$

and we seek to maximize min W_t subject to the same feasibility conditions (10-1) and (10-3). Corresponding to the assumption of utility productivity, I assume that, starting with the same consumptions at times $t + i$ and $t + j$ ($0 \leq i < j \leq m$) the economy is sufficiently productive that generation t will prefer to shift some consumption from $t + i$ to $t + j$, all other consumptions being held constant. The last qualification requires that

$$\alpha^{-(t+i)}c_{t+i} + \alpha^{-(t+j)}c_{t+j}$$

be constant, from (10-10) with equality, which will obviously always hold if there is no satiation in consumption. Hence a small increase h in c_{t+j} must be accompanied by a decrease of $\alpha^{i-j}h$ in c_{t+i}. Since all other consumptions are constant, an increase in W_t is an increase in $\beta_i U(c_{t+i}) + \beta_j U(c_{t+j})$. If in the initial situation $c_{t+i} = c_{t+j} = c$, then a shift to later consumption increases W_t by

$$\beta_i U'(c)(-\alpha^{i-j}h) + \beta_j U'(c)h$$

to a first approximation, which is positive if and only if $\beta_j \alpha^j > \beta_i \alpha^i$. I shall assume this inequality holds for all i and j, $0 \leq i < j \leq m$.

I shall also assume that $\beta_i \geq \beta_{i+1}$, a generalization of the condition $\beta \leq 1$. This represents a nonincreasing concern with increasingly future generations.

THEOREM 3. *Suppose the utility of generation t is given by Eq. (10-22), that $\alpha^i \beta_i$ increases with i for i $\leq$ m, and that β_i is nonincreasing in i. Then the feasible consumption program which maximizes min$_t$ W_t can be characterized as follows. Choose $c_i^*(i = 0, \ldots, m)$ to maximize $W(c_0, \ldots, c_m)$ subject to the constraint*

$$\sum_{i=0}^{m} \alpha^{-i}c_i = \bar{c} \sum_{i=0}^{m} \alpha^{-i},$$

where $\bar{c}$ is the constant-capital level of consumption. Then at the optimum $c_{(m+1)t+i} = c_i^*(0 \leq i \leq m)$. For this policy the following properties hold: $c_i^* < c_{i+1}^*$; $W_t = $ min$_t$ W_t if t is divisible by m + 1; for all other t, $W_t \geq$ min$_t$ W_t and the inequality is strict if $\beta_i > \beta_{i+1}$ for some i < m.

Proof. From the condition that $\alpha^i \beta_i$ is increasing, it follows as in Lemma 4 that $c_i^* < c_{i+1}^*(i < m)$. By construction W_t is the same for all t divisible by $m + 1$. To show that the minimum is attained for all such t, it suffices to show that $W_r \geq W_0(r \leq m)$.

The proposed program for generations $r, \ldots, m + r$ is $c_r^*, \ldots, c_m^*$, $c_0^*, \ldots, c_{r-1}^*$. Then

$$W_r = \sum_{i=0}^{m-r} \beta_i U(c_{r+i}^*) + \sum_{i=m-r+1}^{m} \beta_i U(c_{i-m+r-1}^*)$$

$$= \sum_{i=0}^{m-r} \beta_i U(c_{r+i}^*) + \sum_{i=0}^{r-1} \beta_{i+m-r+1} U(c_i^*);$$

$$W_0 = \sum_{i=0}^{m} \beta_i U(c_i^*) = \sum_{i=0}^{r-1} \beta_i U(c_i^*) + \sum_{i=r}^{m} \beta_i U(c_i^*)$$

$$= \sum_{i=0}^{r-1} \beta_i U(c_i^*) + \sum_{i=0}^{m-r} \beta_{i+r} U(c_{i+r}^*);$$

and $$W_r - W_0 = \sum_{i=0}^{m-r} (\beta_i - \beta_{i+r})U(c_{i+r}^*) + \sum_{i=0}^{r-1} (\beta_{i+m-r+1} - \beta_i)U^*(c_i).$$

Since β_i is monotone decreasing in i and c_i^* increasing in i, we see that $\beta_i - \beta_{i+r} \geq 0$ and therefore $(\beta_i - \beta_{i+r})U(c_{i+r}^*) \geq U(c_r^*)(\beta_i - \beta_{i+r})$. Similarly, $\beta_{i+m-r+1} - \beta_i \leq 0$, $U(c_i^*) \leq U(c_{r-1}^*)$ for $i \leq r - 1$, and therefore $(\beta_{i+m-r+1} - \beta_i)U(c_i^*) \geq U(c_{r-1}^*)(\beta_{i+m-r+1} - \beta_i)$. Further, the first inequality is strict if $0 < i \leq m - r$ and $\beta_i > \beta_{i+r}$, the second if $0 \leq i < r - 1$ and $\beta_i > \beta_{i+m-r+1}$. Since β_i is nonincreasing, we see that if $\beta_j > \beta_{j+1}$ for any $j < m$, then $\beta_i > \beta_k$ for any $i \leq j$ and any $k \geq j + 1$. By considering all possibilities, we see that if $\beta_j > \beta_{j+1}$ for some $j < m$, then one of the inequalities must hold:

$$W_r - W_0 \geq AU(c_r^*) + BU(c_{r-1}^*),$$

where

$$A = \sum_{i=0}^{m-r} (\beta_i - \beta_{i+r}), \quad B = \sum_{i=0}^{r-1} (\beta_{i+m-r+1} - \beta_i),$$

and the inequality is strict if $\beta_j > \beta_{j+1}$ for some $j < m$. Also, $A \geq 0$ and

$$A + B = \sum_{i=0}^{m-r} \beta_i - \sum_{i=r}^{m} \beta_i + \sum_{i=m-r+1}^{m} \beta_i - \sum_{i=0}^{r-1} \beta_i = \sum_{i=0}^{m} \beta_i - \sum_{i=0}^{m} \beta_i = 0,$$

so that $W_r - W_0 \geq A[U(c_r^*) - U(c_{r-1}^*)] \geq 0$, with the strict inequality holding if the β_i's are not all equal.

Thus, the proposed program attains $\min_t W_t$ at $t = 0$ and all other t values divisible by $m + 1$. If it were not optimal, there would be an alternative program $\{c_t'\}$ defining utilities W_t' which would have the property, among others, that $W_t' \geq W_0 + \varepsilon$ for all t divisible by $m + 1$, for some $\varepsilon > 0$. The rest of the proof exactly parallels that of Theorem 2, the infeasibility of the program $\{c_t'\}$ being established by Lemma 2.

We see, therefore, that introducing altruism to generations up to some horizon leads to maximization of a sum of discounted utilities from the origin up to that horizon; beyond that it leads to periodic repetition of the solution with a period equal to that of the horizon.

Remark 1. If the horizon is taken to be infinite or at least equal to the horizon for the human race as a whole, then the maximin criterion becomes simply the utilitarian criterion, maximize $\sum_{t=0}^{\infty} \beta_t U(c_t)$. Under altruism toward future generations forever, the difference between the maximin criterion and the utilitarian disappears.

Remark 2. The assumption that $\alpha^i \beta_i$ is increasing over the horizon might be too strong if we take the view that the horizon is rather short. Since this product is zero beyond the horizon, it might be supposed to get small toward the end. Then c_i^* is no longer increasing, and the reasoning leading to the inequalities $W_r \geq W_0$ becomes invalid. Some of these constraints become binding, so that the nature of the solution must change. It is an open question what the maximin policy is under these circumstances.

Remark 3. Theorem 3 is valid for $m = 0$, the case of no concern for the future. In that case the maximin policy is the constant consumption $\bar{c}$, as is intuitively obvious.

Unproductive Economies

For completeness I also consider maximin policies in unproductive economies. Only the case $m = 1$ (concern only for the next generation) is considered. The economy may be physically unproductive, $\alpha \leq 1$, or unproductive in the utility sense, $\alpha > 1$ but $\alpha\beta \leq 1$.

The case $\alpha \leq 1$ has in effect already been covered by Lemma 3. For any feasible policy it must be that c_t approaches 0 and therefore $W(c_t, c_{t+1})$ approaches its smallest possible value, $W(0,0) = (1 + \beta) U(0)$. In this case the minimum of $W(c_t, c_{t+1})$ may not exist; one can always find a feasible program with $c_t > 0$ everywhere, for example, $c_t = c_0 \rho^t$, for any $\rho < \alpha$ and $c_0 = K_0(\alpha - \rho)/\alpha$. But inf $W(c_t, c_{t+1})$ is defined.

THEOREM 4. *If $\alpha \leq 1$, then inf $W(c_t, c_{t+1}) = (1 + \beta)U(0)$ for all feasible programs.*

The case $\alpha\beta \leq 1$ is more interesting.

THEOREM 5. *If $\alpha\beta \leq 1$ and $\alpha > 1$, then the feasible consumption program which maximizes $\min_t W(c_t, c_{t+1})$ is the constant-capital level of consumption in every period.*

Proof. Suppose Theorem 5 is false. Then there exists a feasible program $\{c_t\}$ such that $W(c_t, c_{t+1}) \geq W(\bar{c}, \bar{c}) + \delta'$ for some $\delta' > 0$.

Since W is concave in its variables and $\partial W/\partial c_t = U'(c_t)$, $\partial W/\partial c_{t+1} = \beta U'(c_{t+1})$, we have

$$W(c_t, c_{t+1}) \leq U'(\bar{c})(c_t - \bar{c}) + \beta U'(\bar{c})(c_{t+1} - \bar{c}) + W(\bar{c}, \bar{c}),$$

so that

$$(10\text{-}23) \quad U'(\bar{c})[(c_t - \bar{c}) + \beta(c_{t+1} - \bar{c})] \geq \delta'$$
$$\text{or} \quad (c_t - \bar{c}) + \beta(c_{t+1} - \bar{c}) \geq \delta, \quad \delta > 0,$$

where $\delta = \delta'/U'(\bar{c})$.

We now prove by induction the following two statements for each t:

$$(a)\ K_{2t} \leq K_0, \quad (b)\ (c_{2t} - \bar{c}) + \alpha^{-1}(c_{2t+1} - \bar{c}) \geq \delta.$$

Clearly, if (b) holds, then by Lemma 1 the program $\{c_t\}$ is infeasible, completing the proof. Also, (a) holds for $t = 0$. We shall show that, for each t, (a) implies (b), and that if (a) and (b) hold for some t, then (a) holds for $t + 1$.

(a) implies (b): clearly (10-10) continues to hold if 0 is replaced by any starting time t, and in particular by $2t$:

$$(10\text{-}24) \quad \sum_{u=2t}^{\infty} \alpha^{-(u-2t)}c_u \leq K_{2t} \leq K_0.$$

In (10-23) replace t by u, multiply by $\alpha^{-(u-2t)}$, and sum for $u \geq 2t$:

$$(10\text{-}25) \quad \sum_{u=2t}^{\infty} \alpha^{-(u-2t)}(c_u - \bar{c}) + \beta \sum_{u=2t}^{\infty} \alpha^{-(u-2t)}(c_{u+1} - \bar{c}) > 0.$$

But

$$\sum_{u=2t}^{\infty} \alpha^{-(u-2t)}(c_{u+1} - \bar{c}) = \alpha \sum_{u=2t+1}^{\infty} \alpha^{-(u-2t)}(c_u - \bar{c})$$

$$= \alpha \sum_{u=2t}^{\infty} \alpha^{-(u-2t)}(c_u - \bar{c}) - \alpha(c_{2t} - \bar{c}).$$

Substitute in (10-25):

(10-26) $(1 + \alpha\beta) \sum_{u=2t}^{\infty} \alpha^{-(u-2t)}(c_u - \bar{c}) > \alpha\beta(c_{2t} - \bar{c}).$

Since

$$\sum_{u=2t}^{\infty} \alpha^{-(u-2t)}\bar{c} = \bar{c} \sum_{u=0}^{\infty} \alpha^{-u} = K_0,$$

it follows from (10-24) that the left-hand side of (10-26) is nonpositive. Therefore, $c_{2t} < \bar{c}$, and, from (10-23), with t replaced by $2t$,

(10-27) $c_{2t+1} > \bar{c}.$

By hypothesis, $\alpha\beta \leq 1$ or $\beta \leq \alpha^{-1}$. From (10-23) and (10-27), (b) holds. (a) and (b) imply (a) for $t + 1$: from (b) and (10-16), $h_t > 0$. From (a) and (10-17), (a) holds for $t + 1$, completing the induction.

References

Dasgupta, P. On some problems arising from Professor Rawls's Conception of Distributive Justice. *Theory and Decision 4*, 325–344, 1974.

Harsanyi, J. Cardinal utility in welfare economics and the theory of risk-bearing. *Journal of Political Economy 61*, 434–435, 1953.

Harsanyi, J. Cardinal welfare, individualistic ethics, and interpersonal comparisons of utility. *Journal of Political Economy 63*, 309–321, 1955.

Rawls, J. *A theory of justice*. Harvard University Press, Cambridge, Mass., 1971.

Solow, R. M. Intergenerational equity and exhaustible resources. *Review of Economic Studies 41*, 29–45, 1974.

Vickrey, W. S. Measuring marginal utility by reactions to risk. *Econometrica 13*, 319–333, 1945.

Vickrey, W. S. Utility, strategy, and social decision rules. *Quarterly Journal of Economics 74*, 507–535, 1960.

11   Extended Sympathy and the Possibility of Social Choice

The domain of the theory of social choice is not in principle the same as that of a theory of justice. In some directions it is clearly wider, since it is supposed to cover all decisions that must be made collectively. On the other hand, it is possible to hold that propositions about distributive justice are not necessarily propositions about collective decisions. Indeed, theories such as Nozick's (1974, chap. 7) argue that justice is the result of individual rather than collective decisions.

Nevertheless, I think it safe to say that the two theories are intimately linked. Suppose we accept the Pareto criterion as part of the definition of a satisfactory theory of social choice. Then in any given feasible set of alternatives, a principle of social choice selects among the members of the Pareto-efficient subset. These constitute the admissible set of redistributions. Further, within this subset any two distributions that yield the same satisfactions to each individual are regarded as indifferent. Hence the principle of social choice selects among alternative distributions of satisfactions. It therefore serves the same function as the principle of distributive justice and may be identified with it.

As for the other direction, I continue to uphold the view that principles of justice are indeed intended as criteria for social decisions. The decision might indeed be to let the actual distribution be governed by some decentralized mechanism; but this is itself a decision. This is the tradition that has been predominant in welfare economics, as in the work of Bergson (1938) or

Reprinted from *American Economic Review Papers and Proceedings,* 67 (1977):219–225.

Samuelson (1947, chap. 8), which I accepted in my own earlier work (Arrow, 1963) and which is also certainly the view of Rawls (1971) and, for that matter, of the utilitarians. A fuller defense of the doctrine that propositions about justice are hypothetical social decisions must await another occasion.

The Structure of Social Decision Problems

I shall simply maintain without discussion the view that the outcome of a social choice procedure (constitution, social welfare function, social decision function, or whatever other term is used) is an ordering (transitive, complete, and reflective relation) of alternative social states. This formulation does not exclude that *some* aspects of resource allocation are reserved to private decision (or to decision by subsocieties). It is simply assumed as given that there is a range of decisions about the distribution of goods which is to be made by society. There are problems with the full formulation of a division of choice between private and social realms (because the decisions may be complementary or substitute), but again these problems will not be dealt with here.

As indicated, I retain the view that the outcome should be an ordering. Presumably, the weakest possible outcome of a constitution would be a choice function, a mapping of each feasible set of alternatives into a chosen subset. Again, one cannot avoid some consistency relations among the choices from different feasible sets. Various conditions weaker than a full ordering have been proposed, but in my judgment they do not lead to interesting conclusions. Unless they are implausibly weak, these conditions do not lead to noticeably greater freedom in the selection of social choice procedures.

What remains is determination of the social ordering. On which data is it based? In particular, how does it relate to individual preferences over social states, what might be termed *individual utilities.* For purposes of this chapter I am accepting the viewpoint of the utilitarians and of welfare economics. It is assumed that each individual has some measure of the satisfaction he draws from each social state and that the social ordering is determined by the specification of these utilities for all possible social states.

I shall return shortly to the measurability properties of utilities; at the moment I use the term in a neutral manner consistent with their being either ordinal or cardinal and interpersonally comparable or not. At this point I want to raise the issue of what properties of the social state are arguments in the individual utility functions. Two leading candidates are (1) a measure of the individual's satisfaction derived from those aspects of the social state that concern him and (2) his evaluation of the extent to which the social state is a just or otherwise socially satisfactory allocation. (Of course, combinations of these two viewpoints are possible.) In my work on the impossibility theorem I regarded either interpretation as permissible, in the sense that the impossibility was valid under either (1963, pp. 17–18). Sen (1977) has argued that my suggested conditions on social choice are more appropriate to the interpretation of choice among principles of justice than to the determination of a just allocation of satisfactions. I remain unconvinced that the same issues do not arise under both interpretations, and I think the results to be presented in this chapter are valid in either interpretation. However, I have the first interpretation primarily in mind here. After all, if we are seeking a concept of justice, it is not very satisfactory to start with the idea that every individual has already formed a concept which enters into the determination of the social outcome.

In this last statement I think I am at one with Rawls. But it is now clear to me that in another way there is sharp divergence: Rawls clearly does not base the just allocation on individual utilities but rather on the distribution of the "primary goods" which permit individuals to maximize whatever utility functions they choose (for his most extended statement of this position see Rawls, 1975, esp. pp. 551–554).

The work I am reporting on here has an ironic relation to Rawls's difference principle. Under certain epistemological assumptions about individual utilities, a social choice approach leads to Rawls's difference principle—but in terms of utilities, not primary goods.

The Invariance of Social Choice under Transformations of Utilities

The new results in social choice theory that I wish to sketch were developed independently by two young scholars, Steven Strasnick, in an unpublished doctoral dissertation in philosophy at Harvard (1975) and Peter J. Hammond, an English economist, in a recently published paper (1976). The works have been influential even in manuscript and have led in particular to an excellent synthesis by the Belgian economists Claude d'Aspremont and Louis Gevers (1977). It is their exposition which I shall largely follow. Most of this chapter will be devoted to the formal theory, although I shall omit proofs; at the end I shall make some comments on interpretation.

In my book I used the preference orderings of individuals over social states as the variables which determined the social orderings. As is well known, an alternative equivalent representation of individual preference would have been a real-valued utility function over social states, which, however, would have meaning only up to a monotone transformation.[1] Since no interpersonal comparisons appeared in my approach, the utility functions of the different individuals could be subject to independent monotone transformations.

The term *meaning,* which may seem to raise frightening semantic issues, has a precise meaning. If we represent individual preferences by utility functions, the social choice will have to be invariant under independent monotone transformations for different individuals.

Let N = the set of individuals and X = the set of possible social alternatives. Any given feasible set of alternatives is, then, a subset of X.

A utility function $u(x)$ is a real-valued function on X. It defines an ordering over X in the usual way—x is preferred to y if and only if $u(x) > u(y)$. A specification of utility functions, one for each individual, $u_i(x)$ $(i = 1, \ldots , n)$, can also be regarded as a single function $u(x,i)$ over the Cartesian product $X \times N$. Let U = the set of real-valued functions on $X \times N$.

From now on, the term *utility function* will refer to any member of U. In these terms a social welfare or constitution (to use my now-favorite term) can be defined in the following way.

DEFINITION. *A constitution is a function f mapping U into orderings of X.*

That is, we associate to each utility function (that is, a utility function for each individual) a social ordering of social states.

Let u be a utility function and let g_i $(i = 1, \ldots , n)$ be n (strictly) monotone functions from real numbers to real numbers. Let a utility function u' be defined by

$$u'(x,i) = g_i [u(x,i)].$$

If we maintain the strictly ordinal approach of Arrow (1963) and also prohibit interpersonal comparisons, then there would be no operational distinction between u and u'; the only evidence we have is the ordering of

---

1. Strictly speaking, not every preference ordering can be represented by a real-valued indicator, but this restriction can be neglected here. It is no restriction if the number of alternatives is finite.

social states for each individual, and that is the same for u and u'. Hence this ascetic viewpoint would require that the orderings defined by u and u' be the same.

• *Ordinal Invariance:* If there exist strictly monotonic functions g_i ($i = 1, \ldots, n$) from real numbers to real numbers such that

$$u'(x,i) = g_i [u(x,i)] \quad \text{for all } x \text{ and } i,$$

then $f(u) = f(u')$.

As is well known (see Arrow, 1963), ordinal invariance, together with the other assumptions usually made about the constitution, implies that there exists no constitution.

The question then arises, are there less demanding forms of invariance which permit the existence of satisfactory constitutions and which can be justified in terms of actual or at least hypothetical observation?

If cardinal interpersonal comparisons of utility differences are regarded as meaningful, then the sum of utilities defines a constitution. The transformations under which the constitution is to be invariant must be such that the truth-value of statements of the form

$$u(x,i) - u(y,i) = k[u(x,j) - u(y,j)]$$

is preserved. This obviously restricts the transformations to linear transformations with the same (positive) coefficient for all individuals.

• *Cardinal-Difference Invariance:* If there exist numbers a_i, $b\,(> 0)$ such that

$$u'(x,i) = a_i + b\,u(x,i) \quad \text{for all } x \text{ and } i,$$

then $f(u) = f(u')$. In that case the condition $\Sigma_i u(x,i) > \Sigma_i u(y,i)$ satisfies cardinal-difference invariance. Ordering by sum of utilities also satisfies the other conditions (independence of irrelevant alternatives, Pareto Principle, anonymity) of the following section.

I want to concentrate, however, on a different invariance principle. This one permits interpersonal ordinal comparisons. That is, we regard as meaningful statements of the form

individual i in state x is better off than individual j in state y.

Whatever one may think of interpersonal comparisons, at least these are ordinal and therefore may be interpreted as hypothetical choice.

In this case $u(x,i)$ may be interpreted as the utility derived by individual i

in state x. Statements of the form

$$u(x,i) > u(y,j)$$

are to be preserved under transformations. Thus, the permitted transformations are monotone transformations of the whole utility function, but not transformations which differ from individual to individual.

  • *Co-ordinal Invariance:* If there exists a strictly monotone function g from real numbers to real numbers such that

$$u'(x,i) = g[u(x,i)]   \text{for all } x \text{ and } i,$$

then $f(u) = f(u')$.

Other Conditions on Social Choice

We retain conditions on social choice like those in Arrow (1963), though restated to be compatible with the present definition of a constitution as a mapping from utility functions rather than from n-tuples of orderings.

Since, for each u, $f(u)$ is an ordering, the notation $x\, f(u)\, y$ means

> x is at least as good as y in the social ordering induced by the utility function u.

The strict preference ordering defined by u will be denoted by $f^P(u)$.

The (controversial) assumption of independence of irrelevant alternatives will be stated here only for preferences, that is, for choice from two-member sets. Only that part of the assumption was used in Arrow (1963).

  • *Binary Relevancy:* If u and u' are such that

$$u(x,i) = u'(x,i)   \text{and}   u(y,i) = u'(y,i)   \text{for all } i,$$

then $x\, f(u)\, y$ if and only if $x\, f(u')\, y$.

The democratic condition that all individuals are to count equally will be here represented in the strong form of symmetry among individuals, instead of the very weak nondictatorship condition.

  • *Anonymity:* Let s be a permutation of N. If

$$u(x,i) = u'[(x,s\,(i)]   \text{for all } x \text{ and } i,$$

then $f(u) = f(u')$.

The Pareto condition used in Arrow (1963) is the weak condition that follows.

  • *Weak Pareto:* If $u(x,i) > u(y,i)$ for all i, then $x\, f^P(u)\, y$.

For certain purposes we shall want the stronger condition that if at least one individual is better off by a change, while none are hurt, the change should be made.

- *Strong Pareto:* If $u(x,i) \geq u(y,i)$ for all i, and, for some j, $u(x,j) > u(y,j)$, then $x f^P(u) \, y$.

Finally, there is an interesting generalization of the Pareto condition, an implication of which has interesting consequences. Up to this point we have taken the range of individuals, N, as given. But suppose we assume that we have a constitution for every set of individuals. We would expect to have some consistency conditions among these constitutions. Indeed, the Pareto principle is one such. If there is only one individual in the world, the social ordering is simply his. Then the weak Pareto principle can be interpreted as asserting that if all one-individual subsets prefer x to y, then so does the whole society; while the strong Pareto principle says that if all one-individual subsets weakly prefer x to y, while at least one has a strong preference, then society prefers x to y. The one-individual subsets are a partition of the entire set of voters. Then it is reasonable to extend the principle to cover all partitions of the voters; for each subset, we are assuming that the constitution prescribes a mapping of the utility function (restricted to the individuals in that subset) into a social ordering.

Since N is now variable,

$$U_N = \text{the set of real-valued functions on } X \times N.$$

A constitution for any given sets of voters N is now supposed to define social orderings for utility functions on every subset of voters.

DEFINITION. *A constitution is a family of functions f_N, defined for all sets of voters N, mapping U_N into orderings of X.*

If $u \in U_N$ for some N, and $M \subset N$, then u_M will be the function u restricted to individuals in M and so belongs to U_M. Hence, for any $u \in U_N$, $f_M(U_M)$ is defined for every $M \subset N$.

- *Generalized Strong Pareto:* (a) If N consists of the single individual i, $f_N(u)$ is the ordering defined by the utility indicator $u(x,i)$. (b) If Q is a partition of N, and, for all $M \in Q$, $x f_M (u_M) \, y$, while for some $M' \in Q$, $x f^P_{M'}(u_{M'}) \, y$, then $x f^P_N(u) \, y$.

This principle, stated by Strasnick, had been used earlier by Young (1974, p. 44).

Here we use the generalized strong Pareto principle only in the special form given next.

• *Elimination of Indifferent Individuals:* Let N be partitioned into M' and M''. Suppose $u \in U_N$, $u' \in U_N$ and $u_{M'} = u'_{M'}$, while for all x and y, $u(x,i) = u(y,i)$ and $u'(x,i) = u'(y,i)$ for all $i \in M''$. Then $f_N(u) = f_N(u')$.

The Theorems

We know of course that ordinal invariance, binary relevancy, anonymity, and the weak Pareto condition are incompatible. If, however, we replace ordinal invariance by co-ordinal invariance, the conditions are indeed satisfied and, in fact, by the maximin principle — that is,

$$x\,f(u)\,y \quad \text{if and only if} \quad \min_i u(x,i) \geq \min_i u(y,i).$$

This condition also satisfies elimination of indifferent individuals and the generalized weak Pareto principle (an obvious analogue of the generalized strong Pareto principle given in the preceding section). It does not satisfy the strong Pareto principle; however, as Sen (1970, p. 138n11) has noted, a simple modification will lead to satisfaction.

• *Lexical Maximin Principle:* For any alternative x and utility function u, rank the individuals in increasing order of $u(x,i)$ and let $i(x,k)$ be the kth ranking individual; ties can be broken arbitrarily. For any pair of alternatives x, y let

$$k(x,y) = \min \{k | u[x,k] \neq u[y,i(y,k)]\},$$

if defined. Then $x\,f^P(u)\,y$ if and only if $u[x,i(x,k(x,y))] > u[y,i(y,k(x,y))]$.

The lexical maximin principle satisfies co-ordinal invariance, binary relevancy, anonymity, and the generalized strong Pareto condition.

It is not, however, the only principle satisfying these conditions. Indeed, the maximax principle,

$$x\,f(u)\,y \quad \text{if and only if} \quad \max_i u(x,i) \geq \max_i u(y,i),$$

also satisfies co-ordinal invariance, binary relevancy, anonymity, and the weak Pareto condition; and clearly, the lexical maximax principle, defined in the obvious way, satisfies all the conditions stated above for lexical maximin.

What is surprising is that these are the only two such conditions; and, by means of a very weak equity assumption, the lexical maximax principle can be ruled out.

I define two more conditions; they will not be regarded as primary, but their relations to the other conditions will be stated.

• *Strong Equity:* For all $u \in U_N$, all x and y in X, and all i and j in N, if $u(x,g) = u(y,g)$ for $g \neq i,j$, and $u(y,i) < u(x,i) < u(x,j) < u(y,j)$, then $x\,f(u)\,y$.

That is, if all but two individuals are indifferent between x and y, and one individual is better off than the other in both x and y, his choice should not be binding. By itself, this amounts to putting a weak version of Rawls right into the axiom system.

The dual assumption to strong equity is

• *Inequity:* For all $u \in U_N$, all x and y in X, and all i and j in N, if $u(x,g) = u(y,g)$ for $g \neq i, j$, and $u(y,i) < u(x,i) < u(x,j) < u(y,j)$, then $y\,f^P(u)\,x$.

The better-off individual *always* prevails.

THEOREM 1. *If the constitution satisfies binary relevancy, anonymity, co-ordinality invariance, and elimination of indifferent individuals, then either strong equity or inequity holds.*

This result may seem surprisingly strong, and its proof takes numerous steps. However, an intuitive sketch can be given for the case of two individuals. In the first place, the assumptions of binary relevancy, anonymity, and elimination of indifferent individuals can easily be shown to imply

• *Neutrality:* If s is a permutation of X, and $u(x,i) = u'\,[s(x),i]$ for all x and i, then $x\,f(u)\,y$ if and only if $s(x)\,f(u')\,s(y)$.

Changing the names of the alternatives does not matter. Suppose, then, both strong equity and inequity fail. The failure of strong equity implies the existence of u, x, y, i, and j, such that

$$u(y,i) < u(x,i) < u(x,j) < u(y,j), \quad y\,f^P(u)\,x.$$

The failure of inequity implies the existence of u', x', y', i', and j' such that

$$u'\,(y',i') < u'(x',i') < u'(x',j') < u'(y',j'), \quad x'\,f(u')\,y'.$$

But from neutrality and anonymity, we take $x' = x$, $y' = y$, $i' = i$, $j' = j$. Then on the set consisting of the four elements, (x,i), (x,j), (y,i), and (y,j), u and u' give the same ordering. By binary relevancy, the ordering over other elements is irrelevant to the choice between x and y. But an ordinal transformation common to the two individuals takes u into u', in contradiction to co-ordinal invariance.

The extension to many individuals is laborious but relies mainly on elimination of indifferent individuals.

On the other hand, as Hammond and Strasnick have shown, strong equity with the other assumptions implies lexical maximin.

THEOREM 2. *If the constitution satisfies binary relevancy, anonymity, co-ordinal invariance, the strong Pareto principle, and strong equity, then it is the lexical maximin principle.*

The strong equity assumption postulates the result for two individuals; the problem in the proof is to extend it to any number of individuals.

Of course, entirely dual to Theorem 2, we have

THEOREM 3. *If the constitution satisfies binary relevancy, anonymity, co-ordinal invariance, the strong Pareto principle, and inequity, then it is the lexical maximax principle.*

If we add the strong Pareto principle to the assumptions of Theorem 1, then Theorems 1, 2, and 3 together tell us we have reduced the range of possible constitutions to two, the lexical maximin and the lexical maximax. To eliminate the second, it is sufficient to deny the inequity assumption, instead of imposing the apparently stronger strong equity condition. An assumption which contradicts inequity is

• *Minimal Equity:* There exist $u \in U_N$, $x \in X$, $y \in X$, and $j \in N$, such that for all $i \neq j$, $u(y,i) < (x,i) < u(x,j) < u(y,j)$, and $x f(u) y$.

That is, there is at least one utility function and one individual such that the individual is better off than anyone else under either alternative and has preferences opposite to all of theirs, and the given individual does not prevail. Since lexical maximax clearly does not satisfy minimal equity, it is clear   from Theorem 3 that minimal equity contradicts inequity. From Theorems 1 and 2, then, we must have lexical maximin.

THEOREM 4. *If the constitution satisfies binary relevancy, anonymity, co-ordinal invariance, the strong Pareto principle, and minimal equity, then it is the lexical maximin principle.*

Evaluation of the Axiomatic Justification of Maximin

Suppose we assume for a moment the meaningfulness of interpersonal ordinal comparisons (see next section). Do we find the results convincing?

There are two reservations which come to mind. The first is narrower, that is, it accepts virtually all of the argument. The whole argument is basically symmetrical in "best-off" and "worst-off" individuals.[2] These are indeed

---

2. Robert Nozick has stressed this point to me.

distinguished from the others; that is an implication of co-ordinal invariance. In effect, the distribution of utilities of the intermediate individuals is not ascribed any meaning, since the magnitudes are not co-ordinally invariant. All we know about the intermediate individuals is that they are intermediate; they might be close to one end or the other.[3] But to exclude letting decisions be made in the interests of the best-off requires some form of direct assumption to the contrary, if only in the weak form of the minimal equity assumption.

That this might not be innocuous can be seen by noting that one could equally well state a minimal inequity condition which would lead to a maximax criterion; after all, an assertion that the best-off individual should *never* prevail does not seem all that weak. The idea that the worst-off should have some preference has to be built into the assumptions; at least with co-ordinal invariance, there is no intrinsic way of distinguishing him from his fortunate compeer.

Indeed, the question can be raised with regard to the original position of Rawls. Why, in that situation, should not the ignorant ones each look to the best rather than the worst possibility? We have to introduce some additional considerations beyond those of formal symmetry. Rawls introduced the familiar notion of risk aversion. But this is getting close to the doctrines of utilitarianism. If we assume diminishing marginal utility (whether in the risk-bearing sense or some other), then we can indeed explain the asymmetric treatment of best-off and worst-off, who are those with higher marginal utility.

But obviously we have now introduced a whole range of considerations beyond those permitted by co-ordinal invariance and also beyond those permitted in Rawlsian theory. Technically, the invariance requirements are being weakened, and more possibilities are being introduced.

Another argument for moving in this direction is the second of the two reservations about the present line of development that I indicated above. It can be put as a continuity requirement. Suppose a change from x to y diminishes the utility of the worst-off by some very small amount but increases the utility of all others by a great deal. Surely it seems reasonable to

---

3. The special role of the extremes has appeared in a parallel context, that of decision making under uncertainty, where we do not wish to ascribe probabilities (directly or indirectly) to the possible states of the world. The states of the world correspond to individuals, the actions to be chosen to alternative social states. Certain approaches imply co-ordinal invariance. See Milnor (1954, theorem 4) and Arrow and Hurwicz (1972).

argue that if the loss to the worst-off is small enough and the gain to everyone else large enough, society should prefer y to x. Indeed, if there were *no* loss to the worst-off and a gain to all others, the lexical maximin rule would call y a strict improvement; hence, by any kind of continuity argument, the preference for y over x should be maintained if the utility loss to the worst-off is sufficiently small.

It may be objected that, utilities being ordinally meaningful, continuity with respect to utilities is not all that natural or even meaningful. But consider instead the distribution of goods which determines the utilities of the different individuals. This may be regarded as a point in a Euclidean vector space or some other topological space. It is perfectly meaningful then to postulate that preferences are continuous with respect to the underlying topology. Thus, if (x,i) is preferred to (y,j), then (x',i) is preferred to (y',j) for all x' and y' sufficiently close to x and y, respectively. With such a restriction on the underlying preferences, we can restrict ourselves to utility functions which are continuous in the social state. Then continuity of the constitution with respect to the utility function is an ordinally invariant and therefore certainly co-ordinally invariant property.

Thus, adding a continuity requirement to the hypotheses of Theorem 4 leads to an impossibility theorem.

This is by no means a "formal" matter. Clearly, the intuition behind the continuity requirement is a small step in the direction of utilitarian ethics; even the worst-off member of the society might be made to suffer if there were enough benefit to others. The assumption of diminishing marginal utility implies with regard to usual policy alternatives that there are better ways of improving the lot of better-off members than by hurting the worst-off.

Nonetheless, there is one striking case, of great practical importance, where our intuition is in favor of utilitarianism in some form as against any maximin rule. I refer to allocation over time. Typically, we expect future generations to be better off than we are. Should we save for them either directly or in the form of public investments? A maximin rule would surely say no. But if investment is productive, so that in terms of goods the next generation gains more than we lose, we usually feel that some investment is worthwhile even though the recipients will be better off than we are.[4]

---

4. I do not find Rawls's theory of just saving (1971, sec. 44) at all clear; it seems to avoid a rigid maximin rule without providing a clear substitute. See Arrow (1973) and Dasgupta (1974).

The Operational Significance of Interpersonal Ordinal Comparisons

The discussion above suggests that, if anything, even interpersonal ordinal comparisons are not sufficient to take account of our intuitions of justice as derived from a social choice framework. The requirement of co-ordinal invariance may still be too strict. In this section I address the opposite question; whether such comparisons have any meaning—in other words, whether the invariance criterion should not perhaps be even stricter.

The possibility of such comparisons has already been defended in different forms by Suppes (1966), Kolm (1972, pt. C), and myself (1963, pp. 114–115). I will comment only briefly, to avoid repeating my earlier arguments excessively.

The concept of a preference ordering or, by extension, of a utility function is related to hypothetical choices. Its usual use is in a complete theory, say of individual behavior, in which the preference ordering and the feasible set jointly determine the chosen alternative. The preference ordering is thought of as given before the feasible set is known and therefore determines choices among all possible pairs of alternatives. The feasible set prescribes which alternatives are in fact available. It makes sense, therefore, to include in our information choices which are not in fact feasible even though they are conceivable.

Now we can say that among the characteristics which determine an individual's satisfaction are some which are not, at least at the moment, alterable. An individual who is ill can meaningfully be said to prefer being well. If in fact there were some medical means of cure, we would test this preference by asking if he would purchase the services. Clearly the preference would be there whether or not medicine was useful.

We may suppose that everything which determines an individual's satisfaction is included in the list of goods. Thus, not only the wine but the ability to enjoy and discriminate are included among goods. It is, in fact, true that only some of the goods so defined are transferable among individuals; others are not. But that consideration enters into the definition of the feasible set, not that of the ordering. If we use this complete list, then everyone should have the same utility function for what he gets out of the social state. This does not, of course, mean that individuals agree on the utility of a social state, since what they receive from a given state differs among individuals.

The location of interpersonal differences in a list of qualities has been defended by Pascal (1965, p. 323):

What is the Ego? . . . Does he who loves someone on account of beauty really love that person? No; for the small-pox, which will kill beauty without killing the person, will cause him to love her no more.

And if one loves me for judgment, memory, he does not love *me*, for I can lose these qualities without losing myself. Where, then, is this Ego, if it be neither in the body nor the soul? . . . For it is impossible and would be unjust to love the soul of a person in the abstract . . . We never, then, love a person, but only qualities.

Let us, then, jeer no more at those who are honored on account of rank and office; for we love a person only on account of borrowed qualities.

Formally, we suppose a space Y which defines the range of possible implications of a social state for an individual. Since the state defines, for every individual, everything that characterizes his satisfactions, the space Y is the same for all individuals. It includes goods, tastes, and the reactions of others to the extent that individuals care about one another. All individuals have the same preferences over Y. Let $u(y)$ be the ordinally defined utility indicator. Each state in x defines implications for every individual. Let $G_i(x)$ $(i = 1, \ldots, n)$ be for each individual a mapping from X to Y, expressing these implications. Then we can identify $u(x,i) = u[G_i(x)]$, and this possesses co-ordinal invariance.

This is at least one way to interpret and defend interpersonal ordinal comparisons. (There are others.)

I cannot conclude without admitting some difficulties. I can think of two, though perhaps they are the same looked at somewhat differently. For one thing, if your satisfaction depends on some inner qualities that I do not possess, then I really have not had the experience which will enable me to judge the satisfaction one would derive from that quality in association with some distribution of goods. Hence, my judgment has a probability element in it and therefore will not agree with your judgment. But it is essential to the present construction that the comparisons of individual i in state x with individual j in state y be the same whether the comparison is made by $i, j,$ or a third individual, k.

The second difficulty is that reducing an individual to a specified list of qualities is denying his individuality in a deep sense. The last line of the quotation from Pascal should give one pause. In a way that I cannot articulate well and am none too sure about defending, the autonomy of individuals, an element of mutual incommensurability among people, seems denied by the possibility of interpersonal comparisons. No doubt it is some such feeling as this that has made me so reluctant to shift from pure ordinalism, despite my desire to seek a basis for a theory of justice.

References

K. J. Arrow, *Social Choice and Individual Values,* 2nd edition, New York, and New Haven, Conn. 1963.

K. J. Arrow, "Rawls's Principle of Just Saving," *Swedish J. Econ.,* 1973, *75,* 323–335.

K. J. Arrow and L. Hurwicz, "An Optimality Criterion for Decision-Making Under Ignorance," in C. F. Carter and J. L. Ford (eds.), *Uncertainty and Expectations in Economics,* Oxford, 1972.

A. Bergson, "A Reformulation of Certain Aspects of Welfare Economics," *Quart. J. Econ.,* 1938, *52,* 310–334.

P. Dasgupta, "On Some Alternative Criteria for Justice Between Generations," *J. Pub. Econ.,* 1974, *3,* 405–423.

C. d'Aspremont and L. Gevers, "Equity and the Informational Basis of Collective Choice," *Rev. Econ. Stud.,* 1977, *46,* 199–210.

P. J. Hammond, "Equity, Arrow's Conditions, and Rawls' Difference Principle," *Econometrica,* 1976, *44,* 793–804.

S. C. Kolm, *Justice et Equité,* Paris, 1972.

J. Milnor, "Games against Nature," in R. M. Thrall, C. H. Coombs, and R. L. Davis (eds.), *Decision Processes,* New York, 1954.

R. Nozick, *Anarchy, State, and Utopia,* New York, 1974.

B. Pascal, *Pensées,* New York, 1965.

J. Rawls, *A Theory of Justice,* Cambridge, Mass., 1971.

J. Rawls, "Fairness as Goodness," *Philosophical Review,* 1975, *84,* 536–554.

P. A. Samuelson, *Foundations of Economic Analysis,* Cambridge, Mass., 1947.

A. K. Sen, *Collective Choice and Social Welfare,* San Francisco, 1970.

A. K. Sen, "Social Choice Theory: A Re-examination," *Econometrica,* 1977, *45,* 53–89.

S. L. Strasnick, *Preference Priority and the Maximization of Social Welfare,* doctoral dissertation, Harvard University, 1975.

P. Suppes, "Some Formal Models of Grading Principles," *Synthese,* Dec. 1966, *16,* 284–306.

H. P. Young, "An Axiomatization of Borda's Rule," *J. Econ. Theory,* Sept. 1974, *9,* 43–52.

12   Current Developments in the Theory of Social Choice

The theory of social choice, as it has developed in the last several decades but with earlier history reaching back into the eighteenth century, seeks to analyze the concept of rational choice as it extends from the individual to a collectivity. The concept of rationality it has typically worked with is minimal in nature, being confined to imposing what may be termed formal conditions. The theory is correspondingly general in its application.

Narrowly construed, the scope of the theory is the analysis of the conditions under which some mechanism or rule can be found which permits a collectivity (government, social organization, labor union, business) to arrive at decisions which, in some way or another, reflect the decisions desired by its members. It is therefore a normative theory of elections and legislative choices.

More broadly, it can be interpreted to provide one aspect of any normative judgment about interpersonal relations which is based in some measure on the satisfaction of individual needs. A theory of justice such as John Rawls's (1971), in which the truth-value of a proposition of the form "state x is just" or, still more in the spirit of the theory, "state x is more just than state y," depends on the truth-values of propositions of the form "state x is better for individual i than state y," or "state x is fairer to individual i than state y," for each individual i, is an example of social choice falling within the purview of the general theory.

Unfortunately, the main results of the theory so far have been negative.

Reprinted from *Social Research*, 44 (1977):607–622.

That is, if we impose some reasonable-sounding conditions on the process of forming social choices from individual preferences, it can be demonstrated that there are no processes which will always satisfy those conditions. Most recent research has been devoted to seeking ways of overcoming this difficulty. Although there is no thoroughly satisfactory resolution, and there probably can never be a truly all-embracing one, some of the recent contributions are illuminating and very likely hopeful.

In the first section of this chapter I shall remind the reader of some fundamental formal criteria for rationality in preferences and choices, of the recurring controversy whether preferences have a cardinal as well as an ordinal significance — that is, does it make sense to speak of intensities of preferences — and of the possibility and meaning of interpersonal comparability of preferences. In the second section majority voting is analyzed as a means of social choice. The reasons it might be judged desirable are stated as criteria for social choice mechanisms. The famous paradox which arises in extending majority voting to choice among more than two alternatives is stated. The next section is a statement of the central result in the theory of social choice, that the paradox arising in majority voting is a general phenomenon which holds for all social choice mechanisms satisfying some reasonable conditions.

The first three sections restate results known by 1952; the remaining ones summarize current attempts to get around the central paradox. The fourth examines a weakening of rationality requirements for social preference, and the last explores perhaps the most fundamental reorientation, that of strengthening the rationality conditions for individuals so as to admit certain kinds of interpersonal comparisons. In one direction, we are led to classical utilitarianism; in another, to criteria closely resembling those of Rawls.

Preference, Choice, and Rationality

The paradigm of rational choice, as it has been elaborated most especially by economists, is the confrontation of a fixed preference pattern over potential alternatives with a varying set of opportunities. There are many alternative states the chooser might conceivably choose among. Only a limited subset of the alternatives is available at any particular time. Thus an individual can conceive of the alternative consumption patterns available to him at an income of $50,000 a year even though his present annual income is only $10,000 and his effective choices correspondingly limited. It is postulated that the chooser has a preference between any two alternatives, to state (in words or actions) which he prefers to the other. (Economists find it necessary to be concerned with the possibility of indifference between two alternatives, but I shall ignore indifference for purposes of this exposition.)

In any concrete choice situation, only a limited number of alternatives are actually *feasible;* the other conceivable or *possible* alternatives are not available, typically because they would require more resources than exist. Then it is assumed in this paradigm that the chooser selects that one of the feasible alternatives which is preferred to all the others.

This sketch leads to an operational interpretation of preference: it is hypothetical choice from a pair of alternatives. That is, the statement "state x is preferred to state y" is interpreted to mean "state x would be chosen if the only two feasible states were x and y."

A formal requirement of rationality applied to preferences and the choices based on them is that the preferences constitute what is known technically as an *ordering.* Specifically, a relation among alternatives is said to be *complete* (or connected) if, for every pair of alternatives, one is preferred to the other; the relation is said to be *transitive* if, for any three alternatives, say x, y, z, if x is preferred to y and y to z, then x is preferred to z. The last is a natural consistency requirement among choices made from differing feasible sets. A relation among alternative states is an *ordering* if it is both complete and transitive.

There is an intuitive and long-held view that more can be said about a preference than its mere existence. We can, it is held, make quantitative statements, about *how much* one alternative is preferred to another. Careful epistemological analysis of the meaning of quantitative statements of this kind, especially as developed by mathematical psychologists such as R. Duncan Luce and Patrick Suppes (see Krantz et al., 1971) shows that they really assert that statements of the following form are meaningful: "The preference for x over y is just as strong (or intense) as the preference for z over w." Clearly, if preferences are measurable, such statements are meaningful; and the converse can be shown to be true.

If such quantitative statements are meaningful, the preference system is said to be *cardinal;* if only simple preference statements of the form "x is preferred to y" are allowed, the preferences are said to be *ordinal.* Both viewpoints have been defended vigorously. The cardinal preference view has received considerable support from comparing uncertainties about alternatives, an analysis which originated with Daniel Bernoulli in the eighteenth century and has been developed in important ways by Frank

Ramsey (1931) and by John von Neumann and Oskar Morgenstern (1947) in the twentieth. Suppose an individual is offered the following two alternative uncertainties: (a) a 50–50 chance of getting alternative x or alternative w; (b) a 50–50 chance of getting alternative y or alternative z. If x were preferred to y and w to z, we would expect that the first would be chosen. To make the choice interesting, therefore, suppose x is preferred to y but z is preferred to w. Suppose further that the individual in fact chooses uncertainty (a). Since (a) is derived from (b) by replacing y by x and z by w, it is plausible to interpret the preference (a) over (b) as meaning that the intensity of preference for x over y is greater than the intensity of preference for z over w. Hence, intensity of preference can be given an operational interpretation and is therefore meaningful.

The issues are complex and unresolved; for example, it can be counter-argued that intensities of preference relevant to choice among certainties should not depend on attitudes toward risk. I merely want to indicate that some case can be made for the cardinalization of preferences.

If preferences among pairs of alternatives can be given quantitative significance, then we can, equivalently, assign numbers to the alternatives themselves in such a way that higher numbers are assigned to more preferred alternatives and that the differences in numbers between two alternatives measure intensity of preference. That is, we can find a utility function $U(x)$, assigning a number to each alternative x with the following properties: (1) $U(x) > U(y)$ if and only if x is preferred to y; (2) $U(x) - U(y) = U(z) - U(w)$ if and only if the intensity of preference for x over y is the same as the preference for z over w. This is done by specifying arbitrarily two alternatives, x_0 and y_0, with x_0 preferred to y_0, and choosing the utility difference between them to be one. Then the utility difference between any two alternatives can be compared with this standard difference; if, for example, x is preferred to y more intensely than x_0 to y_0, then the utility difference must be greater than one. It can be shown, under certain technical conditions, that there is a way of measuring this utility difference as a unique number. The system is completed by taking an arbitrary alternative whose utility is zero.

Notice that the origin and scale unit of the utility function is arbitrary, an act of choice by the measurer. In measuring length, the unit — but not the origin — is arbitrary; in measuring temperature by conventional scales (Fahrenheit or Celsius), both are arbitrary.

If preferences are only ordinal, then under certain conditions we can still find a utility function with property (1) above. However, any other function which numbers the alternatives according to the same ranking is also a utility function. In technical terms, cardinal utility functions can be subject to *positive linear* transformations—that is, if $U(x)$ is a utility function with properties (1) and (2), and $V(x) = a\,U(x) + b$, for any $a > 0$ and any b, then $V(x)$ also has properties (1) and (2). Ordinal utility functions, on the other hand, can be subject to monotone transformations—that is, if $U(x)$ is a utility function satisfying (1), $F(u)$ is an increasing function taking real numbers into real numbers, with $F(u) > F(u')$ whenever $u > u'$, and $V(x) = F[U(x)]$, then $V(x)$ also satisfies (1).

Logically separate from the issue of cardinality is that of interpersonal comparability. Historically, however, the two have been linked in the development of utilitarianism, particularly by Jeremy Bentham and, in a more rigorous form, by Francis Y. Edgeworth and Henry Sidgwick in the latter part of the nineteenth century. The utilitarians assumed that preference intensities of different individuals could be compared—that is, it was meaningful to make a statement of the form "The intensity with which individual 1 prefers x to y is equal to the intensity with which individual 2 prefers y to x" and similar statements. These interpersonal comparisons of preference intensities presuppose cardinal preference for each individual, but the converse is not true. Each individual might have cardinal preferences, yet they need not be interpersonally comparable. As noted above, the unit for an individual's measure of cardinal utility is arbitrary; if the unit can be chosen independently for each individual, then no comparison across individuals is valid. To turn the statement around, interpersonal comparability of preference intensities requires that the utility unit be the same for all individuals.

Curiously, interpersonal comparison of preference intensities, or cardinal-difference comparability, to use a slightly shorter expression, does not require comparability of utility levels. Utilitarianism does not require any statement of the form "Individual 1 is better off under x than individual 2 is under x (or y)." Yet it does not seem unreasonable that if it is permitted to compare the preference gains of movements from one state to another, it is certainly permissible to compare the absolute levels of satisfaction. Of course, it can be argued that even if comparisons of levels are admissible in the sense of being objectively verifiable, it may still be true that they should be disregarded. This is a standard utilitarian viewpoint; even if individual 1 is worse off than individual 2 in a well-defined sense, one should not transfer income from 2 to 1 unless the improvement in 1's welfare is greater than the loss in 2's.

More recently, the suggestion has grown that interpersonal comparisons of level of the form just discussed are permissible and should be the basis of social choice. Cardinal-difference comparisons are not allowed as meaningful, partly on the grounds that the implied cardinality of individual preference has no verifiable meaning. The ideal experiment underlying interpersonal ordinal comparisons is that of changing places, or extended sympathy: "Would individual 1 rather be individual 2 (with all his characteristics) in state *y* than himself in state *x*?" A statement of preference of this kind can be represented by a utility function which can itself be subject to monotone transformations; but the transformation must be the same for all individuals. These comparisons are sometimes called *co-ordinal*. Co-ordinal comparisons are required for John Rawls's "difference principle"; they have also been studied and advocated by a number of writers—Suppes (1966), Serge-Christophe Kolm (1972), myself (1963), and, subsequently, Peter Hammond (1976) and Steven Strasnick (1976a,b).

Majority Voting as Social Choice

Suppose there are a large number of conceivable alternatives, but only two are actually presented. These alternatives might, for example, be candidates for elective office; everyone living (or satisfying certain broad conditions of age and citizenship) is eligible, but only two are actual candidates.

We are seeking a procedure which will work for any set of preferences of the individuals in the collectivity, the *voters,* as we may call them. We do not know in advance what these preferences may be. We want to lay down some conditions that we would expect a good social choice procedure to have.

First, it will be assumed that we wish to treat candidates equally; the social choice procedure should not have a built-in bias toward one alternative or another; this condition will be referred to as *neutrality*. Second, we wish that all voters should be treated equally; we are seeking to model democracy. This condition will be referred to as *anonymity*. The first of these is not always desirable, but the basic social choice dilemmas are not resolved even by relaxing it, or indeed by relaxing the condition of anonymity, unless we go to the extreme of permitting one individual to be a dictator—in which case, of course, the social aspect of the problem disappears.

Now we come to a more basic assumption: the social decision between the two feasible alternatives should depend *only* on the preferences of the voters between them. Preferences among infeasible alternatives or between feasible and infeasible alternatives should have no bearing on the outcome. This condition is usually known as the *independence of irrelevant alternatives.* It is satisfied by every election procedure. It is far from indisputable. But there is clearly merit in it. If Adams and Black are the only two candidates, why should it make any difference what the voters think of Clark? Further, if preferences about irrelevant or infeasible alternatives counted, then the voters might have an incentive to misrepresent their preferences about them; since the infeasible alternatives will not in any case be adopted, they can misstate their preferences without fear of their being adopted.

One more crucial and controversial condition: the preferences of the voters are taken to be ordinal; all that can be asked or are taken to be meaningful are preferences between the two candidates.

Finally, a condition which, while important, is hardly controversial: the social choice procedure should reflect positively the preferences of the voters. Thus, if there is some set of preferences according to which Adams would be elected and if one voter changes his mind so as to favor Adams more highly, then surely Adams should still be elected. This condition may be termed *positive response.*

It is not hard to see that these conditions uniquely specify one social choice procedure, that of majority voting, as first pointed out by Kenneth May (1952). Independence of irrelevant alternatives and the ordinality of preferences together imply that the only information that can be used in making the social choice is the list of voters who prefer Adams to Black and the list with the opposite preference. Because of anonymity, however, only the numbers of voters of the two preferences count. Positive response implies that, if Adams were elected by a certain number of voters, he would be elected by any greater number (and similarly with Black). Now suppose that a bare majority prefer Adams (assume an odd number of voters to avoid ties), but Black were chosen. Now imagine all voters reversing their preferences. By neutrality, Adams would now have to be chosen, but he now has fewer votes than he did in the previous case, a contradiction. Hence, it must be that Adams is elected when a bare majority support him and therefore when any majority support him, and similarly for Black.

Majority voting is then a satisfactory social choice mechanism when there are two alternatives. If we maintain the identification of preference with (possibly hypothetical) choice from a pair of alternatives, we would endow the proposition "x is socially preferred to y" with the meaning "a majority of the voters prefer x to y." But we have suggested that a preference relation, to be regarded as rational, should be an ordering, that is, both complete and transitive. The majority preference relation is certainly complete. But it is not necessarily transitive, and this exemplifies the fundamental paradox of social choice.

That majority voting need not be transitive was first shown as long ago as 1785 by Marie de Caritat, better known under his title of nobility, the Marquis de Condorcet. Suppose there are three voters, Asher, Brown, and Castro, and three candidates, Adams, Black, and Carter. Suppose Asher prefers Adams to Black and Black to Carter, Brown prefers Black to Carter and Carter to Adams, and Castro prefers Carter to Adams and Adams to Black. Then two of the three voters prefer Adams to Black, two prefer Black to Carter, and two prefer Carter to Adams. If we interpret social choice as the outcome of majority voting, we should have to say that Adams is socially preferred to Black, Black to Carter, and Carter to Adams. Social preference can cycle.

To avoid misunderstanding, it is not claimed that majority preference is necessarily intransitive. If our voters had different preferences, the majority preference might in fact be an ordering. For example, if Asher and Brown had the same preference rankings as before, but Castro had the ordering Carter, Black, Adams, then the majority preference ordering would be Black, Carter, Adams — and Black would also have a majority over Adams. But the point is that the system of pairwise majority voting can lead to a cycle in social preferences.

The General Impossibility Theorem

The result of the last section can be stated in a somewhat formal way: Suppose we have a social choice procedure, capable of making choices from any finite number of alternatives, which uses only ordinal information on individual preferences and satisfies the conditions of independence of irrelevant alternatives, positive response, neutrality, and anonymity. Then the implied social preference relation is not necessarily an ordering.

This statement contains most of the philosophical significance of the Impossibility Theorem of social choice. However, since neutrality is not such a transparent desideratum and even anonymity might be challenged, it is worth noting that the general theorem weakens both requirements very considerably. Neutrality can be replaced by the requirement that every social choice is in fact permitted by the social choice procedure:

• *Nonimposition:* For every pair of alternatives x and y, there is some set of individual preferences such that x will be chosen over y and some set of preferences for which y will be chosen over x.

For example, we usually want to require the *Pareto* (or *Unanimity*) *Principle:* If every individual prefers x to y, then the social choice will be x (and vice versa).

Similarly, Anonymity, a requirement of full democracy, can be replaced by the following very minimal condition:

• *Nondictatorship:* The rules of the social choice procedure are not such that there is one individual whose preferences completely determine social preferences for every pair of alternatives.

The contradiction found earlier still holds with these weaker conditions on the social choice procedures.

• *General Impossibility Theorem for Social Choice:* Suppose there is a social choice procedure, capable of making choices from any finite number of alternatives, which uses only ordinal information on individual preferences and satisfies the conditions of independence of irrelevant alternatives, positive response, nonimposition, and nondictatorship. Then there will be some set of individual preferences such that the resulting social preference relation is not an ordering.

As a somewhat technical note, it might be remarked that nonimposition and positive response together imply the Pareto Principle. On the other hand, the Impossibility Theorem remains valid if the conditions of positive response and nonimposition are replaced by the Pareto Principle.

A Weakening of the Social Rationality Condition

A large literature has been devoted to exploring ways of avoiding the unpleasant implications of the Impossibility Theorem. In this and the following section, I will present just two, which to me seem most promising.

One possibility is to weaken the requirement that the social choice procedure yield a rational outcome in the sense defined here. There are several possible weakenings. I concentrate here on just one, weakening the requirement that the choice made from a set of more than two alternatives be completely determined by the preferences among pairs. It is natural to require that the alternative chosen, if there are, say, three alternatives, be preferred to each of the other two. In view of the difficulties found, however, this may be a requirement that will have to be dropped or at least weakened.

To discuss the proposals, it is necessary to introduce now the idea of *indifference* among alternatives. I shall maintain the assumption that individuals are never indifferent (this is in no way a necessary assumption and is made here solely for expository simplicity), but I shall admit the possibility that society may in some sense regard several alternatives as indifferent. That is, it does not care which one is selected. This means that for a given set of alternatives, it may have a *chosen set;* some of the feasible alternatives are selected out as being superior to those not in the chosen set, but no preferential distinction is made among the alternatives in the chosen set.

The proposal, made by Donald Campbell (1976) and Georges Bordes (1976), is simply to regard the alternatives in a preference cycle as indifferent. In the previous example, Adams, Black, and Carter would have to be regarded as indifferent, as is indeed a reasonable solution. There might have been many more candidates, and the three candidates mentioned might have been preferred to them by majority vote without a cycle. In that case, the three candidates would have constituted the chosen set.

This principle can be applied to any way of forming social preferences, in particular to majority voting. The procedure will always produce what is called a *weak ordering:* (1) for any pair of alternatives, either one will be preferred to the other or the two are indifferent; (2) for any three alternatives x, y, z, if x is preferred or indifferent to y and y preferred or indifferent to z, then x is preferred or indifferent to z. A weak ordering ranks all the alternatives, but it permits ties at some of the ranks.

The full principle of rationality in relating choice in a set of alternatives to preferences among pairs can be restated as follows. If T is a set of alternatives and S a subset (that is, consists of some but not all of the alternatives in T), and if one or more of the chosen elements in T belong to S, then the chosen set from S consists precisely of the chosen members of T which remain after cutting the set of alternatives down to S. If, in particular, S contains two members of T, at least one of which is a chosen element, then the principle states that a chosen element of T must be preferred or indifferent to any element. The Campbell-Bordes social choice procedure does not satisfy this condition but does satisfy the weaker one: if T is a set of alternatives and S a subset, and if one or more chosen elements in T belong to S, then the chosen set from S is included in the chosen elements in T belonging to S (but might not contain all of them). In the example, T is the set of all three candidates, and all three are chosen in T. If S consists of Adams and Black, then the chosen alternative is Adams, while both Adams and Black are chosen alternatives in T which belong to S.

The Campbell-Bordes procedure of treating alternatives in a preference cycle as indifferent (technically known as taking the *transitive closure* of the preference relation) also satisfies another weak rationality condition, which Bordes terms "minimality": it is impossible to find a subset of a chosen set such that every alternative in the subset is preferred to every feasible alternative not in the subset.

The main danger in the Campbell-Bordes procedure is that too many alternatives may be treated as indifferent. Nevertheless it does provide an interesting resolution of the social choice paradox with what appears to be a relatively slight weakening of the condition of rationality of social preference.

Interpersonal Comparability

The oldest critique of social choice theory, and indeed of some of the doctrines of social welfare in economics from which it sprang, is that it disregards intensity of preference. Even with two alternatives, it would be argued that a majority with weak preferences should not necessarily prevail against a minority with strong feelings. The problem in accepting this criticism is that of making it operational. Theoretically, is there any meaning to the interpersonal comparison of preference intensities? Practically, is there any way of measuring them, that is, is there any form of individual behavior from which the interpersonal comparisons can be inferred?

Rawls's maximin or difference principle is based, as already noted, on a different kind of interpersonal comparison that does not involve intensities. His position is that the criterion for choosing x over y is that the worst-off individual in x is better off than the worst-off individual in y. The two worst-off individuals need not be the same. To make his principle meaningful, it is required that we can make interpersonal ordinal comparisons as discussed at the beginning of this chapter. If they are permitted, then for each of the states x and y, it is possible to determine the worst-off; and for these two individuals it is possible to compare the well-being of one in state x with that of the other in state y.

Recent work of Peter Hammond (1976), Steven Strasnick (1976a,b), and C. d'Aspremont and Louis Gevers (1977) has greatly clarified the relation of these concepts to social choice theory. Assume that for each individual we have a utility function over all possible alternatives. This can always be found for each individual preference, but the utility function might be meaningful only up to certain transformations monotone or positive linear according as preferences are construed to be ordinal or cardinal; further, the transformations might be required to be the same for all individuals or permitted to vary independently among them, depending on the assumptions about interpersonal comparability.

A social procedure now assigns to each set of utility functions, one for each individual, a social preference relation, required to be an ordering. It is possible to state the condition of independence of irrelevant alternatives and the Pareto Principle in such a way that they make sense in the present formulation. Independence of irrelevant alternatives could be stated as follows: Consider two different sets of utility functions for the individuals i, U_i and U_i', and suppose that for two given alternatives x and y, they coincide, so that $U_i(x) = U_i'(x)$ and $U_i(y) = U_i'(y)$ for individuals i. Then the social preference between x and y should be the same if the utility functions are U_i as if they are U_i'.

If we assume ordinal preferences and no interpersonal comparability, as we have been assuming, then we can state the requirement in the present language as the condition that the social choice remain unchanged if the utility function for each individual is subject to a monotone transformation which may differ from individual to individual. We know that in this case no satisfactory social choice procedure exists.

Suppose we assume cardinal preferences but no interpersonal comparability. In this case social choice should be invariant under a separate positive linear transformation of each utility function. Again, no satisfactory social choice procedure exists, as has been demonstrated by Ehud Kalai and David Schmeidler (1977).

It is perhaps not surprising that some form of interpersonal comparability is needed to secure positive results. The most obvious case is that of cardinal-difference comparability. Here the corresponding invariance condition is that social choice not change if there is a positive linear transformation of the utility functions with the *same* linear coefficient — that is, if for each i, U_i is replaced by $U_i' = aU_i + b_i$, $a > 0$. Then straightforward analysis shows that the resulting criterion is the classical utilitarian sum of utilities — that is, one alternative, x, is preferred to another, y, if and only if $U_1(x) + U_2(x) + \ldots > U_1(y) + U_2(y) + \ldots$

The most recent work has been based on admitting interpersonal comparisons of level rather than of differences. Then the social choice criterion must be invariant under the same monotone transformation of all utility functions. To be more explicit, suppose $F(u)$ is a strictly increasing function which assigns to each real number u a real number $F(u)$. If U is replaced by $F(U_i)$ for each i, the social choice should be unaltered. This property has been named *co-ordinal invariance.* It turns out, remarkably, that the only social choice procedures satisfying the stated conditions and co-ordinally invariant are the Rawls maximin rule, to choose x over y if $\min_i U_i(x) > \min_i U_i(y)$, and the maximax rule, to choose x over y if $\max_i U_i(x) > \max_i U_i(y)$. [The notation $\min_i U(x)$, for example, means the smallest value of $U_i(x)$ as i varies over individuals — in other words, the smallest utility of any individual if x is chosen.]

This result provides an unexpected connection between social choice theory and the Rawls Principle. It remains to be seen whether the interpersonal comparisons required are indeed useful tools of social inquiry.

References

Arrow, K. J. *Social Choice and Individual Values,* 2nd ed. New Haven: Yale University Press, 1963.

Bordes, G. Consistency, rationality, and collective choice. *Review of Economic Studies,* 1976, *43,* 447–457.

Campbell, D. Democratic preference functions. *Journal of Economic Theory,* 1976, *12,* 259–272.

d'Aspremont, C., and L. Gevers. Equity and informational basis of collective choice. *Review of Economic Studies,* 1977, *46,* 199–210.

Hammond, P. J. Equity, Arrow's conditions, and Rawls' difference principle. *Econometrica,* 1976, *44,* 793–804.

Kalai, E., and D. Schmeidler. Aggregation procedures for cardinal preferences: a formulation and proof of Samuelson's impossibility conjecture. *Econometrica,* 1977, *45,* 1431–38.

Kolm, S.-C. *Justice et équité.* Paris: Centre Nationale de la Recherche Scientifique, 1972.

Krantz, D. K., R. D. Luce, P. Suppes, and A. Tversky. *Foundations of Measurement.* New York: Academic Press, 1971.

May, K. O. A set of independent, necessary and sufficient conditions for simple majority decision. *Econometrica,* 1952, *20,* 680–684.

von Neumann, J., and O. Morgenstern. *Theory of Games and Economic Behavior,* 2nd ed. Princeton: Princeton University Press, 1947.

Ramsey, F. P. Truth and probability. In *The Foundations of Probability and Other Essays.* London: K. Paul, Trench, Trubner, 1931, pp. 156–198.

Rawls, J. *A Theory of Justice.* Cambridge, Mass.: Harvard University Press, 1971.

Strasnick, S. Social choice and the derivation of Rawls's difference principle. *Journal of Philosophy,* 1976a, *73,* 85–99.

Strasnick, S. The problem of social choice: Arrow to Rawls. *Philosophy and Public Affairs,* 1976b, *5,* 241–273.

Suppes, P. Some formal models of grading principles. *Synthèse,* 1966, *16,* 284–306.

13 Nozick's Entitlement Theory of Justice

Robert Nozick's sharp and ingenious attack on all patterned views of distributive justice (1974, chap. 7) has attracted much attention, respectful if on the whole sharply critical. It is part of a larger attack on political power in general. The entitlement theory of justice is designed in particular to undermine the view that the state or something like it is needed to ensure redistribution of property in the name of justice.

In formal terms, Nozick does not accept the widespread doctrine that the just distribution of goods is to be regarded as the outcome of a social decision process. Indeed, he would probably go as far as Buchanan (1954) in denying meaning to social decision making. All decisions are individual and are controlling.

This attitude might draw some justification from the difficulties of constructing a thoroughly coherent social choice mechanism. But in my judgment, there is really no way of escaping the notion that justice is a social phenomenon, and some view that it must be the resultant of an impartial procedure is essential. Beyond that, I do not believe that Nozick has constructed a genuinely coherent structure of supporting arguments. Indeed, his case rests primarily on a few dramatic examples, rather than on any systematic argument. Further, there are grave difficulties in any defense of his system as it stands. It can be refuted by examples at least as compelling as his.

It must be admitted, nevertheless, that he does raise serious issues that are

Reprinted from *Philosophia,* 7 (1978):265–279.

neglected in the utilitarian tradition, including such offshoots as social choice theory and welfare economics, and in Rawls's fairness doctrine. These revolve in one way or another about the notions of privacy and property of an individual, his capacity and his scope of decision, which cannot or should not be overridden by social obligations of justice. This modest conclusion, however, is a long way from agreeing that there is no role for socially motivated concepts of justice and for the role of the state and of moral obligation in large redistributions of goods and services.

Where the Nozick System Differs

The tradition of welfare economics, which is in many ways an application of utilitarian principles to a world where goods and services are produced and traded, is to emphasize two stages in the allocation of resources. In the first, individuals hold bundles of goods. In the second, these bundles of goods are traded and transformed into other goods under the motivation of individual improvement at given prices. If the prices are such that supply and demand balance, then the final distribution is efficient in the sense of Pareto: no other resource allocation would have made everyone better off. The final distribution is a function of the initial allocation. Hence, any desire to achieve a more just final allocation can be achieved by a reallocation of the initial holdings; and it should be so achieved in order to maintain Pareto efficiency.

This tradition of welfare economics is a theorem, valid under certain restrictive hypotheses, primarily that the utility of each individual depends only on the allocation of goods to him and that production does not involve increasing returns to scale. If either of these hypotheses is false, the just final allocation has to be made in some other way. Even if the hypotheses are true, the final allocation can be arrived at in practice in some different way — for example, by a computer which has been provided with all the relevant facts, the preferences and production possibilities for all individuals and productive units, and the initial endowments of all factors.

The general criterion of judgment, as opposed to the means of implementation, is based on the distribution of satisfactions resulting from the final allocation. If everyone is better off in one allocation than another, then society is judged better off; if everybody is indifferent between the two allocations, then the two allocations are indifferent from the viewpoint of justice as well as that of efficiency. It is not the specific goods but the levels of satisfaction to which the criteria of justice and efficiency are meant to apply in welfare economics (as, for example, in Bergson, 1938, or Samuelson,

1947, chap. 8, but following on Edgeworth, 1881, 1897, and at least consistent with Sidgwick, 1893).

Nozick's criteria are very much like the welfare economics theorem; but now they are the axioms, not the conclusions, and there are significant differences. There is an original acquisition of property and a transfer, made voluntarily. The concept of justice is assumed to be defined for both original acquisitions and transfers. Then any allocation resulting from just original acquisition followed by just transfers is just.

An individual is entitled to any goods acquired in this manner. Before turning to the content of justice in each of the two modes of acquisition, note already that there is one important difference from the utilitarian tradition. What is acquired is the right to specific goods, not merely to levels of satisfaction. Nozick is very explicit on this matter. A reallocation which hurt no one but which involved an involuntary reshuffling of goods would not be just in Nozick's view.

Pareto optimality does not enter Nozick's story; indeed, levels of satisfaction do not enter in any way. No doubt if transfers are voluntary, we may assume that individuals do not injure themselves, so that the parties involved are at least as well off. But of course there is no guarantee whatever that others are not injured by any definition; if A gives goods to B, B may cease to acquire them from C, who is thereby injured. This possibility exists in a competitive market in any case; but the utilitarian will argue that while efficiency would demand that the market not be interfered with, there may be grounds for compensation to C. Nozick sees no such case; the justice of the original acquisition is not influenced by any effects on the future transfers.

Nozick, unlike the welfare economist, does not assume perfect competition (1974, p. 346n19). Hence Pareto optimality is not implied by Nozick's voluntary, just transfers. Indeed, they may be unilateral, gifts or bequests. Despite the importance of the matter for Nozick's theory, the precise definition of justice in transfers is nowhere presented. Perhaps the best statement is that transfers are just if voluntary or if the individual transforms what is his own to another form by production (p. 160); force and fraud are excluded (p. 152), but no principles are given to justify these exclusions or even to define them properly. (Is offering a product known to the producer to be unsafe a fraud if there is no positive affirmation that it is safe? Is failure to make safety tests a fraud?)

Justice in original acquisition is still more difficult a concept, as Nozick acknowledges. I will not rehearse here the problems which he himself raises, under the name of the Lockean proviso, that the original acquisition not be at the expense of some future individual. As he notes, if taken literally, it can never hold for any scarce good. He suggests a weaker condition, that the original acquisition never made any future individual worse off when the good acquired has scarcity value. I simply make two remarks here: (1) at this point, the idea of rights to individual goods has been replaced by an equivalent-satisfaction concept after all; (2) there really is no reason why even the weaker version of the Lockean provision should be valid. With regard to the second point, suppose a piece of land will eventually be a desired scarce good; then, if this event is foreseen and permanent property rights exist, it will have value today, namely the discounted value of its future use-value.

I will follow Nozick in overlooking completely the role of public goods and externalities, though they are in fact very important. I will also (though this is still harder to swallow) overlook the problem Nozick himself raises, that of rectification of past injustices. The very existence of such a problem in itself shows that a social decision procedure is needed; and once it is granted that it is needed for this purpose, there is no reason not to face the problem of justice itself in that language.

Two Arguments

One might expect some serious arguments for so bold a departure from the usual modes of argument about justice. In fact, the case is remarkably thin. Really, as far as I can tell, there are just two formal arguments, accompanied by three examples whose greatest value is negative, casting doubt on alternative theories of justice. The formal arguments are not in my judgment very strong; the examples are much more effective.

The main argument, not explicitly stated, is the right of individuals to make some private decisions. This is reinforced by appeal to Sen's liberalism paradox (1970, chaps. 6 and 6*): If the right of an individual to make a private choice is interpreted as his right to fix the relative positions of certain alternatives in the social ordering, then a contradiction to the Pareto Principle can be found.

It is not exactly true that privacy requirements are completely neglected by either welfare economists or Rawls (1971). They appear as the limits to redistribution imposed by incentive considerations. The actions needed for the achievement of a just resource allocation may not be possible or desirable to enforce. Thus, an individual with special talents may choose not to exercise them without special reward; if we do not wish to leave the choice to his private decision, for the good of others, we may have to pay him more than what would otherwise be a just reward.

A second argument is that other theories of justice emphasize distribution rather than production. These theories treat "objects as if they appeared from nowhere, out of nothing," whereas in fact "things come into the world already attached to people having entitlements over them" (p. 160).

This argument is not well put. Welfare economics certainly does not imagine that there is no production. A redistributionist would simply hold that the ownership which gave some individuals special claims to products should be modified in the direction of egalitarianism, either by direct redistribution of ownership or by taxation (which has the same effective aim).

What is true is that in welfare economics the ownership of the product is conceived of mainly as control of the purchasing power it generates. If we want to redistribute the income from producing steel, we tax the money income not the steel itself. Nozick instead emphasizes the role of entitlement to the physical product. But in any complex economy with considerable specialization and division of labor, is the entitlement to specific goods of any interest to anyone? The purpose of production is not indeed the production of goods, but the right to acquire other goods. Once it is granted that a producer seeks a value (generalized control over goods) rather than product for its own sake, the choice between receiving the market value and receiving that value less a deduction for redistribution becomes simply a choice between alternative social arrangements. Neither one has the kind of special saliency that Nozick's emphasis on entitlement to specific goods would seem to require.

Three Examples

The Wilt Chamberlain Story

Suppose an allocation of resources deemed just according to some criterion (Rawls's or utilitarian, for example) is achieved. Individuals nevertheless wish to engage in some exchange (in this instance, pay for the services of a basketball player), as a result of which one individual becomes very wealthy. Should this be prohibited?

Actually, if the just allocation of resources were Pareto-efficient, as is usually assumed, this example could not occur (a point which Nozick himself observes, p. 164, note). But a more compelling version of the example would refer to unilateral transfers. Should an individual be forbidden to give money to someone who has already been judged to be getting enough? The most obvious problem here, as Lewis Carroll pointed out long ago (pp. 542–546), is bequest; if an individual is entitled to consume, is he to be denied the right to forgo the consumption in favor of an heir who might not otherwise be entitled to it?

Forced Labor

"The taxation of earnings from labor is on a par with forced labor," Nozick claims. Forced labor is not unknown, at least in the form of compulsory military service; it must be admitted that in situations where the war itself is approved of and most eligible individuals are needed, an overwhelming majority would prefer conscription to voluntary service. But let us not use majority voting as a criterion of ethical theory.

It is worth noting that from the viewpoint of welfare economics, taxes on labor income are *not* ideal. Such a tax distorts the choice between labor and leisure (leisure is a form of income which escapes taxation) and hence leads to inefficient resource allocation. The ideal redistributive tax would be on potential income, the income the individual would earn in the highest-value use of his time for some number of hours fixed in advance, independent of his own choice of occupation and hours of work.

Such a tax is infeasible because it requires information about the individual which the state cannot have. The actual income tax is defended as a best approximation. Hence, in some sense, Nozick's criticism would in fact be met in an ideal application of welfare economics.

Nevertheless, one must concede that actual taxes do fall on labor income. They fall equally on property income, and it is interesting that the rhetorical value of Nozick's example requires a differentiation of the two sources of income which, in general, he is loath to make.

Moreover, it must be remarked that there is a considerable difference between a tax on labor income and forced labor, although there is some resemblance. Once it is recognized that labor is specific in nature and that there are many kinds, it becomes clear that the freedom of choice under a tax is vastly greater than that under compulsory labor. It is surprising that Nozick, who is so concerned over rights to specific bundles of goods, should not take cognizance of this difference. In short, though neither yields absolute freedom of choice, there is a large difference in a quantitative sense between the two situations.

A World of Isolated Individuals

Nozick's refutation of Rawls starts by asking us to consider a world of individuals with no economic interdependence. The production of each is in no way affected by the behavior of others. Suppose in fact the products differ because of personal attributes or sheer luck or whatever. Would there be any obligation on the part of the fortunate to help the less lucky? This is a starting point for Nozick's argument that even with interdependence there is no obligation.

The example clearly has some compelling aspects. However, its hypotheses are somewhat hard to envision. If the individuals did not even know of one another's existence, then the question of obligation would hardly arise. Hence, we must envisage a situation where the individuals, perhaps on separate but neighboring islands or in a frontier situation, know of one another's existence, could transfer goods among themselves, but are self-sufficient.

If there are uncertainties, say of weather, then we would expect a mutually advantageous insurance contract; if communication can take place before the event, there should be a contractual achievement of egalitarianism.

Hence, the only case where one would expect inequality to arise would be when there are personal differences in ability, known in advance. As in the previous example, attention does get focused on one's right to personal ability.

Even if the example is accepted at face value, it does not itself answer the question of obligation when there is economic interdependence in the form of cooperation in production or in mutually beneficial exchange. At most, it suggests that the rights of society to redistribute are restricted to that part of the property of individuals over and above what each could achieve by himself alone. How much of a restriction this is will be touched on later in this chapter.

Some Counterexamples

As already stressed, Nozick's case does not rest on the assumption of perfectly competitive markets, but rather on the freedom to transfer and to enter into mutually agreeable contracts. But then a whole host of possible difficulties arise, some well known in economic theory.

An economic theorist would worry about the possibility of monopolization and collusion. Suppose some individual owns all of a certain commodity—not indispensable to life perhaps, but very useful. Clearly, he can set unusually high prices and engross for himself what most individuals would judge to be an unjust portion of the world's goods. It may be objected that an individual could not arrive at such a position; if he sought to monopolize, he would find, as Nozick remarks, that the price of the good would rise. More precisely, it would rise in a competitive world. But suppose every original owner of the good just happened to give it to one individual. This would be just in Nozick's world, and the outcome would have to be deemed just, although in actuality the monopolist received more value than the donors intended.

Or, to be slightly more realistic, suppose all the owners of some good (a primary good, not one produced) were to collude to charge a higher price. All the actions involved are voluntary; is the outcome just?

Suppose a dominant group, say whites or "Aryans," agreed to trade with the complementary minority only on very unfavorable terms. Indeed, they might not have to agree in any concrete sense: suppose each one happened for his own reasons to resolve to so act. Racial discrimination is very frequently the result of individual free actions, just decisions on the part of the members of the majority in Nozick's theory. Are we to say that the results are just?

In the last case it might be replied that the minority would be free to trade among themselves. If they had the same per capita resources, they would not suffer. If in fact they had inferior resources, then presumably there was a previous injustice which, Nozick would hold, should be rectified. I want to return to this argument; here I note only that in the presence of increasing returns to scale, a minority can suffer from discrimination even with equal per capita resources.

Nozick, it must be admitted, is courageous about the implications he draws: if an individual has discovered a cancer cure, he is entitled to withhold this knowledge, though he cannot prevent others from making the same discovery.

Privacy

One conclusion which Nozick's examples make reasonable is that an individual is entitled to some sphere of decision making on his own. Interestingly enough, Rawls, usually thought of as Nozick's complete opposite, shares this viewpoint as against utilitarians and welfare economists. Rawls's distributional criteria are in terms of what he calls "primary goods," abilities to determine life plans, rather than specific goods or the levels of satisfaction achieved from them. In effect, what an individual does with his primary goods is his private business, and any transfer of them is just.

One may grant that there should be some scope for individuals to make private decisions. One may add to the conditions of justice, conditions of privacy. As far as choice of commodities is concerned, the Pareto Principle implies that there can be no contradiction between the demands of privacy and the demands of justice so long as there are no externalities. What if there are? Can we make a consistent set of privacy judgments which yet permit social decisions? Of course, Sen's paradox shows that we have to sacrifice the universal applicability of the Pareto Principle, but perhaps we can still retain it for the nonprivate parts of the decision.

The question may be posed this way. The total decision space for society may be expressed as a Cartesian product $X_0 \times X_1 \times \ldots \times X_n$, where there are n individuals. X_i $(i = 1, \ldots, n)$ is the space of private decisions available to individual i; if individuals are to be treated symmetrically, these spaces are isomorphic. X_0 is the space of social decisions—for example, some allocation of primary goods in Rawls's sense or, perhaps, some allocation of goods in the ordinary sense, from which the individuals are still permitted to make further trades and unilateral transfers. Whatever rule of social decision making is used will be applied to satisfactions, *given* the private decisions $x_i \epsilon X_i$.

To illustrate, let us use the convenient utilitarian form. Suppose each individual has an interpersonally valid cardinal utility, U_i; in the presence of externalities, U_i will in general depend on all decisions $x_0, x_1, \ldots, x_n$. Then for given x_i $(i = 1, \ldots, n)$, x_0 is chosen to maximize

$$\sum_{i=1}^{n} U_i(x_0, x_1, \ldots, x_n)$$

with respect to x_0 (in some feasible set). Presumably, x_i is chosen by individual i to maximize

$$U_i(x_0, x_1, \ldots x_i \ldots x_n),$$

holding $x_j (j = 0, \ldots n, j \neq i)$ constant.

This description of justice in the presence of privacy involves game-theoretical considerations; the outcome is the equilibrium point (in the sense of Nash) of a certain game. (Though I have chosen a utilitarian formulation for its simplicity, a maximin principle would have a similar form.) Actually, this viewpoint generalizes a principle already found in the theory of justice over generations, thanks to Phelps and Pollak (1968). There they assume that no generation can be bound by desires of its predecessors.

Nozick's formulation, in these terms, amounts to omitting the space of social decisions, X_0, altogether. However, in the presence of externalities, he still requires a game-theoretical construction.

I have tried here to sketch a possible approach to the reconciliation of the claims of justice with those of a private scope for each individual. This has taken for granted that by some process we can defend a set of privacy judgments. There is an alternative approach, implicit in many discussions of the virtues of the price system among economic theorists and others. This is to regard claims to privacy not as primary value judgments but as derived from the inability of others to know everything relevant about an individual. Specifically, an individual knows his own preferences and perhaps his own personal abilities. This knowledge is not directly available to anyone else; others make inferences from the individual's observed behavior, but if it is known that these observations will be used as a basis for inference and therefore for distributive judgments, there is an incentive to behave differently so as to improve the distributive judgment. Gibbard (1973) has shown that there is no general way of formulating a game structure in which individuals may not have some incentive to misrepresent their preferences by their actions.

One can then deliberately factor the decision space into social and private decisions so as to optimize a criterion of justice, where it is assumed that the private decisions are functions of information private to the individual, whereas the social decisions are functions only of public information. This is the argument usually advanced to argue that among the ways of realizing an optimum in accordance with welfare economics, the laissez-faire approach is the best. It happens that under the strong assumptions of absence of both externalities and increasing returns to scale, it yields a Pareto-optimal solution; hence, there is no conflict between the demands of privacy and those of efficiency. If, say, a utilitarian criterion of justice were used, however, the optimal redistribution of income would require an invasion of privacy to establish satisfaction levels. Short of that invasion, one would have to rely on presumptions, for example, of equal possibilities of different utility functions for different individuals. There is room here for a new formulation of the problem of achieving justice in the presence of mutual uncertainty about preferences and other personal characteristics.

One last remark on this approach to privacy as a reaction to lack of information: it does in a way presuppose a basic privacy judgment, that individuals are not required to reveal their preferences and personal abilities as a matter of obligation. It is presupposed that given any revelation mechanism, they will behave selfishly. It is possible to take still another tack — that individuals have an obligation to tell the truth, but that communication is costly. After all, determining one's own preference structure, especially in areas not yet experienced, is none too easy. Hence, privacy may still appear as an economy, rather than a moral requirement or an unavoidable necessity.

Original Acquisition and Personal Abilities

Because Nozick is so concerned to defend property rights, he does not make a case which distinguishes between personal assets (labor, skills, and the like) and material assets. Still, his identification of taxation with forced *labor* suggests an awareness of this difference.

The problem of original acquisition and the difficulties of the Lockean proviso disappear or at least are greatly attenuated when reference is made to personal assets. These do unmistakably and clearly belong to an individual. Both Rawlsian and utilitarian views imply that personal assets are available for redistribution. The degree to which they can be used may be limited by privacy considerations. It may be difficult to know the extent of an individual's talents, and therefore it may be better to induce their use by rewards than to require it.

To strip away an inessential point, it is clear that to the extent that personal talents are developed by the use of scarce resources, they should be paid for. In Nozick's minimal state, this would happen automatically; in a world where education is supplied by the state or below cost, there is no reason why education should not be paid for by the recipient (of course, in ways which allow for difficulties in financing at the time of education and for uncertainties in the future receipt of income).

Further, to minimize the interference with privacy, the use of personal assets should be restricted to taxing the income derived from them.

Even with these constraints, it is still arguable that personal assets should be treated separately from material assets. Personally, I see no consistent argument that individuals with highly valuable natural assets should not share them with others. (This is not the moment to go into a detailed discussion of Nozick's analysis of the arguments for and against this position; let me say simply that the idea of a presumption of equality strikes me as a perfectly reasonable starting point for discussion.) On the other hand, I have some difficulty constructing an airtight argument in favor of such an obligation. It would have to proceed from the moral arbitrariness of the actual distribution of talents, but that may amount to presupposing the result.

If one grants some rights in personal assets to an individual, then for individuals living over time there is some claim to material property. If I perform a service, I may want my reward in the future rather than in the present. Presumably there should be some mechanism for permitting this, if the postponement is advantageous to others as well as myself. Hence, I am paid with some commitment to future goods. But why does it follow from my entitlement to the proceeds of my personal assets that I am also entitled to use this commitment as freely disposable property? I see no reason why, for example, I would be entitled to interest in exchange for the postponement. (There may be grounds in efficiency, and under the Pareto Principle one should accept efficiency until it interferes with justice.)

The Meaning of Property

This leads into the meaning of property, which could be the subject of another paper. I will merely summarize some views, perhaps rather dogmatically. Nozick's concept seems unsophisticated. He continually refers to the ownership of "things," whereas property really refers to rights. The same piece of land may have separable rights, for example to surface use and to mining, and these rights may be separable pieces of property — and indeed are in modern law.

Let me take the activity of covenanting as an example. Suppose I own a piece of land and insist that any sale be accompanied by a provision prohibiting in perpetuity the residence of blacks. That is, not only do I extract this promise from the buyer but I also require that he promise not to sell it without this clause. After a period of time, it may be that no one living wants this clause; but there is no way of getting it released. Such clauses are of course very far from hypothetical and indeed have never been declared illegal; it was only held that the courts, as instruments of the government which was prohibited from discriminating, could not enforce them. Further, covenants with regard to other uses, such as the sale of alcoholic beverages, are still enforced. This appears to be a historical theory of justice with a vengeance.

There is another way of looking at this. The property system is in fact a social construct; not every possible right, particularly with regard to the future, is a possible piece of property. Nozick speaks of everything's coming into existence already owned; but that is merely a particular socially determined property system. Pollution does not come into existence already owned; that is the problem.

The incompleteness of property rights in general creates well-known problems in welfare economics, being in fact the basic component of externalities. In particular, markets for future commitments are relatively underdeveloped compared with those for the present or immediate future. Individuals have to supply for themselves expectations as to future developments in order to make decisions with consequences extending into the future (on investments, for example). These expectations, say, of prices or of supply availabilities, are not "property," but they influence the use of property and are taken into account in the present legal system. An obligation to sell a product for the next few years at a given price is understood in the law to hold only if conditions do not change in a strongly unexpected way; this understanding does not require explicit statement. One of Nozick's own examples would not, in its full implications, be accepted by current legal principles. He supposes (pp. 269–270) that a station wagon was lent to some people for a while and that they became accustomed to it; this creates no obligation that it be given to them. But in fact if someone walks across your land for a sufficiently long period, without interference, he acquires the right to permanent use. The view is that expectations have been created which it would be unjust to deprive him of.

If markets were sufficiently complete, with all future periods and all uncertain contingencies already provided for in the contracts, the concept of property would cease to be problematic. All decisions would have been made in advance, and there would be no further questions of transfers to treat as just or unjust. Because in fact many of these markets do not exist, there are direct nonmarket relations which affect individuals' levels of satisfaction. Voluntary transfers become possible, but not all conceivable transfers can be made. Hence, voluntary transfers become biased in direction, and the possible injustice of the whole system of transfers must be recognized.

Justice and the Core

I noted earlier that Nozick's example of isolated individuals might lead to the conclusion that society was entitled to redistribute only the gains of trade that it produced over and above what individuals could get for themselves without trade (or cooperation in production). This view is indeed attributed to Rawls by Phelps (1976).

Carried a bit further, as suggested by Vickrey to Phelps in the cited paper, this argument might also suggest that any group of individuals within the total should be allowed to keep what this group could collectively achieve. Only the amount above that would be available to society to redistribute.

Formally, this can be stated as requiring that just allocations must satisfy the property that there should not exist a coalition of individuals and an allocation that they could achieve with their own resources such that every member of the coalition would be better off under their own allocation than in the proposed overall allocation.

This is precisely the definition of the *core* of an economy, a now well-known concept in game theory and economic analysis (see, for instance, Hildenbrand and Kirman, 1976, chap. 3; Arrow and Hahn, 1971, chap. 8). If one makes the assumptions of absence of externalities and of increasing returns to scale, then if the number of individuals in the economy is large (and no single one is large on the scale of the economy), the core shrinks to the competitive equilibrium. There is no problem of justice left!

This is not precisely Nozick's conclusion, since he does not wish to assume perfect competition, but it is certainly complementary to it.

My own view is that in some deep sense there are increasing returns to scale. The true basis for division of labor is the value to specialization, not merely in the economy but in society as a whole. Fundamentally similar people become different to complement each other. This vision informs the work of Adam Smith and also Rawls's concept of social union (1971, sec. 79). If this is true, then the core remains large even with many individuals. There are significant gains to social interaction above and beyond what individuals and subgroups can achieve on their own. The owners of scarce personal assets do not have substantial private use of these assets; it is only their value in a large system which makes these assets valuable. Hence, there is a surplus created by the existence of society as such which is available for redistribution.

References

Arrow, K. J., and F. H. Hahn. 1971. *General Competitive Analysis.* San Francisco: Holden-Day, and Edinburgh: Oliver & Boyd.

Bergson, A. 1938. A reformulation of certain aspects of welfare economics. *Quarterly Journal of Economics* 52: 310–334.

Buchanan, J. M. 1954. Individual choice in voting and the market. *Journal of Political Economy* 62: 334–343.

Carroll, Lewis. n.d. *The Complete Works of Lewis Carroll.* New York: Modern Library.

Edgeworth, F. Y. 1881. *Mathematical Psychics.* London: C. Kegan and Paul.

Edgeworth, F. Y. 1897. The pure theory of taxation. *Economic Journal 7.* The relevant portion is reprinted in R. Musgrave and A. T. Peacock (eds.), 1958, *Classics in the Theory of Public Finances,* London and New York: Macmillan, pp. 119–136.

Gibbard, A. 1973. Manipulation of voting schemes: a general result. *Econometrica* 41: 587–601.

Hildenbrand, W., and A. P. Kirman. 1976. *Introduction to Equilibrium Analysis.* Amsterdam and Oxford: North-Holland, and New York: American Elsevier.

Nozick, R. 1974. *Anarchy, State and Utopia.* New York: Basic Books.

Phelps, E. S. 1976. Recent developments in welfare economics: justice et équité. Discussion Paper 75–7617, the Economics Workshops, Columbia University.

Phelps, E. S., and R. A. Pollak. 1968. On second-best national saving and game-equilibrium growth. *Review of Economic Studies* 35: 185–200.

Rawls, J. 1971. *A Theory of Justice.* Cambridge, Mass.: Harvard University Press.

Samuelson, P. A. 1947. *Foundations of Economic Analysis.* Cambridge, Mass.: Harvard University Press.

Sen, A. K. 1970. *Collective Choice and Social Welfare.* San Francisco: Holden-Day.

Sidgwick, H. 1893. *The Methods of Ethics.* Fifth edition.

14 The Trade-off between Growth and Equity

The goals of economic policy are many and varied. Some of them are drawn from outside the economic sphere: national security and power, the achievement of a broad range of social objectives (such as the aesthetic improvement of urban life, social communication, health, internal order, and personal security), or the better development of individuals and of the modes of social interaction. Even within what might loosely be regarded as the endogenous goals of economic policy (perhaps defined as those for which the market is or could be used as a detailed allocative instrument), there is a considerable variety. But perhaps all or virtually all can be reduced in one way or another to three: economic stability, allocative efficiency, and distributive equity.

Where does the goal of economic growth appear in this short list? In some ways economic growth has been a recurrent theme of economic analysis since the days of Adam Smith. But perhaps the period since World War II has seen more emphasis than ever before. This is not surprising, since this period has also seen a more rapid rate of economic growth than anything achieved in the past. This period may be drawing to a close. I have no more belief in the existence of the Kondratiev cycle now than I did when my professors ridiculed the idea, but it still may be true that high productivity growth results from random and unpredictable causes; we may just have had a run of good luck, aided by an arrears of technological development

Reprinted from H. I. Greenfield, A. M. Levenson, W. Hamovitch, and E. Rotwein, eds., *Theory for Economic Efficiency: Essays in Honor of Abba P. Lerner,* pp. 1–11. Copyright © 1979 by the Massachusetts Institute of Technology. Used by permission of the MIT Press.

resulting from the Great Depression and World War II. Further, the exaggerated views of the limits-of-growth proponents do contain a genuine if tautological truth: there are resources, land and minerals, whose total stock is fixed, and continued use must eventually lead to their exhaustion. If these limited resources are indeed essential, growth must become negative.

But resource scarcities are not, in my judgment, a problem that will restrict growth seriously within the next twenty-five to fifty years; and I think it by no means unlikely that the rapid growth of scientifically inspired technology will lead to a resumption of growth of factor productivity. So growth, the attitudes toward it, and the policies that can achieve it—or at least prevent its cessation—are still major issues. But growth is not an elementary goal; it is one derived from the goals of efficiency and equity as applied to choices over time. Specifically, just as we are concerned with possible conflicts between efficiency and equity in resource allocation at a moment of time, so we are also concerned with possible conflicts between efficiency and equity in allocating resources among individuals at different points of time.

From the standpoint of values, this is what the problem of optimal growth policy amounts to. There is also the descriptive problem: identifying both the policies that can affect the distribution of income or that can affect the future evolution of the economy, and the effects of egalitarian policies on growth and of growth-promoting policies on equality of distribution.

Let us start with a review of the problems of reconciling efficiency and equity in a static context. First there is the conceptual question of what is meant by efficiency and what by equity. The answers to both questions have been (and doubtless always will be) matters of dispute as long as humanity, with its inevitable tension between the demands of the individual and those of society, exists. I confine myself to a few observations, to set the basis for subsequent discussion.

Efficiency and equity are both judgments, statements of preference. In the context of economics, the judgments or preferences are about allocations of resources. By an allocation in the full sense, I mean a statement of the inputs and outputs of every production process; of the assignments of final goods to individuals or households; and of the productive resources, labor and property, required of each individual or household.

Interest is clearly confined to feasible allocations. An allocation that requires the use of more of a primary resource than is available or that calls for the distribution to final consumers of more of a commodity than is

produced cannot be considered. Further, the outputs required of any production process must in fact be obtainable from the inputs; the allocation
has to be consistent with the available technological knowledge.

Modern economic analysis has begun to emphasize that there are restrictions on feasibility, in addition to those of resource availability and technology. The very nature of our economic institutions prevents us from achieving any allocation we wish. In an economy based on private property and
free sale of labor services, the initial distribution of skills and ownership of
property determines the distribution of income, which in turn determines
the allocation of consumers' goods. Thus not all technically feasible allocations can be realized. To be sure, the market allocation can be modified by
government actions, either by directly allocating goods or by modifying the
distribution of income through taxation, but the possibilities for reallocation in this manner are limited.

A socialist economy might, in theory, achieve a wider set of allocations,
but it is also subject to limitations. If it relies heavily on the market and its
incentives, then its outcome is similar to that of a capitalist economy. If it
tends more toward direct allocation, then it is apt to be mechanically
egalitarian and give the same bundle of goods to individuals of varying needs
and tastes, not merely for ideological reasons but also for lack of information
to make finer differentiations. Thus the concept of feasibility takes account
not merely of resource limitations and technology, but also of institutional
constraints.

Of efficiency and equity, efficiency is the simpler concept. The usual
definition in economics was first clearly formulated by Vilfredo Pareto: an
allocation of resources is efficient if there is no other feasible allocation that
will make everyone better off. The only ambiguity in this definition is the
meaning of "better off." I confine myself to the individualistic interpretation: each individual is the judge of when he or she is better off, so that we
respect individual decisions in the market and in voting.[1]

Even in a static world, equity is an elusive concept. There is no need to
enlarge on the rival concepts that have always held the field. The differences
among the utilitarian viewpoint, Rawls's principle of benefiting the worst
off, and Nozick's view that any distribution arrived at by free contracting is
just, sufficiently illustrate the variety of views. I will assume simply that

---

1. In the context of time, which is discussed later, this viewpoint may not be entirely
admissible. In education and in other social institutions, we do seek to influence what kind of
individuals will emerge, not merely accept whatever does emerge.

equity means as much equality of income as is possible, that the only reason that can be raised against policies leading to equalization of income is that they impair efficiency (or other desirable aims not considered in this chapter). I have stated this in an extreme fashion for simplicity. All that is really needed for my purposes is that the desirable income distribution is more nearly equal than would be yielded by the natural workings of the system.

To some extent, economic theory can be used to argue that the goals of efficiency and equity can be separated, that any distribution deemed equitable can be achieved without loss of efficiency. The argument is based on important properties of the competitive price system. There are two propositions here: any resource allocation achieved by a competitive price system is efficient; and for any efficient resource allocation, there is a redistribution of initial assets such that the competitive system will, after the redistribution, come to rest at the given resource allocation. These conclusions are valid only under some significant conditions, but for the moment let us assume that the conditions are met. Then the policy implication is that equity should be achieved by redistributing initial assets and then letting the market operate freely to determine production and consumption. In the extreme case an equal division of initial holdings of primary resources would be called for.

It is important that the redistribution of assets not be made dependent on the individual's subsequent actions in the market, for that would amount to a tax on the sales of certain goods, which would impair efficiency. The most important case is that of labor skills, which cannot be redistributed. An alternative would be to redistribute the income arising from their sale, but this amounts to a tax on the sale of skilled labor, as in the case of an ordinary income tax. Since an individual always has the power to reduce his or her offering of labor, the efficiency of allocation is reduced. In short, under a system in which individuals have some control over the total amounts or the particular kinds of labor services they offer, arbitrary redistributions of income are not feasible. Hence there is a trade-off between equity and efficiency.

One important qualification to this last statement must be registered: the undisturbed market system leads to efficiency only under the assumption of perfect competition, but competition is far from perfect. It is therefore conceivable that steps that interfere with the market might improve both efficiency and equity. Antimonopoly policy is a case in point. To the extent that monopolies increase the inequality of income, breaking them up may be a policy in which the efficiency-equity conflict is absent. But one cannot generalize. If antimonopoly policy includes policy against labor monopolies, the effect may be to decrease equity. It is, however, in the context of time that imperfections of competition are most relevant to the efficiency-equity issue.

In considering the relations between efficiency and equity over time, I shall simplify the discussion by ignoring problems of equity within a generation and assume provisionally that all individuals in a given generation are alike.

In the context of allocation over time, there is a new kind of redistribution of resources as compared with the static case: resources can be distributed from the present to the future. This typically takes the form of investment, a sacrifice of current consumption to increase future products. Refraining from consumption of exhaustible resources can be thought of as a special case of investment.

The condition for efficiency in this context is well known; it is the requirement that all investments yield the same rate of return in any given time period. However, among the efficient allocations, there is a distinction between the concept of growth and the concept of equity. If for the moment we assume that growth basically results from capital accumulation, then the greater the capital accumulation the faster the rate of growth. (It is generally recognized that this process cannot continue indefinitely; eventually the rate of growth is conditioned by labor and other fixed factors. But clearly an increase in capital accumulation can increase growth for a period which may be rather long.) However, indefinitely high growth is not necessarily good. Quite apart from problems of exhaustible resources, there is no particular reason why the present generation should sacrifice large amounts of consumption indefinitely to achieve higher rates of growth and higher rates of consumption for its successors. Justice requires a balance between competing values of the current and future generations.

Redistributions in time differ from redistributions at a given moment of time in one important aspect. Usually we think of the latter as reducing total product by reducing incentives. Redistribution from the present to the future, however, is typically productive; we expect such an allocation to yield a return over and above the initial resources invested. In terms of goods, the recipient gains more than the donor loses. Whatever one's exact form of ethics, this clearly is a powerful argument for benefiting the future.

Still, there are two offsetting considerations. One is that present investments tend to make future individuals better off than present ones, so the redistribution is from the present poor to the future rich. To minimize this adverse redistribution, the rate of return required on investments for the future should be higher, as the rate of growth increases. A second—more disputed—consideration is that there is an intrinsic tendency to discount the future. No individual living today can really regard individuals living in the future, particularly the far future, as being equivalent to himself. Indeed, if benefits for all future generations were counted equally, the value of the present would dwindle into insignificance. If we consistently refuse to discount the future, then a current generation should reduce itself to subsistence levels if there is any positive return on investment, no matter how small.

Thus a rough consensus is that a future investment ought to be made if and only if the productivity of the investment is at least as great as the sum of two countervailing effects, the pure futurity or discount effect and an allowance for the greater income of future generations. I call this the investment criterion.

I have spoken so far, for simplicity, as if growth were entirely due to large capital accumulation. In fact, a large fraction of growth in modern society is a result of technological advances that are to a considerable extent at least independent of the usual form of capital accumulation. Hence the future generations may well be richer even if no investment is made today. To that extent the argument for restricting redistribution to the future is strengthened.

Economists typically argue that public investment should be governed by the investment criterion. But actual public investments are not necessarily made in accordance with them. The question may also arise whether private investments are made this way. Indeed, if concern for the future is considered social rather than individual in nature—that is, an expression of justice or of concern for the perpetuation of humanity—then we would expect individuals to save and invest less than the investment criterion requires.

The situation in practice is more complicated than the simple model I have assumed thus far, because individuals live over time and because they are concerned about the futures of their families. Individuals as well as society have reason to save or invest for the future. Their behavior in this regard is parallel to that of the social sector, and they may come up with a rather similar criterion.

To the extent that this is true, we may suppose that the market will lead to something like a just and efficient allocation of resources over time. The theoretical argument might suggest some underinvestment in the future; optimal investment might be more than would be sustained by the preferences of individuals for their own future and for that of their children.

I think a more serious question may be one of imperfections of the capital market. In a world of uncertainty, borrowing cannot necessarily reach the optimal levels. In particular, borrowing for human capital formation, as in education or for development of new technologies, is likely to be restricted, and government intervention for these purposes has been well argued; in the case of education, the need is essentially fully accepted by most nations, possibly even overaccepted.

Today there is a widely dispersed distribution of income. Individuals and institutions, through their decisions, allocate their resources between current consumption and investment and saving for the future. Capital markets, to the extent that they operate, direct the desired saving into different forms of specific investment. The economy of the future is generated from all these decisions, together with the outside forces that also influence growth. The result, as experience has shown, is a restructuring of an economy, generally at a higher average income level but again with a widely dispersed distribution of income.

What, then, is the effect on efficiency and growth of classical redistributive policy through the tax system? There are both positive and negative effects. To start with the latter, the first, and perhaps most important, point is the reduced efficiency of the economic system. This has consequences for growth. The loss in income compared with what might have been means both that there is less available for capital accumulation and that the capital accumulated is used less efficiently. Hence the economy is on a permanently lower level, and perhaps the growth rate is depressed.

A second problem derives from the redistribution itself, apart from the efficiency problems arising from the taxes to pay for the redistribution. It appears that saving by individuals is likely to rise more than proportionately with income. Hence total personal savings will fall as a result of redistribution. Further, to the extent that redistributive taxes fall on the business institutions that form such a large part of the saving mechanism, there may again be a reduction in saving. The income, concentrated in one place and therefore easier to use for saving, is now scattered. In a world of perfect capital markets, this redistribution from firms to individuals would make no difference, but internal financing by firms is to a large extent precisely a compensation for imperfect capital markets.

For these reasons the aggregate volume of capital formation may fall as a consequence of redistribution. There are compensating factors, however. The recipients of the redistributed income may now have better access to capital markets—for example, through mutual funds or even through savings banks. Their incomes may rise to the point where saving becomes worthwhile.

More important is the increased ability of lower-income individuals to engage in forms of capital formation not handled well through the market. I am thinking especially of human capital formation. More schooling may become financially possible. The poor may have a greater chance to choose among jobs the ones for which they are best fitted. Improved conditions in the home are an important, though informal, type of capital formation. Because human capital formation among the poor will not be financed through capital markets, there is special reason to believe it will have an unusually high rate of return.

Taking everything together, taxation-financed redistribution will probably lower aggregate saving, though possibly redirecting part of it into higher-return activities. But such a policy will tend to have a positive effect in reducing the future inequality of income. On the high-income side, the taxes will have the effect of reducing the concentration of wealth. The rich allocate their resources between current consumption and wealth accumulation for themselves and their heirs. If they are taxed, they will in general reduce both. Hence to the extent that income inequality is perpetuated by inheritance, the same policies that redistribute wealth today will reduce inequality tomorrow. On the low-income side, the subsidies will be used for human capital formation, which is largely devoted to affecting income tomorrow. While inheritance can make no significant contribution to improving the income of the next generation of poor, improvement in the household and more schooling can.

Different types of taxes can be used to finance redistribution. Although the ordinary income tax has many merits, it also has some defects. It distorts the choice between labor and leisure, but this is probably unavoidable in any tax system. It imposes a double taxation on saving by taxing both saved income and the return to that saving. We do not know how serious the resulting distortion is, but it might be considerable. It can be avoided by shifting to progressive taxes on total consumption. This will have the additional virtue, from the redistributionist point of view, of taxing consumption derived from gifts and inheritances, which at present are effectively taxed at much lower rates.

It will still be necessary to have annual taxes on wealth, as in Sweden today, to prevent a concentration of wealth by those who consume relatively little out of high incomes. The rate can be low enough to minimize disincentives to save by those who are saving for the purpose of future consumption, while the annual repetition of the tax over a long period of time will fall on those who are accumulating wealth for its own sake or for the sake of the power it conveys.

A policy of income redistribution through taxes and transfers does involve a risk of efficiency losses both at a moment of time and over time. On the other hand, there are some gains in efficiency if the income of lower groups is raised sufficiently to enable them to engage in some rational planning. On the whole, redistribution within a single generation tends to have some positive effect toward equality in the future.

Earlier I singled out the imperfection of the capital markets as the largest element of inefficiency in allocation over time. This raises the question of whether it is possible to counteract these distortions and at the same time decrease inequality. It is evident that the imperfection of the capital market weighs most heavily upon the poor in their human capital formation, and this suggests the proper course of action.

A great part of redistribution should take the form of social capital formation of a kind that will raise the productivity of the poor. The negative income tax will allow the poor the right to choose their own consumption patterns, for example. But I think that it is fairly clear that many kinds of capital formation that will benefit them cannot be carried out at all or at least cannot be carried out efficiently on an individual level.

The most obvious example of social capital formation is education. It may be objected reasonably that this activity is already largely socialized and that there is little possibility of further gains in highly educated countries like the United States and Japan. This obvious lesson has not been learned by many — perhaps even most — developing countries. They have not realized that education provides a means of achieving both high-productivity investment and income equalization.

Even in advanced countries, there is room for improvement. I would judge that the biggest lack is technical education. This becomes especially important in a technologically advancing world where skills have not only to be acquired but also changed. Midcareer shifts should be facilitated by suitable education, as well as updating in the same line of work. The facilities provided are inadequate in most countries. There is another problem. For an individual capable of earning an income, even a young person going to the university, the sacrifice of income is a larger investment than the cost of providing the educational facility. This situation illustrates an imperfection of the capital market; ideally the individual should be able to borrow against future earnings, but cannot.

Providing technical education and financing students is both equalizing and socially efficient in producing appropriate growth. It would be desirable, in my view, that the beneficiary ultimately be responsible for the costs incurred. The best way would be a repayment dependent upon future income. In this way the risks and uncertainties of the benefits are borne by the state, which is an ideal insurer, rather than by the individual. If such a repayment scheme is considered too difficult to achieve, however, I would rather have free tuition and scholarships than no system of technical education or one paid for out of current income.

Similarly, government subsidy to facilitate labor mobility across occupations and across regions would seem an appropriate form of social investment, aimed simultaneously at intertemporal efficiency and equity.

A more speculative idea is subsidizing investment by the poor. Currently in most advanced countries, subsidized housing is provided for lower-income groups. In the United States the program has not worked, possibly for reasons peculiar to the country. This program is investment on behalf of the poor but not by them. An alternative possibility is to enable the poor to own their own homes by subsidizing the investment—for example, by interest-free or low-interest loans. This would constitute a transfer of wealth, not merely of income. In addition to giving the poor a greater stake in the maintenance of their housing, it would offer a chance to make more equal the future distribution of income.

Finally I urge that the government take a much greater role in the development of civilian technology, particularly in the basic steps. It is a familiar argument of economists that in a competitive world, a firm's incentives to innovate will be limited if the innovation will become everyone's property. Patent rights protect only a limited range of innovations. Government addition to the supply of innovative effort will therefore improve efficiency.

The policy of government development of civilian technology will also contribute to equality. In the absence of markets to achieve efficient risk bearing, the resources for technological development come from those already wealthy, and hence technical progress on the whole reinforces the existing distribution of income. If the supply of new technologies comes from the government and is freely available to all newcomers, there is likely to be greater opportunity for equalization of wealth through competition.

I take very seriously the moral obligation to achieve equity in income, now and in the future. This obligation does have to be properly balanced against the requirements of efficient allocation at a given moment of time and over time. No simplistic solution is possible, but recognizing the intrinsic imperfections of competition in a capitalist system affords opportunities to reconcile the two aims.

15 Optimal and Voluntary Income Distribution

The concept of the social welfare function was introduced by Bergson in his classic paper (1938) to express preferences over resource allocations to all individuals in society. Just as the commodity bundles of an individual are supposed to be compared by his or her individual preference ordering, so the alternative allocations of commodity bundles to all individuals can be ordered by a social welfare ordering over this entire space. As with any ordering that satisfies certain regularity properties, the social welfare ordering can be represented by a real-valued function, the social welfare function. Its significance is essentially ordinal, but under additional conditions of separability the function representing an ordering can be chosen to be additive in an appropriate choice of variables.[1]

The optimization of a social welfare function should determine the entire allocation of resources among individuals and therefore includes the normative problems of income distribution. To concentrate on this topic, I will confine attention to the special case where there is only one commodity in

---

1. This point was first made in the context of social welfare functions by Fleming (1953). The classic statement of conditions for additive utility functions is that of Debreu (1960).

Reprinted from Steven Rosefielde, ed., *Economic Welfare and the Economics of Soviet Socialism: Essays in Honor of Abram Bergson* (Cambridge: Cambridge University Press, 1981), pp. 267–288.

the economic system. A resource allocation is then simply a vector with a (nonnegative) component for every individual in the economy.

To confine attention to the simplest normative aspects, I will further abstract from incentive questions. I will simply assume that the total available of the one commodity is given and is not diminished by any transfers.

When we speak of an individual utility function or preference ordering, we usually mean *both* that it is an ordering over the possible commodity bundles for that individual *and* that it is a characteristic of the individual. A social welfare function orders social resource allocations (income distributions in the present limited analysis); but of whom is it a characteristic? One point of view, inherent in the theory of social choice, is that a social ordering is a social construct. In this chapter I will follow Bergson in his view that a social welfare function is characteristic of an individual. Each individual is supposed to have a social conscience, an ordering over income distributions.[2] The social welfare function for a given individual determines the answer he or she would give to the following hypothetical question: For all pairs of income distributions, which would I choose if I were dictator?[3]

If social welfare functions differ from individual to individual, how shall the normative question be posed? We can give one answer by using the criterion of Pareto optimality. We can at least ask for the class of income distributions which are not dominated in the sense that another income distribution will be superior according to everyone's social welfare function. We are thus led into the field of Pareto-optimal income redistribution, which has been the object of considerable study; leading papers are those of Kolm (1969) (unfortunately little noticed, possibly because of the extremely careless printing of the English version), Winter (1969), Hochman and Rodgers (1969), and Archibald and Davidson (1976).

I will not review these papers in detail. Considerable attention is paid in them to Pareto efficiency in the distribution of specific goods, a problem from which I am abstracting. I follow particularly Kolm and Archibald and Davidson in a symmetric formulation of interdependence of utilities.

Since each individual has his or her own social welfare function, we can

2. This position is implicit in Bergson, 1938, and has been made explicit in Bergson, 1966; see esp. pp. 35–36. Pareto, in a little-known paper (1913), also considered social welfare judgments to be made by individuals.

3. Little (1952) attacked the nondictatorship condition in social choice theory on the grounds that social welfare judgments were made by individuals.

incorporate in it any selfish tendencies. It is presupposed that, in a clearly defined sense, an individual will prefer own income to income for others. However, this preference is limited, so that a sufficiently wealthy individual will prefer to give an extra dollar to a sufficiently poor one rather than retain it. Hence, the Pareto-optimality concept includes both regard for others and for self. I make some specific separability assumptions about social welfare preferences; they amount to saying that if redistributions over a limited set of individuals only are permitted, preference by any individual over those distributions is independent of the income levels of the remainder of society. It is further assumed that any individual regards all other individuals symmetrically and that judgments about redistribution among others are the same for all individuals, the product perhaps of a code of ethics.

Under these conditions there is a preferred additive representation of the social welfare function. Let x_i be the income of individual i, n the number of individuals, and $W_i(x_1, \ldots, x_n)$ the social welfare function. I shall show in the first section of this chapter that, under the assumptions made, there exists an altruistic utility function of income, U, and for each individual an egoistic utility function, U_i, such that

$$W_i(x_1, \ldots, x_n) = U_i(x_i) + \sum_{j \neq i} U(x_j).$$

The hypothesis of selfish preference takes the form

$$U_i'(x) > U'(x) \quad \text{for all } i \text{ and all } x.$$

That is, starting from an equal distribution between individual i and some other individual, i would prefer to shift some income to himself.

In the second section I characterize the conditions for Pareto-optimal income distributions with these social welfare functions. From this the following is shown: If the number of members of the economy, n, grows indefinitely with mean income remaining constant, then the Pareto-optimal income distributions converge to the egalitarian.

If the social welfare function is an expression of individual preference, then an individual cannot merely express opinions, but he or she can act on them in the form of giving to others. There has been surprisingly little discussion of the economics of charity, the most extensive being that of Ireland and Johnson (1970). In this chapter I formalize the concept of charity as a noncooperative game. Each individual starts with a specified income, which can be given away to others. At the end of the game any individual's income will equal the original income plus all gifts to him or her less all gifts by him or her. The *i*th individual seeks to maximize W_i. The equilibrium point of the game is completely characterized, and the conditions for it to be Pareto optimal are determined. If the equilibrium is nontrivial, in the sense that some gifts occur, then it is never Pareto-optimal unless there is exactly one giver and all others receive the same final income.

Assumptions on the Social Welfare Functions of Individuals

In a given society an *income allocation* is an assignment of income to th members of the society. If the society is denoted by *S*, then an income allocation is a specification of x_i for all $i \in S$. For convenience, the notation x_S will stand for an income allocation over *S*.

Each individual *i* is supposed to have a preference ordering for income allocations over any society *S*, whether or not $i \in S$. We can certainly imagine a situation in which an individual has some say in allocating income in a society but is not allowed to affect his or her own income.

A "sure-thing" principle will be postulated. That is, a preference ordering for income allocations over some society *S* will not be affected by incomes outside *S*, which cannot be reallocated, or even by the existence of individuals outside *S*.

ASSUMPTION 1. *If $S \subset T$, let x_T and x'_T be two income allocations over T that differ only on S (that is, $x_{T \sim S} = x'_{T \sim S}$). Then x_T is preferred to x'_T by individual i if and only if x_S is preferred to x'_S in i's ordering of income allocations over S.*

Here $T \sim S$ is the set of individuals in *T* but not in *S*; x_S and x'_S are, respectively, the parts of the income allocations x_T and x'_T for individuals in *S*.

A second assumption is that each individual regards all other individuals alike as far as income allocations are concerned.

ASSUMPTION 2. *Let x_S and x'_S be two income allocations over S, where $x'_j = x_{\sigma(j)}$ for all $j \in S$, for σ a permutation of the members of S. Any individual i not belonging to S regards x_S and x'_S as indifferent.*

A stronger assumption is that preferences about income allocations among others are socially formed; specifically, such preferences are the same no matter which individual holds them.

ASSUMPTION 3. *If neither i nor j belong to S, then they have the same preferences over income allocations in S.*

The next assumption states the concept of selfishness; in any redistribution between one individual and another, the first will prefer some degree of inequality in his or her favor to equality.

ASSUMPTION 4. *If S consists of two individuals, i and j, then at any allocations in which $x_i = x_j$, the marginal rate of substitution of i's income for j's according to i is greater than 1.*

Finally, the usual concavity assumptions are imposed.

ASSUMPTION 5. *For any individual i and any society S, if x_S is preferred or indifferent to x'_S according to i, then $(1 - t)x_S + tx'_S$ is preferred to x'_S for any t, $0 < t < 1$.*

Characterization of the Social Welfare Function

Following the standard theorems on separable utility (see Debreu, 1960), Assumption 1 implies immediately that we can choose an additive utility indicator, W_i^S, for individual *i*'s ordering over income distributions over a society *S*:

$$(15\text{-}1) \qquad W_i^S(x_S) = \sum_{j \in S} W_{ij}(x_j).$$

Note that because the society *S* is variable and the preferences are independent not only of the incomes outside *S* but even of the existence of individuals outside *S*, the functions W_{ij} are independent of the set *S*.

The symmetry condition for others, Assumption 2, implies immediately that W_{ij} is the same function for all individuals, $j \neq i$. Let $V_i = W_{ij}$ for $j \neq i$. Consider any two individuals, *i* and *j*, and any set of individuals, *S*, to which neither belong. Then, from (15-1), the preferences of *i* and *j*, respectively, over income allocations in *S* are determined by the utility indicators,

$$W_i^S(x_S) = \sum_{k \in S} V_i(x_k), \qquad W_j^S(x_S) = \sum_{k \in S} V_j(x_k).$$

But from Assumption 3, these two utility indicators must represent the same ordering over x_S's. Since they are additive, one must be a positive linear transformation of the other; without loss of generality they must be the same, which implies that $V_i = V_j$. Since *i* and *j* were arbitrary, we can write $V_i = U$ for all *i*.

Then for any set of individuals S and any $i \in S$,

$$(15\text{-}2) \quad W_i^S(x_S) = W_{ii}(x_i) + \sum_{j \in S \sim \{i\}} W_{ij}(x_j) = W_{ii}(x_i) + \sum_{j \in S \sim \{i\}} V_i(x_j)$$
$$= U_i(x_i) + \sum_{j \in S \sim \{i\}} U(x_j),$$

where we have written U_i for W_{ii}.

Consider in particular the case where S contains two members, i and j. Then $W_i^S(x_i, x_j) = U_i(x_i) + U(x_j)$. The marginal rate of substitution of x_i for x_j is $U_i'(x_i)/U'(x_j)$ in individual i's preference. If $x_i = x_j = x$, then, from Assumption 4, $U_i'(x)/U'(x) > 1$.

Finally, Assumption 5 implies that the functions U_i and U are concave.

THEOREM 1. *Under Assumptions 1 through 5, the preferences of individual i among income allocations over a set of individuals S containing i have as a utility indicator*

$$(15\text{-}3) \quad W_i^S(x_S) = U_i(x_i) + \sum_{j \in S \sim \{i\}} U(x_j),$$

$$(15\text{-}4) \quad \text{where} \quad U_i'(x) > U'(x) \quad \text{for all } x,$$

and the functions U_i and U are strictly concave.

To illustrate the implications of the social welfare function (15-3), we consider the allocations that would be made by an individual i who has dictatorial powers. As the size of the economy grows, the number of terms concerned with the welfare of others grows. One might mistakenly infer that individual i would pay less and less attention to his or her own welfare. In fact, as the economy grows with the same mean income, individual i would allocate more income to himself or herself, although not unboundedly more.

To see this, maximize (15-3) subject to the constraint on total income,

$$(15\text{-}5) \quad \sum_{j \in S} x_j \leq (\#S)\bar{x},$$

where

$$(15\text{-}6) \quad \bar{x} = \text{mean income}$$

$$(15\text{-}7) \quad \text{and } \#S = \text{number of members of } S.$$

Then if we let p be the Lagrange parameter associated with the constraint (15-5),

(15-8) $U_i'(x_i) \leq p$; if $U_i'(x_i) < p$, then $x_i = 0$;

(15-9)   for each $j \in S$, $j \neq i$, $U'(x_j) \leq p$;
            if $U'(x_j) < p$, then $x_j = 0$.

Suppose that $U_i'(x_i) < p$. Since constraint (15-5) is clearly binding, for some $j \neq i$, $x_j > 0$, so that $U'(x_j) = p > U_i'(x_i) = U_i'(0) > U'(0)$ from (15-4), which contradicts the concavity of U. Hence

$$U_i'(x_i) = p.$$

Suppose that for some $j \in S \sim \{i\}$, $U'(x_j) = p$, while for another member, k, of $S \sim \{i\}$, $U'(x_k) < p$. Then $U'(x_j) = p > U'(x_k) = U'(0)$, again a contradiction to the concavity of U. Hence, either

$$x_j = 0 \quad \text{for all } j \in S \sim \{i\}$$

$$\text{or} \quad U'(x_j) = p \quad \text{for all } j \in S \sim \{i\}.$$

In either case, for some x',

(15-10) $x_j = x'$ for all $j \in S \sim \{i\}$.

In the first case, $x_i = (\#S)\bar{x}$ from (15-5), (15-8), and (15-9),

(15-11) $U_i'[(\#S)\bar{x}] = p \geq U'(0)$;

in the second case,

(15-12) $U_i'(x_i) = U'(x')$.

Now define, for both present and future reference,

(15-13) $U_i'[\xi_i(x)] = U'(x)$.

Since U_i' and U' are both decreasing functions, $\xi_i(x)$ is an increasing function of x. It might not be defined for all x. From (15-4), $\lim_{x \to \infty} U_i'(x) \geq \lim_{x \to \infty} U'(x)$. If the equality holds, then ξ_i will be defined for all x. However, if the strict inequality holds, then ξ_i is defined only for $0 \leq x < \tilde{x}$, where $U'(\tilde{x}) = \lim_{x \to \infty} U_i'(x)$.

It follows immediately from (15-4) and the concavity of U_i and U that

(15-14) $\xi_i(x) > x$ for all x.

From (15-11), $x' = 0$ and $x_i = (\#S)\bar{x}$ if

(15-15) $(\#S)\bar{x} \le \xi_i(0)$.

On the other hand, when $x' > 0$,

(15-16) $x_i = \xi_i(x')$.

If $\bar{x} > \xi_i(0)$, then (15-15) cannot hold even if S contains just the one member i. Otherwise, (15-15) will hold for $\#S$ sufficiently small.

From (15-10) and the resource constraint (15-5),

(15-17) $x_i + (\#S - 1)x' = (\#S)\bar{x}$.

From (15-15) to (15-17), x_i and x' will depend only on the number of elements of S for given i. We wish to show that x_i will increase with $\#S$.

For simplicity of notation, let $\#S = n$: we will exhibit x_i and x' as functions of n. There are three possible cases: (a) $(n + 1)\bar{x} \le \xi_i(0)$; (b) $n\bar{x} \le \xi_i(0) < (n + 1)\bar{x}$; and (c) $\xi_i(0) < n\bar{x}$. If (a) holds, then also $n\bar{x} \le \xi_i(0)$. Then, from (15-15), $x' = 0$, both when $\#S = n$ and when $\#S = n + 1$; $x_i(n + 1) = (n + 1)\bar{x} > n\bar{x} = x_i(n)$. If (b) holds, then $x_i(n) = n\bar{x}$, by (15-15), and from (15-16) and the fact that ξ_i is an increasing function, $x_i(n + 1) = \xi_i[x'(n + 1)] > \xi_i(0) \ge n\bar{x} = x_i(n)$. In both cases $x_i(n + 1) > x_i(n)$.

Now suppose that (c) holds. From (15-17) with $\#S = n, n + 1$, respectively, we have

$$x_i(n) + (n - 1)x'(n) = n\bar{x}$$

$$\text{and}\quad x_i(n + 1) + nx'(n + 1) = (n + 1)\bar{x}.$$

Multiply the first equation by $(n + 1)$ and the second by n, and then subtract the first from the second. Simplification implies that

(15-18) $n[x_i(n + 1) - x_i(n)] + n^2[x'(n + 1) - x'(n)] = x_i(n) - x'(n)$.

From (15-14) and (15-16),

(15-19) $x_i(n) = \xi_i[x'(n)] > x'(n)$,

so that the right-hand side of (15-18) is positive and the left-hand side must be. But in case (c), (15-16) holds both for $\#S = n$ and for $\#S = n + 1$. Since ξ_i is increasing, $x_i(n + 1) - x_i(n)$ has the same sign as $x'(n + 1) - x'(n)$; hence, both must be positive.

From (15-17) and (15-19), $x'(n) < \bar{x}$ if $\xi_i(0) < n\bar{x}$; the inequality holds trivially in the opposite case, since then $x'(n) = 0$. Hence, $x_i(n) =$

$\xi_i(x') \leq \xi_i(\bar{x})$ from (15-16), if applicable, or else (15-15). Therefore $x_i(n)$ increases with n but has an upper bound. If we divide through by $\#S = n$ in (15-17), it follows that $x'(n)$ approaches $\bar{x}$, and therefore $x_i(n)$ approaches $\xi_i(\bar{x})$ as n grows large.

COROLLARY 1. *If individual i is a dictator with respect to choice of income allocation, then for given mean income $\bar{x}$, his or her income depends only on the individual's own characteristics and the number of individuals in the economy and is an increasing function of that number. The income of each other individual is also an increasing function of the size of the economy, the same for all such. The income of i is bounded above by $\xi_i(\bar{x})$, the solution of the equation, $U_i'(x) = U'(\bar{x})$, and converges to that limit as the size of the economy grows; the income of each other individual approaches $\bar{x}$.*

This corollary shows that an increase of the size of the economy increases the selfish implications of the welfare function in absolute terms but decreases it relative to the size of the economy.

Characterization of Pareto-Optimal Income Allocations

The allocation determined by setting any individual as a dictator is Pareto optimal, by definition. However, there are many other Pareto-optimal allocations.

I shall assume that Pareto optimality for any economy is defined relative to the members of that economy only and not other individuals.

DEFINITION 1. *For a given economy S, the allocation x'_S dominates the allocation x_S if, for every $i \in S$, $W_i^S(x'_S) \geq W_i^S(x_S)$, with the strict inequality holding for at least one $i \in S$. An allocation x_S is Pareto optimal in S if there is no other allocation over the members of S that dominates x_S and whose total income is the same.*

As all the functions involved are concave, we have the obvious equivalence x_S^* is Pareto optimal in S if and only if there exist $\lambda_i \geq 0$ for all i in S, $\lambda_j > 0$, some $j \in S$, such that x_S^* maximizes $\Sigma_{i \in S} \lambda_i W_i^S(x_S)$ subject to $\Sigma_{i \in S} x_i$ given.

If we substitute for W_i^S from Theorem 1, Eq. (15-3), we see that Pareto-optimal allocations are characterized as maximizing

$$\sum_{i \in S} \lambda_i \left[U_i(x_i) + \sum_{j \in S \sim (i)} U(x_j) \right]$$

for given $\Sigma_{i \in S} x_i$. But

$$\sum_{i \in S} \lambda_i \sum_{j \in S \sim (i)} U(x_j) = \sum_{j \in S} \lambda_j \sum_{i \in S \sim (j)} U(x_i) = \sum_{i \in S} \sum_{j \in S \sim (i)} \lambda_j U(x_i)$$
$$= \sum_{i \in S} \left(\sum_{j \in S \sim (i)} \lambda_j \right) U(x_i) = \sum_{i \in S} (\lambda - \lambda_i) U(x_i)$$

where $\lambda = \Sigma_{j \in S} \lambda_j$. Hence, Pareto-optimal allocations maximize

$$\sum_{i \in S} [\lambda_i U_i(x_i) + (\lambda - \lambda_i) U(x_i)]$$

subject to $\Sigma_{i \in S} x_i$ given. Let p be the Lagrange parameter corresponding to the last constraint. Then a Pareto-optimal allocation satisfies the conditions

(15-20) $\lambda_i U_i'(x_i) + (\lambda - \lambda_i) U'(x_i) \le p$ for all i

with equality if $x_i > 0$. As these conditions are homogeneous of degree 1, we can let $p = 1$ without loss of generality (clearly, $p > 0$). Hence, by a slight rewriting of (15-20), x_S is Pareto optimal (compared with other allocations with the same total) if and only if there exist $\lambda_i \ge 0$, with strict inequality for at least one $i \in S$, such that

(15-21) $\lambda_i [U_i'(x_i) - U'(x_i)] + \lambda U'(x_i) \le 1$,

with equality for such i that $x_i > 0$.

We will eliminate the Lagrange parameters to derive a criterion for Pareto optimality in terms of the proposed allocation x_S alone. From Theorem 1, Exp. (15-4), $U_i'(x_i) - U'(x_i) > 0$. Let

(15-22) $\alpha_i = [U_i'(x_i) - U'(x_i)]^{-1} > 0$, $\beta_i = U'(x_i)$.

Multiplying through in (15-21) by α_i yields

(15-23a) $\lambda_i + \lambda \alpha_i \beta_i \le \alpha_i$ for all i,

(15-23b) $\lambda_i + \lambda \alpha_i \beta_i = \alpha_i$ if $x_i > 0$.

From (15-23a), the condition $\lambda_i \ge 0$ implies that $\alpha_i \ge \lambda \alpha_i \beta_i$, or $\beta_i \lambda \le 1$ for all i.

If we define

(15-24) $\bar{\beta} = \max \beta_i$,

the last condition can be written

(15-25) $\bar{\beta} \lambda \le 1$.

Suppose that there exists a solution to (15-23a–b) with $\lambda_i \geq 0$ for all i; in particular, (15-25) holds for $\lambda = \Sigma_{i \in S} \lambda_i$. I will show that there exists a solution in which it is required that $\lambda_i = 0$ for all i for which $x_i = 0$; in other words, any individual who gets zero income can, without loss of generality, be assigned zero social weight.

Let Σ^0, Σ^+ denote sums for values of i for which $x_i = 0$, $x_i > 0$, respectively, and let $\lambda^0 = \Sigma^0 \lambda_i$. Then

$$\Sigma^+ \lambda_i = \lambda - \lambda^0.$$

Sum (15-23b) over all i for which $x_i > 0$:

$$\lambda - \lambda^0 + \lambda \Sigma^+ \alpha_i \beta_i = \Sigma^+ \alpha_i.$$

Solve for λ:

$$\lambda = (\lambda^0 + \Sigma^+ \alpha_i)/(1 + \Sigma^+ \alpha_i \beta_i).$$

Now try a new solution, $\lambda_i' (i \in S)$, as follows: Let

(15-26a) $\lambda' = (\Sigma^+ \alpha_i)/(1 + \Sigma^+ \alpha_i \beta_i),$

(15-26b)
(15-26c) $\lambda_i' = \begin{cases} \alpha_i (1 - \beta_i \lambda') & \text{if } x_i > 0 \\ 0 & \text{if } x_i = 0. \end{cases}$

Clearly $\lambda' \leq \lambda$. Hence, from (15-25), $\bar{\beta} \lambda' \leq 1$, so that $\beta_i \lambda' \leq 1$ for all i, and therefore $\lambda_i' \geq 0$ if $x_i > 0$; $\lambda_i' = 0$ and therefore $\lambda_i' \geq 0$, if $x_i = 0$, so that $\lambda_i' \geq 0$, all $i \in S$. Also,

$$\sum_{i \in S} \lambda_i' = \Sigma^+ \lambda_i' = \Sigma^+ \alpha_i - \lambda' \Sigma^+ \alpha_i \beta_i = \lambda'.$$

Hence, $\lambda_i' (i \in S)$ is a solution to (15-23a–b), with $\lambda_i' = 0$ when $x_i = 0$.

If we take a solution with $\lambda_i = 0$ when $x_i = 0$, we must have (15-26a–c). If the primes are dropped, condition (15-25) becomes

(15-27) $\bar{\beta} \Sigma^+ \alpha_i \leq 1 + \Sigma^+ \alpha_i \beta_i.$

If this condition is satisfied, then from (15-26), the equations (15.23) are satisfied and the allocation is Pareto optimal.

Let $\mathbf{x} = \min_i x_i$, the lowest income in the allocation. Then, since U' is decreasing, it follows from (15-22) and (15-24) that $\bar{\beta} = U'(\mathbf{x})$. If $\mathbf{x} = 0$, then (15-27) can be written

(15-28) $\displaystyle\sum_{x_i > \mathbf{x}} (\bar{\beta} - \beta_i)\alpha_i \leq 1.$

If $\mathbf{x} > 0$, then Σ^+ is a summation over all i. Sum separately over those i for whom $x_i = \mathbf{x}$ and those for whom $x_i > \mathbf{x}$; note that for the former $\beta_i = \bar{\beta}$. Then (15-27) becomes

$$\bar{\beta} \sum_{x_i=\mathbf{x}} \alpha_i + \bar{\beta} \sum_{x_i>\mathbf{x}} \alpha_i \leq 1 + \bar{\beta} \sum_{x_i=\mathbf{x}} \alpha_i + \sum_{x_i>\mathbf{x}} \alpha_i \beta_i,$$

which again simplifies to (15-28).

THEOREM 2. *Let x_S be an income allocation for the economy S. Let*

$$\alpha_i = [U_i'(x_i) \quad U'(x_i)]^{-1}, \qquad \beta_i = U'(x_i),$$
$$\mathbf{x} = \min_i x_i, \qquad \bar{\beta} = U'(\mathbf{x}).$$

Then x_S is Pareto optimal if and only if

$$\sum_{x_i>\mathbf{x}} (\bar{\beta} - \beta_i)\alpha_i \leq 1.$$

If $x_i > \mathbf{x}$, then $\beta_i < \bar{\beta}$, so that each term, $(\bar{\beta} - \beta_i)\alpha_i > 0$. It follows for any subset of the individuals who receive above-minimum income, the inequality in the optimality criterion is strengthened.

COROLLARY 2. *Let x_S be a Pareto-optimal income allocation for the economy S, and T be any set of individuals for whom $x_i > \mathbf{x}$. Then*

$$\sum_{i\in T} (\bar{\beta} - \beta_i)\alpha_i \leq 1.$$

To illustrate the applicability of the optimality criterion, it will be shown that the upper bound on the income of any individuals found for the dictatorial case in Corollary 1 remains valid for all Pareto-optimal allocations. Consider any individual i. If $x_i = \mathbf{x}$, then by (15-14), $x_i < \xi_i(\mathbf{x})$. If $x_i > \mathbf{x}$, then choose T in Corollary 2 to consist of the individual i alone, so that $(\bar{\beta} - \beta_i)\alpha_i \leq 1$. This implies that $\bar{\beta} \leq \beta_i + \alpha_i^{-1}$. From the definitions, $U'(\mathbf{x}) \leq U_i'(x_i)$; as U_i' is decreasing, the definition (15-13) of ξ_i then implies

COROLLARY 3. *If x_S is any Pareto-optimal income allocation for any economy S, then $x_i \leq \xi_i(\mathbf{x}) \leq \xi_i(\bar{x})$ for all individuals i, where $\mathbf{x}$ is the minimum income in the allocation.*

Pareto-Optimal Income Allocations in Large Economies

It will now be shown that for large economies Pareto-optimal income allocations are approximately egalitarian, provided that the potential members of the successively larger economies are not too different (more precisely, are not arbitrarily selfish). The meaning of the approximation needs a little clarification. Clearly a dictatorial allocation, as characterized in Corollary 1, is always Pareto optimal; hence, we cannot say of any such allocation that all individuals have incomes that are close to one another. What is true is that the number of individuals whose income is above the minimum by any given amount is relatively negligible in large economies.

By the income distribution corresponding to any given income allocation, we mean the proportion of individuals who receive any given income. It will be shown that if we take a sequence of economies of increasing size but the same mean income and select from each any Pareto-optimal income allocation, the corresponding sequence of income distributions converges to an egalitarian distribution. Specifically, for any $\varepsilon > 0$, the proportion of individuals with incomes more than ε above the minimum approaches zero.

Indeed, a stronger statement is true. For any given mean income and any $\varepsilon > 0$, there is a number N such that the number of individuals with incomes more than ε above the minimum never exceeds N, no matter how large the economy and no matter who belongs to it.

To state precisely the notion of a large economy, let us introduce the concept of a *population P* of individuals. Any given economy is a subset of members of P. The population P will be taken to be infinite.

ASSUMPTION 6. *For any $x > 0$, the marginal rate of substitution of i's income for j's according to i when both have income x is bounded above as i and j range over all possible members of the population P.*

Unbounded selfishness is thus ruled out.

For $j \neq i$, the marginal rate of substitution is $U_i'(x)/U'(x)$. Since $U'(x)$ is the same for all individuals, Assumption 6 is equivalent to the following statement:

(15-29)   For any given x, $U_i'(x)$ is bounded above as i varies over P.

Let S be any economy, with mean income $\bar{x}$. For any given $\varepsilon > 0$ and any given Pareto-optimal allocations, x_S, define

(15-30) $S' = \{i \in S | x_i > \mathbf{x} + \varepsilon\}.$

By Corollary 2,

(15-31) $\sum_{i \in S'} (\bar{\beta} - \beta_i)\alpha_i \leq 1.$

Consider the function $U'(x) - U'(x + \varepsilon)$, as x varies over the interval $0 \leq x \leq \bar{x}$. It is everywhere positive. Also, it is continuous everywhere, except possibly at $x = 0$; but if it is not continuous there, it approaches $+\infty$. Hence, $U'(x) - U'(x + \varepsilon)$ is bounded away from 0 on the interval. That is, there exists $\delta > 0$, depending only on ε and $\bar{x}$, such that $U'(x) - U'(x + \varepsilon) \geq \delta$ for $0 \leq x \leq \bar{x}$. If $x' \geq x + \varepsilon$, $U'(x) - U'(x') \geq U'(x) - U'(x + \varepsilon) \geq \delta$. In particular, $\mathbf{x} \leq \bar{x}$, $x_i > \mathbf{x} + \varepsilon$ for $i \in S'$, so that

(15-32) $\bar{\beta} - \beta_i \geq \delta$ for all $i \in S'$.

Also, $\alpha_i^{-1} = U_i'(x_i) - U'(x_i) \leq U_i'(x_i) < U_i'(\varepsilon)$ for $i \in S'$, since $x_i > \mathbf{x} + \varepsilon \geq \varepsilon$. From Assumption 6, in the form (15-29), $U_i'(\varepsilon)$ is bounded above as i varies, the bound depending only on ε. Hence, α_i is bounded below.

$\alpha_i \geq \alpha$ for all $i \in S'$, where α depends only on ε.

Then, from (15-31) and (15-32), $1 \geq \delta\alpha(\#S')$ so that $\#S'$ is bounded above by a quantity depending only on ε and $\bar{x}$.

THEOREM 3. *For any $\varepsilon > 0$ and any mean income $\bar{x}$, there is a number N such that for all economies S and all Pareto-optimal income allocations over S with mean income $\bar{x}$,*

$$\#\{i \in S | x_i > \mathbf{x} + \varepsilon\} \leq N,$$

where $\mathbf{x}$ is the minimum income in that allocation.

COROLLARY 4. *For any $\varepsilon > 0$, any $\delta > 0$, and any mean income $\bar{x}$, there is a number N' such that the proportion of individuals whose income exceeds the minimum by more than ε in a Pareto-optimal allocation is less than δ whenever the economy has more than N' members.*

Although Corollary 4 establishes that the income distribution converges in a certain sense to the egalitarian, it does not satisfy all the conditions that are implied by the usual definition of convergence in distribution. What we really want to prove is that the proportion of individuals whose incomes differ by more than a preassigned value, ε, from the mean income approaches zero. This statement does not follow from Corollary 4. The difficulty is that Assumption 6 does not exclude the possibility that the total income going to individuals whose incomes are above the minimum by ε may remain a nontrivial part of total community income. This can happen only if their mean income approaches infinity. In that case it is possible that the minimum income will converge to a limit below the mean income, $\bar{x}$, and in fact that the proportion of individuals at or near the minimum may not converge to zero.

We now present two examples. The first shows that Assumption 6 is necessary to the conclusions thus far. The second shows that it is not sufficient to imply convergence in distribution and that an additional assumption is needed.

In both examples, it is assumed that the population is a sequence of individuals. In both, it is assumed that $U(x)$, the altruistic utility function, is any strictly concave increasing function.

For the first example, choose two income levels, $0 < \mathbf{x} < x'$, and let $\bar{x} = (\mathbf{x} + x')/2$. Let $\bar{\beta} = U'(\mathbf{x})$, $\beta = U'(x')$. Suppose that the sequence of individuals have egoistic utility functions U_i satisfying the conditions

$$(15\text{-}33) \qquad \sum_{i=1}^{\infty} [U_i'(x') - \beta]^{-1} < \infty, \qquad U_i'(x') > \beta.$$

For example, $U_i'(x') = 2^i + \beta$. Note that if (15-33) is to hold, it must be that $[U_i'(x') - \beta]^{-1}$ approaches zero, and therefore that $U_i'(x')$ approaches infinity as i approaches infinity, in contradiction to Assumption 6. Also note that (15-33) restricts U_i' at only one point for each i. Let S_n consist of the first $2n$ individuals in the sequence; let x^n be the allocation over S_n defined by

$$x_i^n = \begin{cases} \mathbf{x}, & i = 1, \ldots, n \\ x', & i = n+1, \ldots, 2n. \end{cases}$$

Clearly, the mean income is $\bar{x}$, so this allocation is feasible. Also, the income distribution does not converge to the egalitarian, even in the limited sense of Corollary 4, since half the population has income x', which does not get arbitrarily close to $\bar{x}$. We now show that x^n is Pareto optimal. When $x_i > \mathbf{x}$, $x_i = x'$, $U'(x_i) = \beta_i = \beta$, and $\alpha_i = [U_i'(x') - \beta]^{-1}$. The optimality condition of Theorem 2 becomes

$$(15\text{-}34a) \qquad (\bar{\beta} - \beta) \sum_{i=n+1}^{2n} [U_i'(x') - \beta]^{-1} \leq 1.$$

But from (15-33), it must be that

$$\lim_{n \to \infty} \sum_{i=n+1}^{\infty} [U_i'(x') - \beta]^{-1} = 0,$$

and therefore certainly

$$\lim_{n \to \infty} \sum_{i=n+1}^{2n} [U_i'(x') - \beta]^{-1} = 0.$$

Hence, certainly (15-34) holds for n sufficiently large. Thus, if Assumption 6 is violated, there is no convergence to a distribution concentrated near the minimum.

A second example will satisfy Assumption 6, and therefore Theorem 3 and Corollary 4, but will not converge in distribution to the egalitarian. Choose two numbers, x and $\bar{x}$, $0 < x < \bar{x}$. Let the ith individual have an egoistic utility function U_i such that

$$(15\text{-}34b) \quad U_i'[i\bar{x} - (i - 1)x] = U'(x).$$

Note again that this simply restricts U_i' at one point, for each i. This condition is compatible with Assumption 6. Since the functions U_i' are decreasing, it is clear that if Assumption 6 is satisfied at any point x_0, it is satisfied for all $x > x_0$. In particular, then, let $U_i'(x) = V(x)$, for all i, in the interval $(0, x)$. Also, assume that $U_i'(x) > U'(x)$ in that interval. There is no difficulty then in constructing, for each i, the function U_i' for $x > x$ so as to satisfy the conditions that it be decreasing, that $U_i'(x) > U'(x)$, and that (15-34b) hold.

Under these conditions let S_n consist of the first n individuals in the sequence, and let x^n be the dictatorial allocation defined by

$$x_i^n = \begin{cases} x, & i = 1, \ldots, n - 1 \\ n\bar{x} - (n - 1)x & i = n. \end{cases}$$

This allocation is feasible if the mean income is $\bar{x}$. Since $x_i^n > x$ only for $i = n$, it is easy to verify that x^n is a Pareto-optimal allocation for S_n, for all n. Whereas the number of individuals for which $x_i^n > x$ is 1 for all allocations, so that Theorem 3 certainly holds, all other individuals have incomes that are x and therefore remain bounded away from $\bar{x}$. Hence, the distribution does not converge to the egalitarian one concentrated at $\bar{x}$; although in each economy the chosen distribution has only one individual whose income is above the minimum, that income is rising indefinitely above that of the others.

To obviate this possibility, we need another assumption, which reflects the hypothesis of bounded selfishness in a different way.

ASSUMPTION 7. *For every $x > 0$, there is an income $x' > 0$ such that for all individuals i in the population P, i's marginal rate of substitution of i's income for j's is less than or equal to 1 when $x_i = x'$, $x_j = x$.*

Where Assumption 6 measured selfishness by the benefit to others required per dollar of loss starting from equal incomes, Assumption 7 measures selfishness by the number of dollars of income needed to bring Ego to the point of being indifferent between an additional dollar to self or to Other.

Under Assumption 7, $\xi_i(x)$ is bounded uniformly in i for fixed x. In particular, $\xi_i(\bar{x}) \leq \bar{\xi}$ for all i. From Corollary 3, $x_i \leq \bar{\xi}$ for all i in a Pareto-optimal allocation. Divide the members of S into the members of S', as defined by (15-30), and the others. For those not in S', $x_i \leq \mathbf{x} + \varepsilon$, by definition; for those in S', $x_i \leq \bar{\xi}$, as just argued. Therefore, feasibility implies that

$$(\#S)\bar{x} \leq (\#S - \#S')(\mathbf{x} + \varepsilon) + (\#S')\bar{\xi}$$

or, equivalently,

$$\mathbf{x} > \bar{x} - \varepsilon - \{(\#S')/[(\#S) - (\#S')]\}(\bar{\xi} - \bar{x}).$$

By Theorem 3, $\#S'$ is bounded above for fixed ε; hence, for $\#S$ sufficiently large, the last term can be made less than ε, so that $\mathbf{x} > \bar{x} - 2\varepsilon$ for $\#S$ sufficiently large. Thus the number of individuals with income a given amount below $\bar{x}$ can be made zero for $\#S$ sufficiently large.

THEOREM 4. *Under Assumptions 1 through 7, for any $\varepsilon > 0$ and any mean income $\bar{x}$, the minimum income in any Pareto-optimal income allocation exceeds $\bar{x} - \varepsilon$ in all economies with sufficiently large numbers of members. Therefore, the number of individuals with incomes differing from $\bar{x}$ by more than ε in any Pareto-optimal allocation is bounded above uniformly in the economy.*

COROLLARY 5. *Under Assumptions 1 through 7, the proportion of individuals with incomes that differ from the mean income by more than ε in a Pareto-optimal allocation approaches zero as the size of the economy increases.*

Remark. It is easy to see that Assumptions 6 and 7 are independent. The egoistic utility functions of the first example, which violate Assumption 6, could be made to satisfy Assumption 7, whereas that of the second example was chosen to satisfy Assumption 6 but not Assumption 7.

The Charity Game

Consider a set of individuals S with preferences for income allocations satisfying Assumptions 1 through 5. Suppose that they could make no cooperative agreements for income redistribution, through the government or any other way. However, each one starts with a given income x_i^0, and each is permitted to give away any amount to any other individual. Let x_{ij} be the amount given by individual i to individual j, $j \neq i$. The aim of each individual is to maximize his or her welfare.

This is a noncooperative game; the strategies of individual i are the gifts x_{ij}, constrained to be nonnegative; it is permitted to give but not to demand from others. An equilibrium point of the game is one in which individual i is choosing his or her strategy so as to maximize W_i^S, given all gifts of all other individuals.

The final income of individual i, after all gifts have been given and received, is

$$(15\text{-}35) \qquad x_i = x_i^0 + \sum_{k \neq i} x_{ki} - \sum_{k \neq i} x_{ik}.$$

Note that W_i^S depends only on the final incomes. Hence, the effect of a given gift, x_{ij}, works only through those final incomes. Clearly,

$$(15\text{-}36) \qquad \partial x_i / \partial x_{ij} = -1, \qquad \partial x_j / \partial x_{ij} = 1.$$

The requirement that individual i be optimizing for given values of others' strategies can be written (in view of the concavity of W_i^S in the x_{ij}'s)

$$\partial W_i^S / \partial x_{ij} \leq 0, \quad \text{all } j \neq i; \qquad \partial W_i^S / \partial x_{ij} = 0 \quad \text{if } x_{ij} > 0.$$

From Theorem 1 and (15-36), the following statement follows immediately.

LEMMA 1. *The gifts x_{ij}, $i \neq j$, are an equilibrium of the charity game if and only if they satisfy the conditions*

(a) $\qquad U_i'(x_i) \geq U'(x_j) \quad$ *for all i, j, with $i \neq j$*

(b) $\qquad U_i'(x_i) = U'(x_j) \quad$ *if $x_{ij} > 0$.*

Remark. We have not asserted at this stage that the charity game has an equilibrium. The existence does not follow from general theorems, because the domain of the x_{ij}'s may not be compact. Lemma 1 does characterize the equilibrium if it exists; its existence will be argued later.

Suppose that at equilibrium there were an individual j, who both received a gift and gave one (that is, for some i and k, $x_{ij} > 0$ and $x_{jk} > 0$). Remember that, from Theorem 1, Exp. (15-4), $U_j'(x_j) > U'(x_j)$. Then, from Lemma 1(b) applied to the pairs (i,j) and (j,k), it follows that

$$U_i'(x_i) = U'(x_j) < U_j'(x_j) = U'(x_k),$$

in contradiction to Lemma 1(a) for the pair (i,k).

Let G be the set of individuals who give some positive gift, and R be the set of individuals who receive at least one gift:

$$G = \{i | x_{ij} > 0 \quad \text{for some } j\}$$
$$R = \{i | x_{ji} > 0 \quad \text{for some } j\}.$$

It has just been shown that G and R are disjoint.

Let j be any member of R, i be an individual for whom $x_{ij} > 0$, and k be any member of S. Then, from Lemma 1(b) and (a),

$$U'(x_j) = U_i'(x_i) \geq U'(x_k),$$

so that $x_j \leq x_k$. Since k was any member of S, $x_j = \min_k x_k = \mathbf{x}$. Thus

$$(15\text{-}37) \qquad x_i = \mathbf{x} = \min_k x_k \quad \text{for all } i \in R.$$

That is, all receivers at equilibrium have the same final income, which is minimal among all individuals' final incomes.

If $i \in G$, then $x_{ij} > 0$ for some $j \in R$. From (15-37) and Lemma 1(b), $U_i'(x_i) = U'(\mathbf{x})$, or

$$(15\text{-}38) \qquad x_i = \xi_i(\mathbf{x}) \quad \text{for } i \in G.$$

From Lemma 1(a) and the definition of $\mathbf{x}$,

$$(15\text{-}39) \qquad \mathbf{x} \leq x_i \leq \xi_i(\mathbf{x}) \quad \text{for all } i.$$

We will use these facts to characterize the equilibrium in terms of the single parameter $\mathbf{x}$ and exhibit an equation for determining $\mathbf{x}$. We first have to allow for the case where the equilibrium requires no transfers, so the final and original incomes coincide. A necessary condition for this trivial equilibrium is that (15-39) hold, with $x_i = x_i^0$. But if (15-39) holds, then Lemma 1(a) holds for all i and j, whereas Lemma 1(b) is inapplicable. The part of (15-39) which requires that $x_i^0 \geq \mathbf{x}^0$ is, of course, a tautology.

LEMMA 2. *The charity game has the trivial equilibrium $x_i = x_i^0$ (and $x_{ij} = 0$, for all i and j) if and only if $\xi_i(\mathbf{x}^0) \geq x_i^0$, for all i.*

In a trivial equilibrium G and R are empty sets; otherwise, they are not. Clearly, if one is nonempty, so is the other.

For simplicity of notation, let

$$(15\text{-}40) \qquad G_i = \sum_{k \neq i} x_{ik}, \qquad R_i = \sum_{k \neq i} x_{ki}$$

so that, by (15-35),

(15-41) $x_i = x_i^0 - G_i + R_i$.

If $i \in G$, $R_i = 0$, $0 < G_i = x_i^0 - x_i$, and $x_i^0 > \xi_i(\mathbf{x})$, by (15-38). If $i \notin G$, then $G_i = 0$, and $x_i^0 \le x_i \le \xi_i(\mathbf{x})$, by (15-39). Hence G is characterized in terms of original incomes and $\mathbf{x}$:

(15-42) $i \in G$ if and only if $x_i^0 > \xi_i(\mathbf{x})$.

Also,

$$G_i = \begin{cases} x_i^0 - \xi_i(\mathbf{x}) & \text{if } x_i^0 - \xi_i(\mathbf{x}) > 0 \\ 0 & \text{otherwise.} \end{cases}$$

Introduce the notation

(15-43) $$x^+ = \begin{cases} x & \text{if } x > 0 \\ 0 & \text{if } x \le 0. \end{cases}$$

Then

(15-44) $G_i = [x_i^0 - \xi_i(\mathbf{x})]^+$ for all i.

If $i \in R$, then $G_i = 0$, $0 < R_i = x_i - x_i^0$, and $\mathbf{x} > x_i^0$ by (15-37). If $i \notin R$, then $R_i = 0$, $x_i^0 \ge x_i \ge \mathbf{x}$, by (15-39).

(15-45) $i \in R$ if and only if $\mathbf{x} > x_i^0$

(15-46) $R_i = (\mathbf{x} - x_i^0)^+$ for all i.

Conditions (15-42) to (15-46) define the income allocation completely if $\mathbf{x}$ is known. From the definitions of (15-40), it is clear that

$$\sum_i G_i - \sum_i R_i = 0.$$

Then, from (15-44) and (15-46), we see that $\mathbf{x}$ is a root of the equation, $F(x) = 0$, where

(15-47) $$F(x) = \sum_i [x_i^0 - \xi_i(x)]^+ - \sum_i (x - x_i^0)^+.$$

Since ξ_i is an increasing function and also x^+ is a (monotone) increasing function, $[x_i^0 - \xi_i(x)]^+$ is a monotone-decreasing function of x. Similarly, $-(x - x_i^0)$ is a monotone-decreasing function of x. Therefore,

(15-48) F is monotone decreasing

since it is a sum of monotone-decreasing functions. Further, if $x > x_i^0$, then $-(x - x_i^0)^+ = -(x - x_i^0)$ is a strictly decreasing function of x. Hence, if $x > x_i^0$ for at least one i, then F is strictly decreasing.

(15-49) F is strictly decreasing for $x > \mathbf{x}^0$.

If $x = \mathbf{x}^0$, then $x - x_i^0 \leq 0$ for all i, so that $-(x - x_i^0)^+ = 0$ for all i. Hence, $F(\mathbf{x}^0) \geq 0$.

Now choose any $x' > \max x_i^0$. Then $x_i^0 < x' < \xi_i(x')$ for all i so that $[x_i^0 - \xi_i(x')]^+ = 0$ for all i. Also, $-(x' - x_i^0)^+ = -(x' - x_i^0) < 0$ for all i, so that $F(x') < 0$. Since $F(\mathbf{x}^0) \geq 0$ and $F(x') < 0$, the equation $F(x) = 0$ has a root.

Consider two cases, according as $F(\mathbf{x}^0) > 0$ or $F(\mathbf{x}^0) = 0$. In the first case, from (15-48) and (15-49), the root $\mathbf{x}$ is unique, and $\mathbf{x} > \mathbf{x}^0$. Then there is at least one i for which $\mathbf{x} > x_i^0$, so that R and therefore G are nonempty, a nontrivial equilibrium. Given the value of $\mathbf{x}$, the equilibrium is then defined by (15-42) to (15-46). The actual flows, who gives to whom, are not unique, since only the totals given by members of G and received by members of R are specified, but this nonuniqueness is not very interesting.

If $F(\mathbf{x}^0) = 0$, then, from (15-49), it cannot be that $F(x) = 0$ for any larger value of x. In this case, G and R are empty. Indeed, consider the condition that $F(\mathbf{x}^0) = 0$. As already argued, $-(\mathbf{x}^0 - x_i^0)^+ = 0$ for all i. Hence, from (15-47), the condition $F(\mathbf{x}^0) = 0$ requires that

$$\sum_i [x_i^0 - \xi_i(\mathbf{x}^0)]^+ = 0.$$

For a sum of nonnegative terms to equal zero, it is necessary that each one be zero, so that $[x_i^0 - \xi_i(\mathbf{x}^0)]^+ = 0$ for all i, or $x_i^0 \leq \xi_i(\mathbf{x}^0)$ for all i, precisely the condition of Lemma 2 for the existence of a trivial equilibrium.

THEOREM 5. *The charity game always has a unique equilibrium. If the original income of individual i is x_i^0 and $\mathbf{x}^0 = \min_i x_i^0$, then the equilibrium is trivial if $x_i^0 \leq \xi_i(\mathbf{x}^0)$ for all i. (If x_i is the equilibrium income for individual i, the equilibrium is trivial if $x_i = x_i^0$ for all i.) If $x_i^0 - \xi_i(\mathbf{x}^0) > 0$ for some i, then the unique equilibrium is nontrivial. In that case the minimum equilibrium income, $\mathbf{x} = \min_i x_i$, is the unique solution of the equation*

$$\sum_i [x_i^0 - \xi_i(\mathbf{x})]^+ - \sum_i (\mathbf{x} - x_i^0)^+ = 0.$$

The givers are precisely those individuals for whom $x_i^0 > \xi_i(\mathbf{x})$, and the total gifts of a giver are $x_i^0 - \xi_i(\mathbf{x})$. The receivers are precisely those individuals for whom $\mathbf{x} > x_i^0$, and the total gifts received by a receiver equal $\mathbf{x} - x_i^0$.

Is the equilibrium point of a charity game Pareto optimal? Suppose first that the equilibrium is nontrivial. For any $i \in G$, $x_i = \xi_i(\mathbf{x}) > \mathbf{x}$. Since $U_i'(x_i) = U'(\mathbf{x})$,

$$U_i'(x_i) - U'(x_i) = U'(\mathbf{x}) - U'(x_i),$$

from which it follows immediately that

$$(\bar{\beta} - \beta_i)\alpha_i = 1 \quad \text{for } i \in G.$$

However, $\Sigma_{x_i > x} (\bar{\beta} - \beta_i)\alpha_i \leq 1$ for a Pareto-optimal allocation, so the equilibrium allocation can be Pareto optimal only if there is exactly one member of G and no other individual whose equilibrium income is above the minimum.

This is a condition on the equilibrium allocation of final incomes. It is useful to restate it as a condition on original incomes. Suppose that individual 1 is the sole member of G. Then $x_i^0 \leq x_i = \mathbf{x}$ for all $i > 1$. Clearly, $x_1^0 > \xi_1(\mathbf{x}) > \mathbf{x} \geq x_i^0$ for $i > 1$, so that individual 1 must in fact have the largest original income. Label all the individuals now in decreasing order of income, so that x_2^0 is the second-highest original income. Since $x_2^0 \leq \mathbf{x}$ and $F(\mathbf{x}) = 0$, it must be that $F(x_2^0) \geq 0$, since F is decreasing by (15-48). Clearly, this condition is also sufficient that individual 1 be the sole member of G and the sole individual whose equilibrium income exceeds $\mathbf{x}$.

Since $x_1^0 > \xi_1(\mathbf{x}) \geq \xi_1(x_2^0)$, $[x_1^0 - \xi_1(x_2^0)]^+ = x_1^0 - \xi_1(x_2^0)$. For $i > 1$, $x_i^0 \leq x_2^0 < \xi_i(x_2^0)$, so that $[x_i^0 - \xi_i(x_2^0)]^+ = 0$ for $i > 1$. For $i = 1, 2$, $x_2^0 - x_i^0 \leq 0$, so that $(x_2^0 - x_i^0)^+ = 0$. For $i > 2$, $x_2^0 - x_i^0 \geq 0$, so that $(x_2^0 - x_i^0)^+ = x_2^0 - x_i^0$. Hence, from (15-47),

$$0 \leq F(x_2^0) = x_1^0 - \xi_1(x_2^0) - \sum_{i>2} (x_2^0 - x_i^0)$$

or $\quad x_1^0 \geq \xi_1(x_2^0) + \sum_{i>2} (x_2^0 - x_i^0).$

The highest original income must be so high that if the holder brings everyone else up to the second-highest income, he or she would be at least indifferent to giving up further income to the others.

THEOREM 6. *A nontrivial equilibrium of a charity game is Pareto optimal if and only if the final income allocation has exactly one individual above the minimum income or, equivalently, if and only if the original incomes satisfy the condition*

$$x_1^0 \geq \xi_1(x_2^0) + \sum_{i>2} (x_2^0 - x_i^0),$$

where individuals 1 and 2 have the highest and next-highest original incomes, respectively.

In the case of a trivial equilibrium, less can be said beyond the Pareto-optimality criterion itself. By Lemma 1(a), $U_i'(x_i^0) \geq U'(x^0)$, and therefore $U_i'(x_i^0) - U'(x_i^0) \geq U'(x^0) - U'(x_i^0)$, from which it follows that

$$(15\text{-}50) \quad (\bar{\beta} - \beta_i^0)\alpha_i^0 \leq 1,$$

where the superscript means evaluation at original incomes. Further, for fixed x^0, we can vary x_i^0 until equality holds in (15-50), for any i for whom $x_i^0 > x$. Also, for those i, $U'(x_i^0) < U'(x^0)$, so that $\bar{\beta} - \beta_i^0 > 0$ and can be made arbitrarily small, and hence $(\bar{\beta} - \beta_i^0)\alpha_i^0 > 0$ and can be made arbitrarily small. If $x_i^0 > x^0$ for no or one value of i, then clearly the Pareto-optimality criterion is satisfied. Otherwise, let $m = \#\{i | x_i^0 > x^0\}$. Then, by suitable choice of x_i^0, we can make

$$(15\text{-}51) \quad \sum_{x_i^0 > x^0} (\bar{\beta} - \beta_i^0)\alpha_i^0$$

vary from as close to zero as desired up to m, without changing the level of x^0, the number of individuals for whom $x_i^0 > x^0$, or the triviality of the equilibrium. But if $m > 1$, then (15-51) can be made to be below or above 1, and the income allocations may be Pareto optimal or they may not.

THEOREM 7. *Suppose that the distribution of original incomes satisfies the conditions for the existence of a trivial equilibrium in the charity game. If there is at most one individual whose original income is above the minimum, then the allocation is Pareto optimal. Otherwise, the allocation may or may not be Pareto optimal.*

COROLLARY 6. *Any equilibrium allocation of the charity game (trivial or not) for which at most one individual has above-minimum income is Pareto optimal.*

The reason the charity game so rarely leads to a Pareto-optimal allocation is that the income of others is a public good. If there are two or more givers, then each would benefit by the other's giving; but the charity game does not permit mutually advantageous arrangements. Even if there is one giver and one additional individual above the minimum, the benefit to the latter from the former's giving to those with minimum income is never given representation.

References

Archibald, G. C., and D. Davidson. 1976. Non-paternalism and the Basic Theorems of Welfare Economics. *Canadian Journal of Economics* 9:492–507.

Bergson, A. 1938. A Reformulation of Certain Aspects of Welfare Economics. *Quarterly Journal of Economics* 52:310–34.

Bergson, A. 1966. *Essays in Normative Economics.* Cambridge, Mass.: Harvard University Press.

Debreu, G. 1960. Topological Methods in Cardinal Utility Theory. In K. J. Arrow, S. Karlin, and P. Suppes (eds.), *Mathematical Methods in the Social Sciences, 1959.* Stanford, Calif.: Stanford University Press, pp. 16–26.

Fleming, J. M. 1953. A Cardinal Concept of Welfare. *Quarterly Journal of Economics* 66:366–84.

Hochman, H. M., and J. D. Rodgers. 1969. Pareto Optimal Redistribution. *American Economic Review* 59:542–7.

Ireland, T. R., and D. B. Johnson. 1970. *The Economics of Charity,* Part 2 (by D. B. Johnson). Blacksburg, Va.: Center for Study in Public Choice.

Kolm, S. C. 1969. The Optimal Production of Social Justice. In J. Margolis and H. Guitton (eds.), *Public Economics.* New York: St. Martin's Press, pp. 145–200.

Little, I. M. D. 1952. Social Choice and Individual Values. *Journal of Political Economy* 60:422–32.

Pareto, V. 1913. Il massimo di utilità per una colletività in sociologia. *Giornale degli Economisti,* pp. 337–40.

Winter, S. G., Jr. 1969. A Simple Remark on the Second Optimality Theorem of Welfare Economics. *Journal of Economic Theory* 1:99–103.

Index